The Complete Idiot's Reference Card

Wine Store Evaluation Checklist

- ➤ Does the store carry a large selection of wine?
- ➤ Are the wines well organized on the shelves?
- ➤ Are the wine clerks knowledgeable?
- ➤ Do they provide courteous and patient service?
- ➤ Are the prices competitive?
- ➤ Is the store display area cool?
- ➤ Is the wine storage area air conditioned?
- ➤ Are the better wines stored on their sides?
- ➤ Does the store feature many wines on special or discount?
- ➤ Does the store feature private labels or direct imports to provide savings?

Restaurant Wine Service Evaluation Checklist

- ➤ Does the restaurant have a well-rounded wine list or is it a limited one made up by its supplier?
- ➤ Does the wine list offer overaged and potentially dead famous wines at astronomical prices?
- ➤ Does the restaurant have a sommilier?—if not, are the waiters knowledgeable about the wine?
- ➤ Are the wine glasses large enough?
- ➤ Are there different-shaped wine glasses for different kinds of wine?
- ➤ Are the wines stored in a refrigerated wine cellar?
- ➤ Are the white wines pre-chilled? If so, ask for a bottle to be chilled especially for you.
- ➤ Are the wine prices more than double retail?
- ➤ Can you bring your own bottle for a reasonable corkage fee?
- ➤ Can you take home what's left in the bottle?
- ➤ Does the restaurant offer several premium wines by the glass?
- ➤ Does the wine list feature half-bottles?

Vintage Chart

	95	94	93	92	91	90	89	88	87	86	85	84	83	82	81	80	79	78	77	76	75
BORDEAUX RED	8a	7a	7a	6b	6b	9a	10b	8a	8c	8a	8c	5d	7b	10b	6c	6c	7c	7c	6d	7c	9b
BORDEAUX WHITE	8a	7a	7b	6b	6b	9a	10c	6c	4d	8c	8c	3d	6d	6d	6d	5d	8d	8d	*	*	8d
BORDEAUX WHITE SWEET (SAUTERNES)	8a	7a	7b	6b	5b	10b	10b	9b	2d	8b	6b	5c	7b	7c	7c	7c	9c	8c	*	8c	10b
BURGUNDY RED	8a	6a	8b	6b	6b	10b	8b	9b	7c	6d	7c	6d	8b	6d	7d	7d	7d	9c	5d	9c	4d
BURGUNDY WHITE	8a	9a	6b	8b	6c	8c	8c	7c	7c	8d	7c	6d	8d	8d	7d	7d	6d	8d	6d	8d	5d
ALSACE	8a	6b	7b	7c	7b	9c	10d	8c	6d	6d	8d	5d	10d	5d	7d	6d	*	10d	*	10d	*
RHÔNE RED	8a	7a	4c	6b	7b	10b	10b	8b	5c	7c	9c	6d	8d	8c	7c	6d	7d	7d	*	7d	7d
CHAMPAGNE	-	-	NV	NV	NV	10b	10b	7c	NV	6c	10c	NV	7c	*	NV	NV	*	*	NV	8d	7d
GERMAN RHEINGAU	7b	8b	7c	7c	5c	9c	8b	7c	5d	6c	7d	6d	8c	8c	8d	*	7d	*	*	10c	8c
GERMAN MOSEL-SAAR-RUWER	7b	9b	7c	6c	6c	9c	9c	7c	5d	6d	7d	6d	8d	*	8d	*	7d	*	*	9c	8c
ITALY—PIEDMONT	8a	8a	8b	6c	6c	9b	8b	9b	6c	8c	9b	5d	7c	9b	6c	7c	8c	9b	*	*	*
ITALY—TUSCANY	8a	7a	8c	7c	6c	9b	6c	9b	6c	8c	8c	5d	8c	9c	7d	7d	8c	9c	*	NV	*
PORTUGAL—VINTAGE PORTO	-	-	NV	9a	9a	NV	NV	NV	NV	NV	9a	NV	8b	7b	NV	7b	NV	9b	9b	NV	7c
CALIFORNIA RED (NAPA/SONOMA CABERNET SAUVIGNON)	8a	9a	8b	8b	8b	9b	7c	6c	8c	8c	8c	7c	8d	8c	8c	9c	8c	9b	7c	8b	7c
CALIFORNIA WHITE (NAPA/SONOMA CHARDONNAY)	8b	9b	6c	8b	8b	8c	6c	7c	8d	8d	9d	8d	9d	8d	9d	8d	7d	8d	8d	8d	9d

Try it; you'll probably pour it out, but you may be surprised.

Key

10—Exceptional
9—Outstanding
7-8—Very good
6—Good
5—Average
4—Poor
1-3—Very Poor

a—Too young to drink now
b—Can be consumed now but will improve with aging
c—Ready to drink now
d—May be too old
NV—Non-vintage

The COMPLETE IDIOT'S GUIDE TO Wine

by Philip Seldon

alpha books

A Division of Macmillan General Reference
A Simon & Schuster Macmillan Company
1633 Broadway, New York, NY 10019

This book is dedicated to Pretty Lady and Sir Hillary and to the memory of Princess, Dustbin, Gus, and Ginger Snap, all fabulous felines.

Copyright © 1996 Philip Seldon

International Standard Book Number: 0-02-861273-6
Library of Congress Catalog Card Number: 96-084605

98 97 96   8 7 6 5 4 3 2 1

Interpretation of the printing code: the rightmost number of the first series of numbers is the year of the book's printing; the rightmost number of the second series of numbers is the number of the book's printing. For example, a printing code of 96-1 shows that the first printing occurred in 1996.

Printed in the United States of America

Publisher
Theresa H. Murtha

Editor
Lisa A. Bucki

Copy/Production Editors
Lori Cates
Beth Mayland
Christine Prakel

Cover Designer
Mike Freeland

Illustrator
Judd Winick

Designer
Barbara Kordesh

Indexer
Becky Hornyak

Production Team
Heather Butler
Angela Calvert
Tricia Flodder
Jason Hand
Daniel Harris
Daniela Raderstorf
Beth Rago
Pamela Woolf

Contents at a Glance

Contents

7 Stomp Your Feet—We're Making Wine Here

8 Wine Jargon and Other Gobbledegook

18 Bubbles and More 199

19 Fortified Wines 215

Part 4: Wine and You

20 Wine Bottle Secrets

25 The Art of Matching Wine with Food　　299

26 Wine and Your Health　　309

Acknowledgments

First I would like to acknowledge my thousands of friends in the world of wine who helped me acquire the in-depth knowledge of wine necessary to write this book. They answered intrusive questions honestly and helped me learn how to taste a wine like a professional—an education that could not be obtained in any school and which would have required decades of experience in the wine trade to learn by assimilation.

Many thanks to my able colleague, Lesley Pratt, who provided invaluable assistance and moral support in writing this book. I would also like to acknowledge the guidance and patience of my editor, Lisa Bucki, who helped me get over the hurdles and keep within the guidelines of this series. The publisher of the series, Theresa Murtha, deserves a debt of gratitude for letting us produce a longer, more useful book than originally planned and for making it possible to include the coupon for Philip Seldon's Wine Advisor computer software that is part of this publishing package, as well as for permitting the vendors to include discount coupons in the back of the book. My agent, Burt Holji of James Peters Associates, deserves a special note of gratitude—without his able efforts, this book would not have been a reality.

Above all, I would like to honor the memory of the late Alexis Lichine, a good friend whose classic and monumental book, *Alexis Lichine's Encyclopedia of Wine,* was my ready reference whenever I needed specific information or statistics about a particular wine or wine region.

Foreword

When I first started my winery in 1966, there were only 16 wineries in Napa Valley and a hundred or so wineries in all of California. Today there are 600-plus wineries in California, and over 200 wineries in Napa Valley alone. Wine country is on the map as a popular tourist destination. Indeed, over four million persons visit Napa Valley every year. Over the past three decades, interest in wine has grown dramatically as American consumers have discovered the delicious taste of wine and how it adds to the quality of life, including its beneficial effect on health. And with the advent of new winemaking technology, affordable, quality wines are getting better and better with each passing year.

There are more than 30,000 wines available in the United States. While it is wonderful to have such choice, new wine consumers often feel like they are in a foreign country when visiting a wine store. There is a compelling need for a wine book that demystifies wine and explains wine in a straightforward language all consumers can understand. *The Complete Idiot's Guide to Wine* fills that need. Philip Seldon has written a marvelous book in direct, down-to-earth language ideal for introducing wine to novice wine enthusiasts. It is one of the best introductory books ever written; it demystifies wine and debunks notions that fine wine is something to be reserved only for special occasions and celebrations. It encourages individuals new to wine to take pleasure in a glass of wine with every meal as part of a rich and rewarding lifestyle. Furthermore, it emphasizes that wine is the beverage of moderation.

Philip Seldon touches on a subject that has been very close to my heart for more than six decades; specifically, the fact that moderate consumption of wine is beneficial to most people's health. He correctly points out that regular consumption of wine reduces the incidence of heart attack and stroke. Wine has the potential to add years to one's life, as well as enhancing one's pleasure in living.

Philip Seldon is a leading figure on the international wine scene. I recall his early visits to my winery when he first founded *Vintage Magazine*. His questions were astute and to the point. He never left a stone unturned in his quest for knowledge about the wine industry and its numerous diverse products. He is to be commended for writing *The Complete Idiot's Guide to Wine* and bringing to the bookshelf a much-needed introduction to the complex subject of wine.

Robert Mondavi

Founder, Robert Mondavi Winery

Introduction

Do you sometimes find yourself paralyzed when confronted with a wine list? Does a wine store seem like a foreign country? Do you wonder why some wines cost so much more than others? Do you wish that you could recognize a great wine when you taste it? Have you ever wanted to reject a bottle in a restaurant but weren't sure of your ground? If so, this is an essential book for you.

No matter who you are—an ordinary consumer or an experienced gourmet with a fair knowledge of wine, there's something valuable in this book for you. You need practical, down-to-earth information written in plain English...not the arrogant proclamations found in some other wine books.

I'm putting the language of wine into basic, everyday street lingo instead of the exalted and sometimes condescending verbiage found in some other wine books. I want *you* to understand this book and develop the love and appreciation of fine wine that has given me so much pleasure over the years.

This book is written from the trenches, not from an ivory tower. As founder of *Vintage Magazine*, I have developed a keen sense of what the person new to wine needs to know and what about wine is confusing and complicated. Thus, I have written this book to make a very complicated subject easy to understand and remember.

I wrote this book for *you*. I have been inside the wineries, the wine cellars, and the warehouses of the distributors and major retailers. I have asked the questions and received the answers, some true and others not so true. Over the course of 25 years I have tasted over 200,000 wines and have seen the improvement in quality and consistency all over the world as modern winemaking technology has replaced antiquated "traditional" winemaking methods. I impart what I learned to you, so that you can benefit from the wine bargains that have entered the marketplace as a result of these developments.

This book will help you:

➤ Untangle the complicated world of wine.

➤ Find the best wines and the best wine bargains in your local wine store.

➤ Order wine in a restaurant with confidence.

➤ Build your own wine collection and maintain a wine cellar.

➤ Know when it is appropriate to reject a bottle in a restaurant or return it to the retail store.

But most important, this book will help you *relax* when you are in a restaurant, a wine store, or with wine-knowledgeable friends who fancy themselves as connoisseurs.

How to Use This Book

If you are looking for a no-nonsense book that will finally help you understand the complicated world of wine, you've come to the right place. Here's where you'll find the information you need in this book:

Part 1, "The Basics of Wine," provides you with some need-to-know information about wine—how to open a bottle, how to swirl the wine in the glass to get the benefit of the bouquet (its lovely aroma), how high to pour the wine in the glass, the correct temperature to serve a wine, all about corkscrews and which one is the best, how to store your wine in your home, and much more.

Part 2, "Why Wine Is Wine," goes into the fine art of tasting wine like a pro and what to look for. It explains the different grape varieties and how wine is made, providing information that will give you a greater understanding of what is in the glass.

Part 3, "The Kinds of Wine," describes wines from all the major wine-producing regions in the world, providing the kind of details you need to know to knowledge-ably select a bottle of wine.

Part 4, "Wine and You," reveals the secrets of the wine bottle and the wine label. You will learn how to interpret the vast amount of information (or lack thereof) that is on the wine label. You will learn how to evaluate a wine store or restaurant wine list. And you will be given specific information on the wine magazines and newsletters—which are worthwhile reading and which are not. You will learn that wine ratings are not all they appear to be. You will also learn which advanced wine books you should read to obtain a knowledge of topics that go beyond the scope of this book.

Part 5, "Wine at Home," tells you how to entertain with wine, how to conduct wine tastings, stock your wine cellar, and get the fullest enjoyment from the wines you drink. You will also learn the fine art of matching wine with food. Also revealed is the little-known fact that wine is indeed good for your health and that drinking a glass or two of wine will reduce your risk for heart attack and increase your longevity.

Extras

Throughout the book, you'll find helpful boxes that provide you with extra information. Here's what you'll find in each type of box:

Wine Wisdom
These tips will give you some of the insider's view of the wine world and may save you money.

Grape Alert
These alerts will caution you about practices in the wine world that can cost you money.

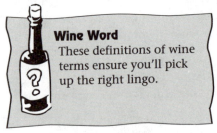

Wine Word
These definitions of wine terms ensure you'll pick up the right lingo.

HEY!

Important Things to Know

These boxes highlight important, more challenging things you should know about the topic of wine.

Trademarks

All terms mentioned in this book that are known to be or are suspected of being trademarks or service marks have been appropriately capitalized. Alpha Books and Macmillan General Reference cannot attest to the accuracy of this information. Use of a term in this book should not be regarded as affecting the validity of any trademark or service mark.

Part 1
The Basics of Wine

Even if you don't need to be told which end of the corkscrew to use to open a bottle, if you are brand new to the subject of wine you probably need to know just about everything else. This part provides a solid introduction to the subject of wine. You will learn that while wine occurs naturally if grape juice is left on its own, the making of wine as we know it requires the expertise and artistry of a skilled and experienced winemaker. You will learn that there are many kinds of wine and many qualities within each wine type.

This part discusses everyday wines, premium wines, and noble wines, and you will discover that all that's labeled champagne is not Champagne. You will also learn why different wines cost so much or not so much.

This part will also provide you with solid information on storing wine, corkscrews, wine glasses, and how to swirl and taste a wine, along with the basics of serving wine for all occasions.

Chapter 1

If You Know Nothing About Wine, Start Here

> **In This Chapter**
>
> ➤ A basic knowledge of wine will make wine drinking more enjoyable
>
> ➤ Wine is the fermented juice of grapes or fruit
>
> ➤ Wines range in quality from ordinary to works of art
>
> ➤ The types of wine
>
> ➤ The quality categories of wine

In this chapter you'll find out why wine is more than just an ordinary beverage. Wine is the fermented juice of grapes or other fruit, although in this book we'll be concentrating on grapes. Through a combination of centuries-old tradition and late 20th century technology, these unassuming-looking fruits can be turned into anything ranging from a simple and enjoyable drink to a complex and noble tribute to the winemaker's art. Wine comes in many types and qualities, and this chapter will provide an introduction to the awesome but thoroughly accessible world of wine.

Why Do I Want to Know Anything About Wine? I Already Know How to Drink

Simple drinking is fine if you regard wine as a thirst-quenching beverage whose taste varies little from bottle to bottle, and the worst experience you can envision is to place a glass to your lips and say, "This tastes flat." However, if you drink wine from that perspective, will you ever have a peak wine experience?

To a true wine enthusiast, drinking wine is much more than quenching your thirst with a beverage that has a pleasant taste or an alcoholic kick. Wine is delicious with many variations of style and taste. A glass of wine makes a meal more enjoyable. Parties are enhanced by wine, as are quiet evenings at home with a glass or two. Drinking wine can be like listening to a great piece of music. Sure, you can listen while you're dressing for work, paying your bills, or microwaving popcorn. But is it the same as sitting back, attuning your mind, and savoring the intricate flavors and harmonies that separate style, composer, and interpreter?

This Book Is About Wine

If you're serious about increasing your knowledge of wine, you've probably got a lot of questions. For example, what distinguishes a mediocre wine from a great wine? Try the following analogy:

Have you ever heard Beethoven's Fifth Symphony played by a high school orchestra? The orchestra diligently rehearsed so everyone was in time and on key and the result was pleasant enough to listen to. But if this was your first exposure to Beethoven, you wondered why so many generations have been so awed by the scowling, shaggy-haired maestro.

On the other hand, if you've heard the same symphony played by a truly great orchestra, you can probably figure out what was missing from the high school orchestra: subtlety, style, and flavor. A great conductor knows how to accent the subtle nuances of orchestration, to draw on the talents of each musician. Each orchestra has its own unique style, which further sets it apart from the mainstream. The flavor lies in the rich harmony of sounds, and it makes you want to hear more. Instead of applauding politely, you want to stand up and yell, "Bravo! Bravo!"

Wine Wisdom
These are three keywords to remember when learning about wine: subtlety, style, and flavor.

Analogies go only so far. But here's an exercise for you to bring the point home:

1. Go through your CD collection. It doesn't matter whether your preference is classical, jazz, rock, or any other idiom.

2. Pick out a really superlative recording—one where all the elements add up to produce nothing less than state-of-the-art. Then pick out another one that is so-so. Your choice.

3. After listening to both of them, make a list of all the things that make the super recording stand out and all the things that the mediocre version lacks.

Chances are that with slight modification, you'll be able to apply your list to tasting wine.

Learning About Wine Isn't Going to Be Simple, but It Will Be Fun and Exciting

Learning about wine isn't easy. It's a lot more complex than remembering which foods go with red wine and which go with white wine. One objective in learning about wine is to free yourself from other people's decisions. We live in a rapidly changing society where rigid ideas of how things should be done aren't acceptable anymore. Think of learning about wine as a tool for empowerment. The next time some know-it-all insists that red wine has no place with seafood, you can disagree heartily, knowing you can back up your stance with vigor and confidence. You'll be feeling good on two counts: You'll have the pleasure that comes from being able to fully appreciate the qualities of a good wine, as well as defending your own taste buds and not nodding meekly to the know-it-all's passé assertion.

What Is Wine?

At the most basic level, wine is fermented fruit juice. In simple terms, fermentation is the conversion of sugar—in the case of wine, grape sugar—into alcohol by the interaction of yeast. Wine can be made from a number of fruits—from apples to pomegranates—but the focus of this book is wine that is made from grapes.

The complexity of wine lies in the fact that good wine does not just appear naturally, although grapes will ferment into wine on their own and then turn into vinegar.

Three factors interact to determine the character of a wine: 1) the grape variety and how it's grown, 2) the climate and soil where it is grown, and 3) the vintner's (winemaker's) creative or commercial objective and winemaking skills. The odds are not stacked in the winemaker's favor. In an ideal world, a superior grape planted in a favorable environment would automatically produce a great wine. In the real world of winemaking, it is surprisingly easy to turn a potentially great wine into an expensive bottle of ordinary table wine, if not a very expensive bottle of awful-tasting microbiological disaster.

> **Wine Words**
> A wine with *complexity* is a wine with more than one simple flavor. A complex wine has layers of flavors and nuances that make it more interesting and enjoyable than a simple wine. The flavor of a complex wine might be described as "tasting of raspberries with hints of chocolate."

5

The vintner has the dual role of scientist and artist. Europeans tend to favor the artistic element, while New World winemakers accent the scientific. This distinction may not be surprising in light of the fact that we live in a society where Microsoft is more of a household word than Michelangelo. It may also have to do with the fact that the growth of the American wine industry has coincided with the technological advances of the past 30 years. Globally, winemakers today have sophisticated technology that enables them to make good quality wine at the lowest price (a good thing to know when you feel like telling off snobbish acquaintances). Technology serves as the background for artistry, enabling winemakers to infuse their wines with the subtle differences in flavor and style that distinguish the products of one vintner from another, grapes and environment being the same.

HEY!

Important Things to Know

Research studies have revealed that drinking wine in moderation is good for your health, but that does not mean that you should cancel your health insurance and buy more wine with the money you save. A glass or two of red wine a day will reduce your cholesterol level and lower your risk of heart disease. One or two glasses of any kind of wine a day will reduce the risk of heart attack from other causes. However, keep in mind that drinking any alcoholic beverage in excess can cause serious health problems, including cirrhosis of the liver.

Wine Words

A wine is said to be *harmonious* if all its elements are in proper relation to each other. The acidity does not overpower the flavor. The body seems right for the other elements of the wine. The aftertaste does not fall short. More on this to come when we discuss wine tasting in Chapter 6.

What Kind of Wine Is My Wine?

Understanding things like harmony and subtlety is essential to fine wine appreciation, but that understanding doesn't address the practical considerations that separate a superb wine from the merely good, and the good from the mediocre. For example, why do some German Rieslings stand head and shoulders above those wines made from the same grape variety in California? Conversely, why does a Napa Valley Cabernet Sauvignon sometimes run circles around an Italian Chianti Classico? There is nothing inherently "better" or "worse" about European or New World wine. A number of factors are involved, and the quality of the end product depends on the interaction between them.

To help you understand what to expect from a particular wine, you need to understand what kind of wine it is. Next, I'll cover the basic types of wine: table wine, sparkling wines, fortified wines, and apéritif wines.

If Wine Is Not Made Out of Wood, Why Do They Call It Table Wine?

If the term "table wine" evokes the image of a bottle or carafe sitting on a red and white checkered table cloth, you have the right idea. Table wines are reds, whites, and rosés that are produced to accompany a meal. Most of the wines we drink and will discuss in this book fall into this basic category.

Important Things to Know

Table wines range in alcohol content from 9 to 14 percent.

Wines with more than 14 percent alcohol (that is, fortified wines) are subject to higher taxation and are therefore classified separately.

Wineries are required by law to state the alcohol content on the label. This simple government regulation has one minor idiosyncrasy: The stated amount may vary within a range of 1.5 percent. That is, a wine designated as 12 percent alcohol may actually have 10.5, or it may have 13.5 percent. Some labels are very accurate. When you see a number like 11.2 percent or 12.6 percent, chances are the winemaker is giving you a precise reading—would you make up a number like 11.2 percent?

Do Varietal Wines Belong in Variety Magazine?

Varietal wines are named for the primary grape used to make the wine. Some varietal wines use one grape exclusively, while others blend the dominant grape with other grape types. When more than one grape is used, the minimum percentage of the designated grape is regulated by law. There's considerable variety in the regulatory legislation.

For example:

➤ In California and Washington, the minimum percentage of the named grape is 75 percent.

Wine Wisdom
Most U.S. wines bear varietal names. You've probably noticed that California wines are labeled Chardonnay or Cabernet Sauvignon, while their French equivalents are called Burgundy or Bordeaux. Most European wines are named for the wine region instead of the grape, although this is starting to change as winemakers capitalize on the power of marketing varietal names.

➤ In Oregon, it's 90 percent (with the exception of Cabernet, which can be 75 percent, like its northern and southern neighbors).

➤ In Australia and the countries of the European Union, the percentage is 85 percent.

Sparkling Wine—More than Champagne

Sparkling wine is wine with bubbles—like soda but not artificially carbonated. Sparkling wine was first perfected in Champagne in the eighteenth century by the Benedictine monk and cellarmaster Dom Perignon. Upon seeing the bubbles in his glass, the good brother eloquently captured the essence of his discovery with the words, "I am drinking stars."

In the United States, the terms *champagne* (remember that lowercase c) and sparkling wine are often used synonymously. Legally, winemakers in the U.S., Canada, and Australia are allowed to use the appellation champagne for their sparkling wines with one catch: the bubbles must be produced naturally during the fermentation process and not added through artificial carbonation. Within that qualification, the choice of grape varieties is up to the producer, and champagne can be made by several methods (not necessarily those used by the French).

In France, the home of the Champagne district (appellation), the story is entirely different. Understandably, the French are not happy to think that the name of their fine and cherished creation can be used generically for effervescent wine like Coke is for cola. Only sparkling wines made from grapes grown in the Champagne region may bear the name Champagne or anything resembling it. The same is true for all member nations of the European Union. The New World, as usual, makes up its own rules.

> **Wine Wisdom**
> Personally, I don't approve of the way the Champagne name has been co-opted for generic usage. When buying domestic sparkling wines, remember that those labeled sparkling wine are superior quality to those labeled champagne. Resist the temptation to go for the champagne name at a cheap price.

Fortified Wines—Strong and Powerful

Fortified wines are wines whose alcohol content has been increased by the addition of brandy or neutral spirits. They usually range from 17-21 percent alcohol by volume. Ports, Sherries, Marsalas, and Madeiras are all fortified wines. In the U.S., they are often regarded as an acquired taste. Dessert wines are almost always fortified wines. They are not always sweet, although most of them are. They are best suited to drinking alone or after a meal. The terms *fortified wines* and *dessert wines* are often used interchangeably.

Apéritif Wines—Great for the Cocktail Hour

Technically, apéritif wines are white or red wines flavored with herbs and spices to give them a unique flavor (and often, a unique color). Vermouth falls into this category. Lillet is another example. Lillet is a lot more popular in Europe than the U.S.

Wine Wisdom
Apéritif wines are too commonly used as mixers. Try enjoying them for their own unusual taste.

What Color Is My Wine?

The three basic colors of wine are white, red, and pink. Within each color category, there are a variety of gradations. These can sometimes provide clues to the wine's taste quality (such as lightness, fullness, clarity, brilliance) and age. More importantly, the appearance of the wine can reveal flaws that should place you on guard when you take that tasting sip.

Wine Wisdom
A wine's color can be a clue to its quality and taste, so it should be drunk from clear glasses. Chapter 2 provides more information about selecting your wine glasses.

HEY!

Important Things to Know

Like people, wines look best in natural or incandescent lighting. Unless you're drinking your wine at the office party, fluorescent lights should be avoided because they give the wine an erroneous color. Fluorescent lights give off a bluish cast that distorts the color of red wines, giving the wine a brownish cast and the false impression that it has aged past its prime.

If White Wine Is Not White, Why Don't They Call It Yellow?

White wine essentially means that the wine lacks red pigment. If wine shops had swatch books for customers like paint emporiums, white wines would cover a spectrum from pale straw, to light green-yellow, through yellow to deep gold.

White wines attain their color (or lack of color, depending on your perspective) in one of two ways. Most frequently, they are made from white grapes. Of course, white grapes are actually green or yellow or a combination of the two.

White wine comes in a number of styles such as "light-bodied and refreshing," "soft and mild," "full-bodied," or "oaked and complex." We will go into greater detail about wine styles and qualities later in this book.

Important Things to Know

HEY!

White wine can also be made from the juice of red grapes. In fact, the red pigment resides only in the grape's skin, not in the juice. Therefore, when wine is fermented without the skin, the wine remains white regardless of the grape variety.

Red Wine Is Sometimes Red

Red wine is easily identified by its deep red color. Without even making the association, you may have, at some time or another, used the name of the most famous red wine region—Burgundy—to describe the color of a scarf or sofa or dress or the upholstery of the car with the six-figure price tag. To many people, the very color of red wine denotes richness.

Important Things to Know

HEY!

In the swatch book, red wines would cover a spectrum from pale brick to deep ruby, through purple to almost inky. In winemaker's language, the grapes they are made from are black grapes (although I will continue to refer to them as red). During the fermentation process, the skins are left in contact with the colorless juice, and voilà!—red wine.

The Tannins in Red Wine Make You Pucker

The skins of red grapes also contain tannin, which is the key to the major taste distinction between red and white wines. The longer the juice is left in contact with the skins and wooden casks, the higher the tannin content of the wine. If you're not used to the taste of a strong red wine, you may find yourself puckering up. You may have had a similar sensation the first time you tasted strong tea (which, like wine, contains tannic acid) or even lemonade (citric acid). Once you're used to the taste of tannin, you miss it when it's not there.

In wine language, tannins produce the firmness of a red wine. A wine with a high tannin content may taste bitter to even the most seasoned wine lover. This is one reason that red wines are matched carefully with a meal. A wine that tastes unpleasantly bitter on its own may be the perfect complement to a steak or roast beef dinner.

Wine Words
Tannin is an astringent acid derived from the skins, seeds, and stems of grapes, and even the wooden casks in which wines are aged.

A Rosé Is a Rosé Is a Rosé Is a Rosé...

The third shade (type) of wine is recognized by its pink color—and no, it is not made by mixing red and white wine together. Rosé wines are made from red grapes that are left in contact with the skins for only a few hours—just long enough to absorb a tinge of color and very little tannin. Technically, what are now called blush wines are lighter than rosé wines. However, the wine industry knows what sells and what doesn't. Blush wines sell; rosé wines don't. Until consumers demand change, a rosé was a rosé is a blush. (That is, today winemakers are using the trendier term, "blush," to refer to both blush and rosé wines.)

Rosé Goes with Everything, but Not Always

Because the skin contact in rosés is minimal, their tannin content is low. No puckering up. Like white wines, rosés are served chilled and go better with lighter foods. They make a refreshing summer drink and a good party beverage.

What Quality Wine?

Wine comes in several qualities but the wine industry and many authors differentiate only two categories—everyday or jug wine and premium wine, with the premium category encompassing wines ranging from a low of $7 a bottle to wines selling for several hundred dollars a bottle. Thus, their premium category is meaningless for explaining all these wines. For the purpose of explaining wine quality, I devised a scheme of wine categories by dividing the premium category into three categories (simple, mid-, and super-premium) and adding a new category, noble wines, for those rare wines that evolve into magnificent works of art when fully mature. The term "fine wine" is used by the wine industry to describe wines that are bottled in glass and closed with a cork (as opposed to a screw cap, plastic bottles, or boxes). Now that many everyday wines are bottled with corks rather than screw caps, this term should refer to wines that are in the mid-premium quality category or better.

Wine Words

A *jug wine* is an inexpensive wine sold in a large bottle. Generally, jug wines sell for less than six or seven dollars a bottle and are suitable for everyday drinking.

Wine Words

A *magnum* is a wine bottle that contains two regular-sized bottles of wine. In quantity, this is 1.5 liters.

Grape Alert

Premium wines are a varied lot. As you go up the ladder, each one gains in style and finesse. Simple premium wines have more personality than jug wines, mid-premiums more so, and so on. Just because a producer describes his wine as a "premium wine" on his label does not necessarily mean that you are getting something much better than a jug wine—price is not always an accurate guide.

Jug Wines and Everyday Wines—For When You Are on the Cheap

What does the term "jug wine" invoke? A dorm party? A big ol' jug on the floor of the car or pickup when you were just barely old enough to drink (or drive)?

Actually, jug wines don't always come in jugs. Many now come in magnums. Over the years, they've gotten a lot of bad press. Jug wines are simple wines made for immediate consumption. They're not really bad—just ordinary. Like the high school orchestra playing Beethoven, it's still Beethoven. Just don't look for a lot of complexity or finesse.

Good jug and everyday wines can be tasty, pleasant, and refreshing. They offer vinous (grape-like) flavor, along with body, balance, and straightforward appeal.

Premium Wines—Good Value for Everyday

Premium wines have more character and finesse. They have texture and complexity, and evoke the flavors and aromas of the grape variety (or varieties) of the region of origin. Unlike jug wines, which have a short aftertaste, the taste of premium wines lingers on the palate, which adds another dimension to the wine tasting experience—frequently new flavors appear in the aftertaste. Premium wines span the price range from $7 to $35 per bottle, with a similar range in quality. I will use the term "super-premium" frequently in this book to describe the higher-quality end of the premium category with the hope that the wine industry adopts it. It should—it's a very useful descriptive term for wines that are close to noble quality but not quite there.

Noble Wines—When You Made the $1,000,000 Deal

In my scheme of wine quality categories, noble wines are the best of the best of fine wines. To simply call them "fine wines" would be like calling Japan's prized Kobi beef prime beef or a throughbred racehorse an ordinary nag. The producers of noble wines spare no expense or effort in producing them, and the result is a wine of breathtaking beauty. Noble wines have distinctive characteristics that set them apart from all other libations. "Breeding" is a good word to describe them, and it's not meant for snob appeal. They are like a symphony in perfect harmony with every note and orchestral nuance clearly discernible. It's in their nature to be complex; for example, "delicate, yet assertive." They're multifaceted, like diamonds. In the world of wine, noble wines are truly works of art.

Wine Wisdom
Identify premium wines by the varietal (Cabernet Sauvignon) or regional (Bordeaux) designations that appear on the label as part of their name. Premium wines offer the appeal of a fine wine-tasting experience without putting a strain on the budget.

Important Things to Know

The unique qualities of noble wines are enhanced with prolonged aging. Like great artists, their performance gains in stature as they mature. Noble wines are the ones cloistered in climate-controlled cellars, aging into works of art.

What Is "Estate Bottling"?

An estate is a wine plantation where the grapes are grown, fermented, and ultimately, bottled. This all-in-one approach to winemaking is a good way to ensure quality. No part of the winemaking operation is farmed out to someone who might be content to give less than an all-out effort. The winery controlling the vineyards is responsible for the whole deal, from the raw materials through the end product.

With estate bottling, there are no gaps in the chain of accountability. Winemakers take pride in their operation and strive toward a product that satisfies customer tastes. Most estate-bottled wines say so on the bottle, but not always.

Grape Alert
A winery making jug-quality or inexpensive wines that controls all its facilities and the winemaking process qualifies to legally use the estate-bottled term, although that kind of estate-bottled wine remains a simple wine. The term "estate-bottled" frequently connotes a quality wine, but doesn't always.

Why Do Wines Cost So Much?

As noted before, wine is the midpoint between grape juice and vinegar. Noble wines like Chateau Lafite-Rothschild don't just happen by accident, and there's not much market for noble vinaigrette.

The more expensive wines are the product of superior grapes, technical expertise, artistic indulgence, and tender loving care. A lot of personal involvement goes into the process, along with skills, flair, and finesse.

Harmony, symmetry, complexity, finesse, and elegance are some of the adjectives defining the unique character of a noble wine. Close your eyes and see what images those words invoke. That's why some wines cost so much.

And Not So Much?

Barring a natural disaster, it's relatively simple for a competent winemaker to produce a decent jug wine. There's no need for split-second timing in harvesting, no subtle blending, no anxious nail-biting during fermentation. The result is simple and pleasant and virtually guaranteed.

Producing a competent wine is less labor-intensive, less chancy, and consequently less expensive than producing an extraordinary wine. They cost less to make, so they cost less to buy.

The Least You Need to Know

➤ Wine is the fermented juice of grapes or fruit.

➤ Learning about wine isn't easy, but is definitely worth the effort.

➤ Wine comes in several kinds—"table wine," "apéritif wine," "dessert or fortified wine," and "sparkling wine." It also comes in three colors—white, red, and rosé.

➤ Wine comes in several qualities—"jug wine," "premium wine," and "noble wine."

➤ Better wines cost more because they are more expensive to make. Inexpensive wines cost so little because the basic procedures in making a good wine are not expensive.

Chapter 2

Serving Wine

In This Chapter

➤ How to open a bottle

➤ Choosing the right wine glass

➤ The proper temperatures to serve wine

➤ Breathing and decanting

➤ Keeping an open bottle

In this chapter you'll become acquainted with those strange-looking gadgets called corkscrews and those crystalline bowls on stilts known as wineglasses. In addition to having its own accessories, serving wine also requires some background knowledge. You'll learn the best temperatures for serving red and white wine and be able to join the debate between "breathing" and "non-breathing" (that is, letting it stand before serving or serving it on opening). You'll learn that a decanter is more than a decorative item and find out how to keep an open bottle without having to use it as salad dressing. Opening and serving wine may not be as simple as pouring a Coke but it is not the ominous task you might think—and it's certainly very rewarding.

So You Want to Get the Wine Out of the Bottle

Unfortunately, wine bottles don't come with pop tops. Some do come with screw caps, although these tend to have a negative image. Many people associate screw caps with cheap wine and corks with high quality. This may or may not be the case.

It's possible that part of the cork's elite image is due to the trouble it takes to open one. You figure with all the effort involved, there has to be something worthwhile inside. That's one good reason to increase your wine know-how. It increases the chances that the beverage inside the impossibly sealed bottle will really be worth drinking.

Removing a cork should not require the brain of Albert Einstein or the body of Arnold Schwarzenegger. But it does require some skill and intelligence and an instrument of some sort.

Important Things to Know

The reason for using a cork seal is not to make wine lovers feel like klutzes. Cork has some unique properties. It is light in weight and contains millions of tiny cells. Each cell is separated by a strong, impermeable membrane. A cork can be compressed for insertion, and once in place, it will expand to create a tight fit. Most wine producers prefer a straight, untapered cork at least one and one-half inches long.

There is one practical reason for the traditional association of corks with quality wine: Only a cork provides the permanent seal necessary for prolonged aging. Corks used for noble wines are longer (two inches) and less porous than those used for many premium wines.

If you'd like to serve up some esoteric knowledge along with your wine, try this: Most corks used throughout the wine world come from Spain or Portugal, which provide close to 90 percent of the world's total supply. The tree used for cork is the cork oak, Quercus suber, which grows in warm climates.

If a cork is extremely dry or even crumbles when you try to remove it, it is a sign that the wine has not been stored on its side to keep the cork moist. Most of the time, the wine may be OK, but if it isn't you have a good reason to return the bottle or reject it in a restaurant. Sniff the cork to see if it smells like wine—if it smells of vinegar or something else, you know the wine is spoiled.

Foiled by the Foil?

Before you even get to the blasted cork, the foil (called the capsule) has to be removed first. The foil can removed in three ways.

➤ Cut through it with a knife below the lip area at the top of the bottle.

➤ Slice through the foil around the neck and rip the whole thing off in one fell swoop.

➤ Use the screwpull foil cutter, which makes cutting the foil a breeze.

Grape Alert

After the foil is sliced off and the capsule removed, you may find a moldy-looking substance on the cork's surface. No need to fear for the contents inside. The green-grey stuff is usually a harmless build-up of cellar muck or seepage (I know that sounds awful, but I guarantee you it's nothing). Just remove it with a damp cloth.

I prefer removing the foil entirely. That way you can see the length of the cork and the chateau name or trademark printed on it before you open the bottle. Sometimes the vintage date or even the brand may be different from what is on the label. In this case, go with the cork!

Pulling a Cork with One of the Good Corkscrews

For years, the choice of corkscrews was very limited. Today, we're all lucky. There are a variety of corkscrews on the market. Some are great and some are not so good. It's a matter of personal choice, too. You can select the corkscrew that best suits your own wine-opening style.

The most popular corkscrew is the waiter's corkscrew, which looks like a shiny, scaled-down Swiss Army Knife without the red handle. The waiter's corkscrew has a helix type worm (spiral screw) which works well because it grips the cork firmly, allowing for easy removal. The opposite of the helix type is the augur type, with its point set dead-center. With the augur type, the cork is more likely to self-destruct instead of emerging intact.

The waiter's corkscrew has a device for leverage and a knife for cutting the foil. It takes some skill to use it efficiently, but once acquired, it has simple, traditional appeal. It's all very simple—once you screw in the cork, you place the lever arm on the edge of the bottle and use the base of the corkscrew as a lever to pull the cork.

The "Ah-So" (you can invent your own reason for this unusual appellation) or Pronged Corkpuller, is not a corkscrew at all, but a two-pronged device developed in Germany. One slender steel leg is gently pushed down until it goes below the top of the cork, and the other leg is gently placed opposite. The cork is secured by a rocking motion used to get the prongs fully inserted around the cork. (You have to be very careful not to push in the cork.) The cork is then removed by gently twisting and pulling upward.

Waiter's corkscrew.

The Ah-So is a difficult gadget, but it's the only way to get the cork out when the cork-screw drills a hole in the cork. Not only does it demand a tender touch, but it does not work on all corks. When it works, the Ah-So has two major advantages. The first is the reasonable ease and speed of operation. The second is that the cork is removed intact and can be reinserted easily.

The drawbacks are that the Ah-So requires much more skill than most corkscrews, and is severely challenged by a dried-out cork. If the cork is at all loose, the Ah-So pushes it into the wine before it can be gripped. This is the nightmare of many wine novices (and non-novices). If the thought of it makes you sweat, try another device.

Ah-So corkpuller.

At first glance, the twin-lever and twin-screw corkscrews look like Rube Goldberg inventions. They are somewhat clumsy in size, but both are simple to use. Both gadgets rely on the principle of mechanical advantage to make removing the cork easier.

The twin-lever works by twisting the screw into the cork and then using another lever to pull it out. If the device is made well, it really will be effortless. To use the twin-lever corkscrew, follow these simple steps:

1. Place the corkscrew over the wine bottle.

2. Turn the handle attached to the screw to get the worm into the cork.

3. Turn the second handle attached to the cylinder. The cork glides out of the bottle.

A twin-lever corkscrew.

This is the catch with the twin-lever—depending on the manufacturer, it can be excellent or awful. Twin-levers come in either wood or metal. Look for a sharp point and a wide-helix worm.

Avoiding the Bad Corkscrews

A fashionable item a decade ago was a device with a needle, which pumped air to force out the cork. This ostensibly clever gadget should have seen an early demise. Instead, it seems to have proliferated. Pick up any wine accessories catalog and I'm sure you'll see one. This devilish device is antithetical to wine in virtually every respect. First, it pumps air into the wine, which can stir up the sediment, especially in an older wine. Second, the needle simply pushes a loose cork in. Third, if a cork is no longer airtight, the air simply escapes and the cork stays put. The last drawback can be disastrous. In a case where the cork is tight and the bottle defective, the pressure can cause the bottle to shatter.

Pulling the Best Corkscrew

The Screwpull is the patented name of a sculptural-looking item that minimizes leverage pressure and offers great strength and durability for long-term use. This nifty piece of design comes with a long, powerful worm and a strong plastic design for the needed leverage. Its self-centering action removes corks with minimal human effort.

The Screwpull makes it easy for even the most inept to pull any cork like a pro, using the following steps:

1. Simply put the Screwpull over the bottle's top, centering the worm over the cork, and turn the handle on the top counter-clockwise.

2. After the worm is in the cork, keep turning and the cork moves out of the bottle into the device.

3. After the cork is out of the bottle, hold on to the cork and turn the handle counter-clockwise some more—the cork will pop right off the worm.

The Screwpull also comes in a completely automatic lever version, which is my favorite. It makes pulling the cork a breeze in a two-step process. You place this gadget over the bottle and pull the lever—the screw goes in and the cork comes out in one simple operation. Then you pull the lever again and the cork slips off the screw. Really neat!

The screwpull.

Which Glass Is the Right Glass?

Does it make a difference what kind of glass you drink your wine in? Indeed it does. This section provides some simple guidelines for choosing the right glass, once you've chosen the right wine. Crystal glasses are ideal but not necessary—their beauty and clarity make the wine sparkle with a true radiance. Ordinary glass wine glasses are fine and less likely to break in a dishwasher. (Some crystal is so delicate it shatters if you even give it a gentle bump.) You can find good, ordinary glass wine glasses for about $50 to $75 a dozen. Crystal wine glasses start at around $75 a dozen and the sky is the limit—$40 a stem is not unusual, and the best sell for upwards of $100 or more a glass.

The Correct Color Is No Color at All

Colorful Art Deco glasses are not the vessel of choice for your wine. The wine's color is a clue to its body, richness, and quality. You'll never be able to weed out wines with imperfections when viewing them in a colored glass, and a glass that masks or changes the wine's true color will certainly not enhance your sensory experience.

Wine Wisdom
Red wines in particular look awful in colored glasses, and the richer the wine, the worse it will look.

Of course, if you insist on using blue, red, or green glasses, you may come up with new phrases for wine tasting: Ah yes, the color of Mississippi mud, this is no doubt a fine vintage Lafite Rothschild…

I still recommend that you stick with the old rule of clear, colorless glasses.

Is the Shape So Important?

Some are fatter and rounder and some are elliptical. Is there really a reason, you ask? And why do they all have that long stem that makes breakage so easy, if not inevitable?

There is a reason that wine glasses have a long stem (and it's not to make glass makers rich as you keep replacing them). The stem is there to keep you from touching the bowl, which can result in a temperature change of the wine from the heat of your hand. It also keeps fingerprints off the bowl. Remember, enjoying wine is a parasensory experience. Do you really want to be looking at thumb whorls as you examine the deep, rich color of a tawny Port?

The capacity of the glass should be ample. This is hardly surprising when you consider that your nose is going to dive part-way in.

The actual shape of the glass is less important. But there is one rule to follow: The rim of the bowl should curve in slightly to help capture the aroma you generate by swirling.

Wine Wisdom
A 12-ounce bowl is a good capacity for an all-purpose glass. The glass should always be less than half full, with plenty of room for swirling the wine before sniffing and tasting (see Chapter 3). A 12-ounce bowl allows for a good four- or five-ounce serving.

The All-Purpose Glass

If you don't want to splurge on five or six types of glasses, or you don't have the room to store them, you're in the company of most wine drinkers. The usual all-purpose glass is a round-stemmed glass with an eight- or 12-ounce capacity. Either the classic Bordeaux or Burgundy glass also makes a fine all-purpose wine glass. The one exception to this is Champagne, which deserves its own glass. In short, get two types of glasses and you'll be set.

The Burgundy Glass

The Burgundy glass is a large, round-stemmed wine glass with a large, curved bowl and a width approximately the same dimension as its height. It has a large opening, and is particularly suitable for capturing the exquisite perfume and bouquet of a fine Burgundy. A typical size will be 12 or 16 ounces, although many come 24 ounces or larger. Of course, it's good for any kind of wine and it is ideal for wine with very complex aromas.

The Burgundy glass.

The Bordeaux Glass

The Bordeaux glass is quite different from the Burgundy glass in that its height is much higher than its width. It generally has a smaller opening than the Burgundy glass to capture the vinous quality of a fine Bordeaux. It is also a good glass to choose if you must choose only one wine glass.

The Bordeaux glass.

The Champagne Flute

To fully appreciate the bubbles, Champagne should be poured into glasses with a high, narrow tapering bowl like the traditional Champagne "flute." It usually comes in a six- to eight-ounce size that can be filled to the top. You usually shouldn't swirl Champagne (see Chapter 3 for more about swirling). Its forceful bubbles exude the wine's flavor, so you don't need to have a large space above the wine like regular table wines. You should not use the typical wedding glass—the flat saucer with hollow stem. You'll watch in dismay as the bubbles you paid for quickly fade from sight.

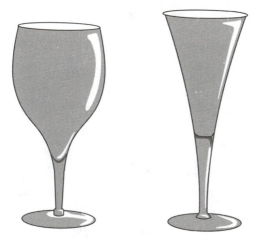

Champagne flutes.

Other Glasses

If you're a whitewine enthusiast, you might want to try the tall, slender Hock glass, originally intended for Rhine wines. If your choice is red, a big Burgundy balloon glass can add some variety to your table, although some wine drinkers find it too unwieldy.

There's also a Sherry glass, called a copita. It's a small glass with a narrow taper and a small opening. The Sherry glass is made to capture the wine's aroma, and it's also perfect for enjoying other cordials.

No doubt you've seen the oversized Cognac or Brandy snifters. Their large size enables devotees to capture the wine's essence, slowly funneling it to your nose. Snifters add an elegant touch to your table, and this is one case where bigger is definitely better. A 16-ounce snifter is actually meant to hold no more than one or two ounces.

Wine Wisdom
There are a few contraptions on the market for heating Brandy or Cognac. They may add a little thrill to your life if you like fires, but they ruin the flavor by scorching it. Avoid them.

The Special Care of the Wine Glass

Regardless of whether you opt for the basics or set aside room for a wine connoisseur's collection of glassware, caring for wine glasses requires special attention, not only to keep from breaking them, but to keep your wines looking and tasting like they were intended.

Wine glasses must be absolutely clean. This is especially true if they've been resting in the cabinet for a while and have picked up dust or off-odors. You should always wash your glasses prior to use. Choose a good dishwashing detergent, and be sure to rinse them thoroughly several times to remove all detergent residue. You don't want to hear a guest saying, "This is a fine Burgundy with just a hint of lemon."

The best way to be sure your glass is really clean is to gently exhale into the glass and then smell it. It's not only the smell of Palmolive or Dove, but any other odors that remain which will come through when you pour the wine into the glass. Don't be afraid to smell the glass when dining out, either. Unfortunately, some of the best restaurants are notorious for stale glasses. You're paying enough for your wine; the least you deserve is a clean, unadulterated glass.

Pouring Wine—Can I Look Like an Oaf?

You've been practicing with your corkscrew and foil cutter, now what? Some restaurateurs insist that their staff pour wine by holding the bottle at the bottom with the thumb in the indentation. First of all, not all bottles you'll be serving have indentations. Second, with a heavy bottle, this may not be the best idea.

There's no standard technique for pouring wine in your home, except to get the contents into the glass. Hold the bottle so you feel comfortable with it. If you feel insecure holding it from the bottom, just be sure your fingers are far away from the lip. Aim for the center of the glass and pour slowly, keeping your eyes peeled for that all-important one-third to one-half full—wine glasses should not be filled to the top. When you've poured the desired amount, give the bottle a slight twist as you raise it to avoid drips.

Is Room Temperature the Temperature of My Room?

The rule of "room temperature" for serving red wines originated long before central heating or air conditioning. When you're talking about wine, room temperature is about 70 degrees (some wine devotees even prefer 65 degrees). If you're taking your bottle out of a specialized wine storage area, chances are it's ready for serving as is. If your home or apartment is overheated or you've just brought a bottle home on a hot day, don't be afraid to put your red wine in the refrigerator. A short cool-down will bring it down to the 70 degree mark without damaging its contents.

Important Things to Know

If you've left your wine in the fridge for a bit too long, or you're finishing up last night's bottle, there's a shortcut to waiting for it to warm—put it in the microwave. Just be sure that you're using microwave-safe glasses, not crystal, which contains lead and may crack. Set it on a very low power level (two or three on most microwaves) and try 20 or 30 seconds, or until you feel it's up to room temperature. It's best to zap it twice rather than use a setting that's too hot or too long and risk burning your wine

You Should Chill White Wines but Not to "Brrr"

White wines taste best when served chilled, but too much chill interferes with the flavor instead of enhancing it. Quite a few restaurants are guilty of over-refrigeration. This goes for rosé wines as well as whites. If your fingers start to stick to the glass, let it stand a while to warm up.

When Should I Open the Bottle?

It's tempting to say, "when you're ready to drink it, of course." However, there is some debate on this issue, and it's been going on for years. Read on.

Wine Wisdom
Try your own taste test. Take a sip of the wine immediately after chilling. Let it stand for a few minutes. Then taste it again. You'll see for yourself how overchilling the wine puts some of the flavor to sleep. This type of comparison test is a good way to acquaint yourself with the subtle nuances of flavor that emerge when wine is served at its best temperature.

Should a Wine Breathe?

The debate overwhen to open the bottle rages between the "breathers" and "non-breathers." The breathers insist that exposure to air makes the wine come to life because the aromas are unleashed. Actually, one of two things may be happening: 1) certain flavor components in the wine may erupt with exposure to air; and 2) some odors that block our perception of more delicate smells dissipate with airing, allowing the more subtle odors to come through.

While it's true that breathing allows some off-odors to dissipate, the non-breathers maintain that the same thing is accomplished by swirling. Breathers also argue that breathing time enhances the flavor of young (recently vinted) wines, although I've never been totally convinced.

Grape Alert
Many old wines seem to "die" in the glass a few minutes after the cork is pulled. Breathe at your own risk.

I'm not really trying to take sides, although I admit I'm more of a non-breather. There are no hard-and-fast rules. Try it both ways and see which you like best. You'll probably find your breathing time varies with the type of wine, the vintage, or even the particular bottle.

If you opt for breathing, I suggest you open the wine bottle 15 to 20 minutes before serving. Then pour some into glasses a few minutes before you and your guests are seated. If breathing really brings improvements, they will be more likely to come along in good-sized wine glasses than in the bottle with its tiny opening.

What Is Decanting?

Decanters can be beautiful, decorative objects, but are they necessary? Decanting does have a purpose, and that purpose is not just to impress your friends with your elegant taste in cut glass. Decanters are made for old wines, which collect sediment during the aging process.

Bottle-aging wines for 10 or more years (sometimes even less) can build up a deposit. When this sediment is mixed with the wine, the taste is bitter and unpleasant. In its mildest form, the sediment will mask the subtle nuances that have been developing over the years. The last thing you want is a bottle of very expensive sludge.

Wine Wisdom
When you decant wine, pour it slowly and carefully, without stopping, into another container. This slow, steady motion allows the sediment to remain in the bottle without being stirred back into the wine.

Not all aged wines have deposits. The ones that do were usually made with minimal filtering, so the flavors become more intricate and complex during aging. All the more reason to get rid of the sediment before drinking.

Since wine should be stored on its side, the sediment collects on the side of the bottle. Therefore, long before you serve your wine (a day or two is fine), you may want to stand the bottle upright, allowing the sediment to fall to the bottom. Then you decant the wine.

Incidentally, decanting also aerates the wine (lets the wine breathe). While the decanters sold in wine shops and catalogs are sure to get compliments from your friends, you can actually use any vessel as a decanter. Just be sure it's clean and free from any off-aromas.

During decanting, you should have a source of light illuminating the bottle's neck so you can see when the sediment is close to being poured. Once any sediment is near the neck, stop. If your decanter has a stopper, replace it until you are ready to serve the wine. Bring the bottle with you to the table. It's an impressive touch, and your guests will want to know the wine they are enjoying.

How Do I Aerate My Wine?

If you decide that you want to aerate your wine, there are several ways to do it. The traditional method is to simply open the wine an hour or so before you plan to drink it. Or you can decant it and leave the stopper off the decanter. Some wine drinkers like to aerate their wines in the glass, but if the wine needs several hours or more of aeration (some wines will benefit from prolonged aeration), this is not practicable. Depending on the circumstances, all methods have their benefits.

How Do I Keep an Open Bottle?

Theoretically, wine begins to deteriorate due to the effect of air on the wine (oxidation) immediately after opening, and a bottle of wine is best consumed within a few hours. (Isn't that a great excuse to have more than one glass?) But if you're enjoying your wine by yourself, or the two of you really don't want half a bottle each, there are ways to keep wine for several weeks without losing too much flavor.

As a general rule, the more ordinary the wine, the better it will keep. Jug wines, made with thoroughly modern techniques, have no microorganisms in the wine to culture and spoil, and they usually come with screw caps, anyway. Finer wines are more of a risk.

Chill It

Like any perishable food, wine will keep longer if it's chilled. However, unlike your cottage cheese or orange juice, wine does lose some of its flavor in cold storage, but in a decade of experiments, I have found that there is very little flavor deterioration even with fine wines if it is well-chilled in the refrigerator for as long as three weeks.

The best way to keep a wine after it is open is to cork the bottle and put it into a cold refrigerator. This will prevent the air that has been absorbed by the wine after it has been opened to oxidize the wine. It's the oxidation of the wine that impairs the flavor in most cases. Also, chilling the wine prevents the formation of vinegar, the natural by-product of wine.

Freeze It

Believe it or not, wine can be frozen for prolonged storage after it has been opened. In one experiment, I froze some of the finest grand cru Bordeaux and Burgundies after a massive wine tasting of premier cru wines. That was 16 years ago, and in my experiments, the wine retained its character from the time it was frozen—the wine did not age. I still have a few bottles in the freezer and will let you know in a decade or so how long a wine can be kept frozen. Incidentally, the wine can be thawed out and refrozen with little flavor impairment.

Carbon Dioxide (CO$_2$) Systems

There are systems that dispense wine by using CO$_2$ under pressure. Because the gadget is inserted into the bottle immediately after opening, there is little risk of oxidation and the wine will keep for several days. This is an excellent method of always having a bottle available for a glass or two without having to keep it in the refrigerator. Some of the units are highly attractive and make a fine addition to a bar or dining room.

Wine Keeper Gadgets

There are gadgets that purport to preserve the wine by removing the air from the bottle or prevent oxidation by squirting CO$_2$ into the bottle after it has been opened. In my experiments, I have found these methods to be useless—once the air has been absorbed by the wine, the damage has been done. What will preserve the wine is not a vacuum or CO$_2$ in the bottle, but a procedure that will prevent the absorbed oxygen from acting on the wine. As iron does not rust much in the winter, you can similarly impede the oxidation of the wine by keeping it chilled. Forget these gadgets—simply refrigerate your wine for future drinking.

Don't Rebottle It

Some wine experts advise that you pour the leftover wine into a smaller bottle. Or do this when first opening the wine. This also serves no useful purpose as the wine has already absorbed air and will oxidize if not refrigerated. As I have said before, if you want to preserve a bottle after it has been opened, keep it in the refrigerator.

The Least You Need to Know

➤ Wine bottles are sealed with screw caps or corks. Only the least expensive wines use screw caps—a cork can be a sign of quality.

➤ Corks are not easy to get out but, once you get the hang of it, it's not so hard.

➤ You need only one or two wine glass styles. Choose only clear glasses, not colored ones, so you can see the wine's color and clarity.

➤ Red wine should be served at slightly below room temperature; white wines should be served chilled, but not overchilled.

➤ You can keep an open bottle of wine in the refrigerator for several weeks without losing much flavor.

Chapter 3

Getting Into Wine

In This Chapter

➤ How to become a good wine taster

➤ Evaluating wines

➤ Why wine is vintage dated

I'm sure that this is what you've been waiting for—how to taste your wine. In this chapter you'll find out what to look for when you bring the glass to your lips, and why your nose is as important as your taste buds. You'll learn how to tell a great wine from one that is merely competent and what all those vintage dates really mean. We'll also cover the basics of matching wine with food so your taste experience is enhanced.

What's in the Glass?

Yes, it's wine, but it's more than just a beverage—it's something wonderful to behold. The rest of this section covers important things to do when you savor your wine, whether you're just tasting different wines to become familiar with them, or you're enjoying a bottle you've just opened for dinner. Chapter 5 will cover what is in the glass and how to identify different wine characteristics in detail.

Swirling the Wine

Now that you've chosen your implement for releasing the prize from the bottle and you're ready to try out your skills, it's time to get down to the basics of tasting. The first step in this venture is swirling. Before you actually get down to tasting wines, you should practice swirling just to become comfortable with the act. This is where the shape of the traditional wine glass makes a difference—swirling wine in your glass helps bring the aroma and flavors up to the surface where they are trapped by the curved design of the glass.

Wine Wisdom
The goal in swirling is to vaporize the wine within the container of the glass. It defeats the purpose if you swirl, pause, and then sniff into the glass. Think of it as a continuous motion. Give the glass a few swirls, then bring it right to your nose.

For your initial practice session, try swirling with water. Fill the glass roughly one-third of the way (slightly over is fine, but be sure it's no more than one-half full). Hold the glass parallel to the floor, and use your wrist to make a subtle, circular motion. The trick is to keep the motion minimal and the glass straight rather than tilted. One way to practice this is to try it first with the glass still on the table. When you feel secure, try it at waist level. Now you know why I suggested water. When you graduate to the real thing, try it this way: Pale white wines first; deep red wines last.

Important Things to Know

HEY!

After you swirl the wine, you may notice rivulets of wine cascading down the side of the glass. These are called "legs" or "tears" and are a sign of a wine with a full body or high alcohol. It is caused because the different liquids in the wine evaporate at different rates. Sometimes the legs are caused by glycerin in the wine as well. Legs are a clue that the wine is a quality wine, but like most other things in wine, this is not always the case.

Color Tells the Story, Too

You've probably noticed that wine lovers always check the color and appearance of the wine. Examining the way the wine looks will reveal any obvious flaws (for example, brown color in either a white or red wine is a sign of over-oxidation, cloudiness a sign that the wine is spoiled), but it's not a good idea to get hung up on appearances. The custom of checking the wine's appearance comes from the old days when wines were not often made clean and were clear because of poor winemaking techniques. Today, with improved techniques and quality standards, there's less chance of this happening.

Remember that lighting is important. Natural or incandescent lighting allows you to see how the wine really looks. Soft lighting is fine, especially if you're enjoying your wine as part of a romantic dinner. Fluorescent lighting makes a red wine appear brown and should be avoided.

Important Things to Know

The main points to look for are clarity and color. The wine should be free from a hazy or cloudy look. Haziness is usually a sign of a biological instability or a bacterial or chemical taint, usually from faulty winemaking. Tasting will reveal this for sure. When a wine is flawed, you will always smell and taste the defects. On the other hand, a wine with gemlike brilliance is truly a beauty to behold.

The Nose Will Tell

You've diligently practiced your swirling. You've mastered whites, rosés, and reds, and you're even keeping the tablecloth on the table clean. The question is now: What do you look for when you place your nose in a glass?

Important Things to Know

Wine is the only natural beverage that offers a complex array of aromas, fragrances (there is a difference between the two; I'll get to that in a moment), and flavors. Orange juice, whether fresh, frozen, homestyle, grovestand, or original, always smells like orange juice. Milk, in all of its forms, still smells like milk. Vodka—despite what the advertisers would like us to believe—is purely one-dimensional.

Inhaling a fine wine is like the prelude is to a full orchestral experience. You can pick out the different melodies, harmonies, counterpoint, and even individual instruments as they work toward the whole effect. In the same way, you can taste the individual components and flavors that contribute to the structure of a wine.

You might call wine a sensory symphony. The range of smells and fragrances is almost unlimited. Wines can be vinous, winelike, and grapey; they can be multifaceted with layers upon layers upon...you get the picture. You can come up with your own metaphors.

The scent of a wine is referred to as its *nose*. *Aroma* is used to describe the scent of a young, undeveloped wine. For an older, more complex wine, the term to use is *bouquet*. This distinction is easy when you think of the image that goes with each word.

Wine Word
In wines, the soft and supple fragrances that develop with aging are called *esters*.

➤ When you think of aroma, you tend to think of a single item like coffee.

➤ A bouquet, in contrast, is an intricate arrangement whose fragrance results from the delicate interaction of its components.

I hate to bring up the bad part first, but it's important to know what you don't want to smell in a wine. Some of these agents are so powerful your nose won't even get near the rim of the glass before you know something's wrong. Others are more subtle, so it's even more important you know what they are to tell a good wine from a flawed one.

➤ Vinegar is an obvious one, indicating your wine bottle has been open too long or something has gone wrong in the winemaking.

➤ The smell of raisins or cooked or baked qualities are also indications that something is wrong, usually that the wine is too old. (Have you ever heard anyone describing a fine wine as "raisiny"?)

There are a number of faults that are signs of microbiological contamination. The most frequently encountered ones are

➤ Sulphur dioxide (think of the smell of a just-struck match).

➤ Hydrogen sulphide (rotten eggs).

➤ Dekkara (the smell of rancid corn chips).

➤ Volatile acidity (vinegar).

➤ Ethyl acetate (acetone or nail polish remover).

➤ Mercaptins (range in smell from garlic and onion to skunk).

➤ Smells of decay (wilted lettuce, dead leaves, mucus, manure, vomit).

➤ Petrochemical smells (diesel fuel, Vaseline).

➤ Geraniums (from bacterial spoilage).

➤ Potassium sorbate (believe it or not, this one smells like bubble gum).

➤ Corky (actually, the scent of a particular mold that grows in corks; wines with this flaw are said to be "corked").

Important Things to Know

Most wines contain sulphur dioxide, a harmless preservative. Sulphur dioxide is sort of a wine wonder drug (which works as an antibacterial, antioxidant) and anti-yeast agent (which keeps sweet wines from refermenting in the bottle). Winemakers are required by law to have the words "Contains Sulfites" on the labels of all wines with sulphur dioxide that are sold for U.S. consumption to caution those rare persons who are hypersensitive to sulphites.

Prudently, winemakers opt for the minimal levels of this additive, and any residual smell should dissipate with airing. Occasionally, wines get an overdose and airing the wine won't help. In this case (as with all of the flaws mentioned above) you're justified in returning the wine.

The nose of a wine can be "nonexistent," "weak," "moderate," or "intense." Closed-in refers to a nose that is weak because it has not had the chance to develop. The other taste components provide the clues to whether the nose is closed-in or simply weak. It takes some experience to interpret these clues, but it's not a job for Sherlock Holmes.

Besides intensity, you should examine the nose for its structure and its balance, the relationship of flavor, alcohol, and acidity. A young white wine high in acid can be "refreshing"—a positive attribute. An equally acidic red will be "unpleasant," even "flawed." Some wines are simple in their flavor. You might describe them as "straightforward" or "one-dimensional."

Wines that display an array of flavors both on the nose and on the palate, usually with subtle or supple undertones, are *complex*. When the various elements work in harmony, the wine is said to be *balanced*. When one element dominates all the rest, the wine is unbalanced. The balance is described in relative terms that resemble a ratings quiz. For starters, here are a few terms that experts use, grouped accordingly:

Superlative	Adequate	Inadequate
harmonious	good	poor
excellent	normal	acidic
perfect	average	heady
		unbalanced

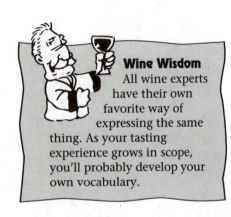

Wine Wisdom
All wine experts have their own favorite way of expressing the same thing. As your tasting experience grows in scope, you'll probably develop your own vocabulary.

Many wine scents may seem strange at first:

➤ The scent of a fine Burgundy frequently resembles wild violets, tar, or truffles.

➤ An aged Bordeaux smells pleasantly "roasted," like in pot roast.

➤ A Late Harvest Riesling smells nutty and honeyed.

➤ A young Riesling or a Muscat resembles pine oil.

➤ American labrusca varieties, referred to as "foxy," have a pungent odor all their own.

Some wine smells require getting used to. Others require getting used to the fact that they're just plain unusual.

The Taste Is What It's All About

Now that your nose is back in place and you've prepared all your adjectives, it's time to take a sip.

➤ Take a sizable sip, filling your mouth with wine.

➤ Roll the wine over your tongue and palate to get the feel, or the *body*, of the wine.

➤ Savor and evaluate the wine.

Body is determined by the wine's alcohol, glycerin, and extract. It's either light, moderate, or full, and may or may not be in balance with the flavor and other components. The body appears firm with sufficient acidity, or it may be "flabby" when acidity is lacking. It may feel "heavy" from residual sugar, or may feel "harsh," "rough," "coarse," "silky," "velvety," "smooth," or "creamy," depending on its structure.

The tannins in red wines frequently add a necessary and pleasing astringency to fine wines. It may not seem so pleasing at first pucker, but as your wine experience progresses, certain wines will begin to seem flat and dull without it.

Gurgling to Make It Better

You've swirled and sniffed and it's time to gurgle. You've got the wine in your mouth. Now, purse your lips and draw air into your mouth, slightly gurgling the wine to vaporize it. The result is a "whooshing" sound that identifies experienced wine tasters. It isn't really bad manners, although I wouldn't suggest it for formal gatherings.

Gurgling the wine permits the full flavor of the wine, warmed by the mouth, to flow through the nasal canal to the olfactory bulb. In short, it's tasting and sniffing rolled into one. It does have a purpose (other than startling your guests). It enables you to fully experience every nuance of flavor.

It's really a simple motion: Purse your lips as if you are going to whistle, then suck in the air over the wine.

Swallowing Slowly for a Lingering Aftertaste

Continuity is the sign of a well-structured wine. There should be no conflict between what you taste and what you smell. The flavor in your mouth should confirm your initial olfactory impression.

After you swallow the wine, you will usually notice a lingering aftertaste, known as the *finish*. The finish is described as "long," "lingering," "fleeting," or "nonexistent." Accompanying these temporal adjectives are "complex," "acidic," "sharp," or "dull." Often, the wine's finish will be a taste experience in itself, adding new dimensions and flavors. Professionals evaluate the finish in terms of the time (usually in seconds) that the flavor lingers.

You can tell when a wine is beginning to pass the peak of maturity by its finish. There may be a hint of dead leaves, or a lack of vinous flavor, which is called "dried out."

HEY!

Important Things to Know

Scents, flavors, body, alcohol, acidity, and astringency provide the total "impression" of a wine, all of which make up its structure. Here are a few adjectives to use when describing a wine's structure:

- ➤ Well-defined.
- ➤ Firm.
- ➤ Broad.
- ➤ Tightly-knit.
- ➤ Good backbone.
- ➤ One-dimensional.
- ➤ Multifaceted.

When all the elements of structure, flavor, and complexity attain a perfect harmony—sometimes virtually indescribable—the result is "breed" or "finesse." These terms are frequently used to describe classic noble wines.

Why Does Wine Come in Vintages?

The structure of a high-quality wine is often dependent on its vintage. A famous wine property might produce one-dimensional wines in a poor vintage and glorious, multifacted wines in a superb vintage. For that reason it is important to know what vintage the wine came from. We've all seen it in the movies. One way to show that the hero or heroine is elegant and sophisticated, the party is chic, or the occasion momentous, is to have someone hold up a bottle announcing, "Lafite '61." Or '45 or '72 or '59.

The truth is, we've all been sold a bill of goods. American consumers have been led to believe that a vintage date means quality, and that only inferior or inexpensive wines are not "vintaged." In reality, having a vintage date on a bottle often has very little bearing on the quality of its contents although, as I said, knowing the vintage is important with high-quality wines.

A declaration of vintage on a label merely indicates when the grapes were harvested and when the wine was made.

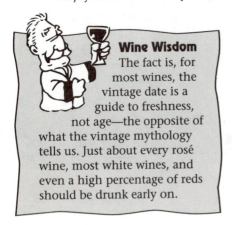

Grape Alert

The mythology attached to vintages and the general lack of information on the part of consumers enhances the merchant's potential to sell mediocre wines at excessive prices. One mark of a savvy wine buyer is understanding just what a vintage date on a wine signifies and what it is that makes a good vintage.

➤ California law requires that at least 95 percent of the grapes be picked that year.

➤ In France, the minimum is generally 80 percent and in Germany, 75 percent.

➤ Each country or region establishes its own standards for determining vintage.

A vintage date declares when the wine was made, but not how or under what conditions. In short, if you're not familiar with the reputation of an individual producer or vintage, all the label reveals is the wine's age or freshness. Most wines—probably at least 80 percent—do not improve with "cellaring" (prolonged aging). They were meant to be enjoyed two to three years after the vintage date.

Wine Wisdom

The fact is, for most wines, the vintage date is a guide to freshness, not age—the opposite of what the vintage mythology tells us. Just about every rosé wine, most white wines, and even a high percentage of reds should be drunk early on.

There are factors that make one vintage better or worse than another. The grapes, climate, and winemaker are all important and they're all interrelated. The one factor determining the quality of the finished product is ultimately the climate.

An ideal vintage means that certain weather conditions were met the entire year. The perfect winter has ample rainfall and enough cold to let the vines have the grapes' equivalent of REM sleep. The spring is mild and free from frosts, rains, or other assaults. The mid-season begins cool and heats up slowly, without any environmental mood swings. The ripening period is neither too hot nor too rainy.

The gradual heat over the late mid-ripening period increases the grapes' natural sugars. Incremental warming with cool evenings let them retain high acidity. The absence of rain in the mid- or late-season keeps the berries from becoming diluted, or swollen with water.

No matter how skilled or experienced, the vintner's role always includes some high-stakes gambling.

➤ For those with conservative leanings, when the vines are pruned in midwinter to control vine growth, they can be pruned to produce a small crop of guaranteed high-quality fruit.

➤ Growers (vineyardists) can bet that the vintage will bring warm (but not hot) and dry conditions so they'll get equal quality from a larger crop.

The better growers understand the unique capabilities of each grape variety they work with. If they hold out for a good or excellent crop both quantitywise and qualitywise, they can lose out to the unpredictable nature of climate on both counts. If they play it conservative and prune drastically for a small crop, a spell of bad weather can mean a complete wipeout.

Harvesting is always a crucial decision. Vineyardists generally harvest too early rather than too late. Picking too late has too many risks: rains, hail, un-wanted molds from high humidity. Sometimes the decision is a wise gut reaction (which sounds like a contradiction in terms, but for the experienced grower, it's not). Sometimes the motive is fear, pure and simple.

Wine Wisdom
There are charts available that tell you which are the best years and which years are so-so for quality wines. And remember, for most wines below the super-premium level, freshness—not age—is the key to optimum flavor. My vintage chart is on the tearout card in the front of this book.

One other decisive factor in vintage quality is whether a vineyard, variety, or the whole crop is picked in one fell swoop or whether the process is staggered, based on the peak ripeness of the vineyard, row, or single vine. For example, the vine's age makes a big difference. Young vines typically ripen early, producing a light "small" crop. Really old vines also produce small crops, but they take much longer to ripen. Average-age vines (7 to 25 years), not surprisingly, yield average-size crops.

All of this barely touches the surface of the intricate mechanisms involved in coming up with a great (or not-so-great) vintage. Even in so-called "great vintages," producers can make a mistake or two and the quality is below par. Fortunately, all you have to do is read a label.

The Least You Need to Know

➤ The aroma of a wine will give you a good idea of its taste. The aroma is one of the things that makes wine so enjoyable.

➤ The color of a wine can give you a clue about its condition.

➤ For high-quality wine, the vintage year is a sign of the wine's quality in that vintage; for most other wines (mid-premium and below), the vintage date is a sign of freshness and drinkability.

Keeping Your Wine Cache

Storing wine in your home, or "cellaring," is considered by many wine enthusiasts to be a vital part of wine serving and entertainment. You really don't need a castle or monastery or a deep dark hillside cavern (although if you should have one, you'll no doubt be the envy of your wine-loving friends). All you really need is a place that's away from direct sunlight, free of vibration, and has a temperature that does not fluctuate drastically over a short period of time. But wine racks or wine closets make the storage task easier to manage, and a beautiful assemblage of wine racks or a fine furniture wine closet is a beauty to behold. This chapter introduces you to the best methods for keeping your wines in good condition.

Do I Need a Wine Rack?

Whether or not you need a wine rack depends on your cellaring needs. Wine bottles must be stored lying on their sides to prevent the cork from drying out. This makes it difficult to keep your wine on a shelf or on top of a cabinet—you don't want your wines rolling around. If you prefer to keep only a few cases or bottles on hand for occasional use, there's no need to invest in elaborate storage units or racks. Many people keep a few bottles of wine on hand just so they won't have to go running to the local wine shop at the penultimate moment. Others begin that way, until one day they realize that wine bottles are taking over the bookcase and dresser. If you find yourself emerging carefully from your bed to avoid being assaulted by a protruding wine bottle, you know it's time for a special storage unit.

If you're still in the stage of short-term storage, the cardboard boxes or wooden cases the wines come in will serve sufficiently for storage units. Simply tilt them so that the wine is lying on its side. But beware—they are not made for stacking. If you try to stack them too high, the bottom row will collapse. Do you really want a stream of deep crimson leading a path from your living room?

Wine Racks

Wine racks hold wine bottles in the perfect "lying down" orientation, and come in a variety of sizes and structures and materials. There are inexpensive materials like white pine and expensive ones like clear Lucite and polished brass. Some designer-decorated homes boast of a "wine wall," a built-in rack that can cost up to several thousand dollars. The type of rack you choose will depend on your needs, taste, and budget. If you're thinking of going for glitter, remember this: If properly located away from bright light and heat, your wine rack will rarely be on public display.

Where to Buy Wine Racks

You can find wine racks in most department or houseware stores and, in states where wine dealers are allowed to sell merchandise in addition to alcoholic beverages, many wine stores offer a fine selection. There are also several wine accessory catalog companies that sell wine racks, wine rack wall units, and wine storage furniture by mail-order. Refer to Chapter 22 for details.

Wine Wisdom
When buying your wine rack, always check to see if it's sturdy, easy to assemble, and has openings large enough to house a Burgundy or Champagne bottle. Believe it or not, some wine racks are not made to accommodate the most popular bottle sizes. If your rack comes unassembled, you might want to check to see that the instructions are easy to follow and are in English.

What Kind of Wine Rack to Buy

Wine racks come in two basic configurations—the 12-bottle shelf and the much larger bookcase style. Unless you're really thinking of getting serious fast and you've got a lot of extra space, the bookcase style may be a bit much. Many small racks are very well-designed, and are easily stacked without danger of toppling. They fit easily into closets, on bookshelves, or in other convenient nooks, and they allow you to add on as needed.

Bookshelf-style wine racks come either with openings for single bottles or with square or diamond shaped ports that hold from six to a dozen bottles. You can find attractive models in fine furniture hardwoods, wrought iron, brass, chrome, or Lucite. The single-bottle models are generally more expensive. It's not necessary to splurge, but if you decide to pull out all the stops…well, why not?

> **Grape Alert**
> Be sure to check that the unit is stable and will not be top-heavy when fully loaded.

Wine Storage Vaults

If you really want to go all out, there are completely self-contained, temperature regulated wine cabinets that are like having your own private storage vault, the urban equivalent of a monk's cellar.

These storage vaults are available as fine furniture and come in a variety of styles, woods, and finishes. Prices range from several hundred dollars to several thousand. If you would like an impressive and attractive way to show off your wine collection, you should consider investing in one of these units.

Different models make use of different types of cooling units. Some use refrigerator units or air conditioners, which are unsuitable, while the best use state-of-the-art devices intended specifically for wine coolage. Since vibration is a serious enemy of your wine because it can prematurely age your wine, you should determine what cooling method is used and whether the manufacturer guarantees the unit to be vibration-free. You do not want your wine to be shaken up like a milkshake.

Another factor to consider is whether the bottles are stored in front of each other. In some models, you have to remove the front bottles first to get to the others. You may find it a real nuisance—or you may not.

The companies making storage units range from highly reputable manufacturers to fly-by-night operations. A number of years ago, one of the leading mail-order wine storage unit companies took off to points unknown with hundreds of thousands of dollars of wine lovers' money. Beware. Before buying, always consider the longevity of the firm, its reputation, its warranty, and whether they have local service agents in case of trouble.

Personally, I recommend buying an expensive unit only from a local department store, a reputable furniture store, decorator with a high profile, or one of the mail-order companies mentioned in Chapter 22. Buying from someone you trust will guarantee that your wine cellar stays user-friendly.

What Temperature Should I Store My Wine At?

Storing your wine at 55 degrees is often emphasized as essential (not necessarily so), but a uniform temperature is more important. The ideal temperature should not change by more than 10 degrees Fahrenheit in either direction over the course of a week or two.

Grape Alert
Extreme heat makes wine mature precociously and will deteriorate before it reaches its peak. A number of years ago when my apartment building's air conditioning failed during a 100 degree heat wave, my wines roasted for nearly a week. Champagne bottles exploded and most of the wines were ruined. But, some of the more sturdy Bordeaux and California Cabernet Sauvignon survived and were in good shape years later.

Wines can be stored at temperatures up to 65 or 70 degrees without damage, but fine wines do not develop their full potential if stored at too high a temperature. If your home has a fruit cellar, it might be ideal for storing your wine. Be careful when storing wine in your basement because the furnace might make it too hot. Check its temperature in the winter!

What if the Temperature Varies?

The general rule is that a cellar should be a constant 55 degrees. This is a good ideal to strive for, but if it's not practical for you, don't despair. As long as the changes in temperature are gradual and there are no extremes of heat and cold, your wines won't damage. If your storage conditions vary from, say 50 degrees in winter to a high of about 70 degrees in summer, you don't have to worry.

The Least You Need to Know

➤ You don't need a wine rack if you keep only a few wines.

➤ Wine racks should have holes large enough to accommodate a Champagne bottle.

➤ Wine should be stored at a cool temperature (55 degrees Fahrenheit or so), with the bottle lying on its side.

Part 2
Why Wine Is Wine

You can think of wine as a cross between a beverage, a food, and an experience. With Mother Nature assisted by skilled and dedicated winemakers, the seemingly simple process of fermentation produces a marvelous result, a multidimensional product with a unique identity and exquisite beauty.

In your quest to enhance your enjoyment of wine, you'll learn how to apply words like bouquet *and* aroma, breed *and* finesse. You'll discover a world where the scent of tar or rubber can coexist with berries, butter, roses and violets. You'll find yourself swirling and sniffing and even spitting—and being commended for your know-how instead of rebuked for what may seem to be bad manners. There are many ways to enjoy wine, and this part of the book will start you along on your journey.

Chapter 5

The Goût of Wine

In This Chapter

➤ Fermentation creates new and marvelous flavors not found in other beverages

➤ What makes a wine taste so good

➤ Taste and aftertaste

➤ Finesse and breed

➤ Matching wine with food basics

Adding alcohol to your grape juice won't turn it into wine. Grape juice is made up of simple flavors that stay simple. The process of fermentation makes wine a multi-dimensional product, intriguing and intricate, hence our title for this chapter—goût is derived from the French verb "goûter," which means (among other things) tasting, relishing, and enjoying. Many of the scents and flavors created by the transformation of grape juice into wine cannot be found anywhere else in nature. Wine writers try to describe wines by evoking comparison to various berries, bell peppers, leather (like a fine leather glove), chocolate, and so forth, but the flavors they are seeking to describe are unique to wine. Describing a wine is frequently like describing a banana—you have to taste it to know what it tastes like.

The Scents of Wine

Very often, what we call "taste" is actually our perception of a particular scent or scents that enter the olfactory canal through the mouth. In fact, we experience most flavors through our sense of smell. Think of the way food tastes when you have a cold. With a stuffed-up nose there's not much difference between your favorite chocolate chip cookies and the cardboard box they come in.

Allowing enough room in the glass to stick your nose halfway in while drinking is not just a neat trick used to sell bigger glasses. Of the more than 300 components of wine that have been identified, scientists believe at least 200 are odor-producing.

We detect smells through a complex of nerve endings called the olfactory bulb, which is located in the upper part of the nose. This little bulb is a very acute sensor. Its nerve endings get particularly sharp when air is inhaled, which is why wine should be sniffed in order to experience its full flavor.

Scientists have yet to tell us what handy mechanism allows us to experience the vast warehouse of scents and aromas we can sense. We do know that certain weak flavors can be detected despite the presence of a dominant one, or that certain substances can mask the smell of others. The olfactory sense also becomes used to a scent after it is experienced, and, after a short time, it loses its impact. As you progress in your wine-tasting and learn to pick out subtle aromas, all this will fall into place.

Premium and noble wines contain numerous aromatic and flavor compounds. These compounds are not usually present in jug or ordinary wines, and they contribute to the wine's character by providing its bouquet—an aromatic or perfumed scent. The finest wines contain myriad complex and often delicate nuances of flavor, making them comparable to fine works of art or music. Scientists are still trying to find out what makes this possible as the chemical compounds responsible frequently defy identification, even with sophisticated laboratory equipment. Wine is a thing of many wonders.

Taste and Aftertaste

You learned long ago in grade school that the primary organ of taste is the tongue. Of course, schools are not allowed to teach wine-tasting to children or to encourage kids to stick their noses in milk, but essentially, your teacher was right. The tongue has four specific areas that correspond to our four basic tastes: sweet, salt, bitter, and sour. The sweet sensation is strongest on the tip of the tongue, saltiness and sourness on the sides, and bitterness on the back. These tastes reach our brain through receptor cells inside the taste buds.

The taste buds themselves are contained within the papillae, those tiny cell-like structures that seem to pave our tongues. Sensations pass through the pores of these sensitive little cells and travel via nerve endings to the cortex of the brain. Not surprisingly, these nerves end very close to where the "smelling" nerves end. It's not difficult to see how the two processes of taste and smell are intertwined.

Two things govern the way our senses work when confronted with taste and aroma. The first, of course, is the character of the taste and scent. The second is our individual ability to perceive the taste and scent. Debates have been raging for years in wine circles over whether tasters are made or born. The answer is both. Some people do smell and taste things more acutely than others. For the most part, though, tasters are made. It's like learning to appreciate art. If you're not familiar with modern art and you see a Picasso for the first time, you may wonder why the eyes are in such a weird place or why those funny lines go through somebody's cheekbone. You may miss the subtleties of color and form entirely. But once you learn what to look for in a painting—how to really see what is on the canvas— it's like having a new pair of eyes (although maybe not eyes quite like Picasso's version).

Wine Wisdom

If wine classes are given in your locality or if there is a wine club or restaurant that conducts wine tastings, it would be a good idea to participate. You will have the opportunity to taste many wines with commentary by an expert who will describe each wine in the terms you need to learn. You will find your taste perception improving dramatically after only a few sessions.

Important Things to Know

HEY!

One wine book that was recently published describes which part of the tongue is responsible for discerning flavor, acidity, and so on, but suggests that because these receptors are either in the front or back, you should taste the various components in a progression like step one, step two. This is nonsense—when you taste a wine, all the taste and scent receptors are attacked at once—the wine does not slowly glide through your mouth like lava. Your perception of a wine is immediate, but you should concentrate on the attributes of a wine—its color, scent, and taste—in progression to appreciate a wine's full potential.

You've probably noticed that your ability to taste and smell isn't always the same. The most obvious blocker to getting your full flavor quotient is having a cold or allergy. Mood and mental state are two other factors. If you're even mildly fatigued, familiar objects like your briefcase or gym bag can feel a lot heavier. Images start swimming across the page or computer screen. It's the same thing with taste and smell, although you may not be as aware of it.

Most of us use metaphors that reflect the connection between mood and taste perception, although we usually don't give them much thought. For example, if you're feeling sad or depressed you might say, "Food doesn't taste the same anymore." It's not just a figure of speech—your taste buds are just feeling like the rest of you. The company you're with also has its effect. You can try your own taste test the next time you have dinner over at the house of those relatives you don't like.

Hopefully, the idea of tasting wine will put you in a good mood that will wake your taste buds up to peak performance and you'll enjoy the company of your tasting partners.

To get the full flavor of the wine, you should approach the tasting process with an open mind. Remember, taste is an individual thing. If you read the tasting notes of three wine experts, you may think they've all been sipping different bottles. Only the color is agreed upon—and that's not always the case either. Just because someone waves their glass at you excitedly saying, "Ah! The outdoors! This wine tastes of fresh leaves and wild flowers!" doesn't mean you're a philistine because you can't taste a single daisy. People's perceptions are different.

On the other hand, wine tasting is not totally a free-association process, and the outdoorsy flavors are not entirely on the taste buds of the beholder. Listening to an experienced taster describe the wine you are drinking can help you discover more of your own tasting capacity.

Fresh leaves and wild flowers actually are often associated with wine. So are raspberries, ripe cherries, cinnamon, sage, and rosés. When the flavor is less distinct, you might just say it tastes "fruity." It's a positive quality, although not a particularly sharp one.

A good wine is characterized by continuity. Your taste buds confirm what your nose has alluded to, and you experience a lingering aftertaste when you swallow. The aftertaste or finish may be fleeting or barely perceptible, or it may evoke a whole new vocabulary of adjectives. Most often, the aftertaste will add new perceptions of taste that didn't seem to be there when the wine was still in your mouth. The following are qualities you should look for when savoring a wine.

Body

The body is the fullness (or lack of) that you feel when you roll the wine over your tongue and palate. Body is the product of the wine's alcohol, glycerin, and extract. It is either light, moderate, or full, and may or may not be in balance with the flavor and other constituents.

Viscosity

No, we are not talking about motor oil. A wine characterized by viscosity is thicker, fuller, and has a heavier body than the average wine. The term to use for a full-bodied wine high in alcohol and glycerin, and with more flavor than acidity is "fat." A wine with viscosity will frequently display "legs," formed by wine clinging to the side of the glass.

Acidity

Acidity refers to the non-volatile acids in wine, which are principally tartaric, malic, and citric. These acids provide the wine with a sense of freshness and (hopefully) balance.

Sufficient acidity gives a wine firm body, while lack of acidity may make it feel "flabby." (And no, despite what you'd like to hear, drinking acidic wines will not provide firmness for flabby thighs and abdomens.)

Balance

Balance refers to the proportion of the various elements of a wine in relation to one another. For example, acid against sweetness, fruit flavors against wood, and tannic alcohol against acid and flavor.

When all the components are working together, like the instruments in a world-class orchestra, the wine is balanced. Harmonious is the prime adjective of choice. When wines are imbalanced, they may be acetic, cloying, flat or flabby, or even awkward. Ever wonder why negative descriptions always outweigh the good ones? Many wine writers compare a wine to their vision of perfection rather than appreciate the wine for what it offers. Don't fall into that trap.

Backbone

The backbone is the structural framework of a wine provided by the alcohol, acids, and tannins. A wine with good backbone leaves a positive impression on the taste buds and olfactory sense.

Mouthfeel

The mouthfeel of the wine is its texture, while body is the wine's weight or viscosity. Never neglect to savor it fully, rolling the wine over your mouth. And if the tasting environment permits, don't forget your gurgling. The texture and feel of the wine in the mouth is part of the beauty that makes wine so exciting. Overall, the adjectives used to describe mouthfeel are tactile (the same ones you use to describe textures): silky, velvety, rough, coarse, or smooth. The one exception to this rule is the "pucker" of tannic red wines. The puckering quality may seem strange at first, but as your wine tasting experience progresses, certain wines will seem flat or dull without it.

Harmony

Harmony refers to the interplay of the wine's constituents. Harmony means smooth, flowing, and compatible. When everything is in sync, the result is a balanced wine.

Finesse and Breed

These are two descriptors that speak for themselves, like Katherine Hepburn and Cary Grant emanating from your wine cellar. If you can't think of a contemporary star who measures up, don't worry about it. Wines with breed and finesse are the loveliest, most harmonious, and refined wines. The classics. These are the wines that age gracefully and wondrously. Finesse and breed are not usually the qualities of mid-premium or lesser wines. Wines with breed and finesse are those rare noble wines in which all elements of structure, flavor, and complexity combine to a peak of almost indescribable perfection. For these noble beauties, fermentation is merely the beginning of a long life culminating in a wine comparable to the finest work of art.

It's hard to speak of finesse and breed without throwing in at least a touch of romanticism. Technically, finesse is the quality of elegance that separates a fine wine from one which is simply good. Breed goes up even higher. Breed is the term we use to describe wines that achieve "classical proportions." It's star quality at its utmost. The quality is usually elusive to describe, but you'll know it the moment you experience it. Noble wines such as Chateau Lafite-Rothschild, Chateau Y'quem or the legendary Burgundy, La Tâche, have finesse and breed.

Matching Wine with Food—A First Look

Now that we know what to look for in a wine, the next step is to know how to match wine with food. The following is a first look—for a more complete discussion, see Chapter 25.

So Rosé Doesn't Go with Everything

When it comes to rosés, there are two extreme ends of the advice spectrum. There are the marketing experts who claim that rosé goes with everything. Then there are the snobs who claim that rosé is passé—don't listen to either of them.

As in most situations, it's best to ignore the extremists on both sides. Because the grape skin contact in making rosés is minimal, they don't have the tannic quality that makes red wines heavier and harder to match with foods (and sometimes harder to drink on their own) than whites. Like white wines, rosés are drunk chilled and make a good summer beverage. They can be great for barbecues and outdoor parties. Most rosé fans recommend them with the same dishes you usually pair up with light white wines.

Things like fish or seafood, or vegetarian favorites, go well with rosés. A good dry rosé, like a French Tavel, goes beautifully with ham, white meat, and poultry dishes as well as Asian foods.

Important Things to Know

Rosés are light wines in taste as well as color. They're thoroughly over-powered by steaks, chops, and roasts. They may not be the best match for very sweet or salted tidbits, or anything too assertive in taste. Think of the foods you tend to enjoy in warmer weather, and chances are, you'll be able to come up with some good matches for rosé.

What About Whites?

Contrary to popular assumption, white wines are actually a varied lot. They range from pale and delicate young wines, which are in danger of being overpowered if your chef salad has too much Roquefort dressing, to tawny grandes dames (or grands hommes) that can give any red a run for its vintage.

Wine Wisdom

White wines are usually served chilled, and virtually any white wine you enjoy will taste fine all by itself. Whites are excellent with dishes served in cream sauce if that's your style.

And the Reds?

All right, I admit it. The best way to impress people with your wine expertise is still the tried-and-true method of showing them how well you can choose the perfect red wine for dinner. With their influence on the tannic taste buds, red wines can be tricky critters. The finest red wine without a proper pairing can make your cheeks hollow in seconds.

Important Things to Know

HEY!

Reds that are high in tannins are perfect with high-protein foods like beef or cheese. A well-chosen red wine is a superb complement to a cheese platter (equally well-chosen). In general you'll want to avoid sweet or excessively salty foods, which tend to make tannic wines taste even more tannic. Remember, most red wines are best served slightly cooler than room temperature.

Light young reds like Beaujolais Nouveau (serve this wine chilled) are a good choice with the same type of foods you'd usually pair with white wine. This is a handy thing to know if you have a guest with an allergy to white wines (white wines contain more sulfites than reds, and some people have an unusual sensitivity) or one who simply prefers red.

The Least You Need to Know

➤ Wine's unique flavors are a by-product of fermentation.

➤ The important characteristics of wine that you should look for in its taste and aftertaste include body, viscosity, acidity, balance, backbone, mouthfeel, and finesse.

➤ Some foods go best with white wines; others best with reds. Rosé wines do not go with everything.

Grape Varieties

Of those 8,000 grape varieties, a select few are now on display at your local wine shop. That's good because it gives you less wine names to memorize. But don't get too complacent—there are still many grape varieties to consider. While many of these grapes became famous by turning up in the right place—that is, in a famous wine named after a wine place name, such as Corton-Charlemagne—they became popular in their own right, and appear on wine bottles named as varietal wines. White grapes are listed here first, then reds. It's not an order of rank or preference, just a convenience.

The Most Popular White Grape Varieties

Most white wines are made from white grapes. There are hundreds of white grape varieties that are made into wine, but only a handful are seen on wine labels as varietal wines. This section reviews some of the most popular.

Chardonnay

Chardonnay is the haute varietal of the white wine grapes. It is known as the king of white grape varieties. Power and finesse are two qualities of this white vinifera, which yields the world's finest white wines.

In northern Burgundy, Chardonnay is responsible for Chablis. It's also the key player in many wines from Champagne, especially those called "Blancs de Blancs," which are made entirely from white grapes. Some people call Chardonnay the "Champagne grape." It's accurate on two levels: Chardonnay is the primary grape variety in the finest Champagnes, and both Chardonnay and Champagne are names that evoke images of high quality.

Wine Words

The grape variety is technically known as a *cultivar*. You'll see this term frequently in wine literature. Its a fancy name meaning a specific vine variety or clone. A *clone* is a grapevine that has been produced by grafting to retain the genetic characteristics of the mother vine.

In California, the styles of Chardonnay vary widely. Some made from ripe grapes are fermented and aged in French oak barrels to yield round, rich wines—flavorful, powerful, and oily in texture. Others approximate the same style to a lesser degree. A few non-oak versions capture the direct fruitiness of the Chardonnay in a crisp style. Most California Chardonnays tend to be fuller in body and higher in alcohol than their French cousins.

It's impossible to discuss Chardonnay without mentioning oak. Most Chardonnay receives a restful yet invigorating treatment in an oak bath. The best Chardonnays get their spa treatment inside the traditional French oak barrel. Less expensive wines have to be content with soaking in oak chips or in liquid essence of oak.

The flavors imparted by oak have a vanilla, smoky, spicy, or nutty character. That's easy to associate—they're all woodsy qualities. The Chardonnay flavors and scents are rich and fruity. You can name any fruit you like, from apples to mangoes, and chances are you'll taste at least a hint of it in a cool glass of Chardonnay.

HEY! Important Things to Know

Chardonnay grows successfully in many different countries, but it is synonymous with the celebrated white wines from France's Cote d'Or region of Burgundy. There, it's identified with such legendary names as Montrachet, Meursault, and Corton-Charlemagne. If these sound like the sites of ancient battles, they'll become more familiar to you as your wine knowledge grows.

Pinot Grigio (Pinot Gris)

Pinot Grigio, or Pinot Gris, is a white vinifera, related to the Pinot Noir. It's known as the Tokay in Alsace, and the Rulander in Germany.

The skin of Pinot Grigio is strikingly dark for a white variety, and some of its wines are unusually deep in color. They're medium- to full-bodied, somewhat neutral in flavor and low in acidity when well made. When picked before fully ripe they can be high in acidity and undistinguished. Often dismissed as without distinction, some Pinot Grigios from Italy are beginning to take center stage. Pinot Grigio wines are inexpensive and, when well made, are easy to drink.

Northeastern Italy is the primary stomping ground for this grape. It's grown in small quantities in the U.S., mainly in Oregon, although it's becoming more popular in California.

Sauvignon Blanc

Sauvignon Blanc is an adaptive white vinifera. It's a fairly productive grape that ripens in mid-season. Harvested at full maturity, it offers wines with a characteristic herbaceous, sometimes peppery aroma. Picked early, the grape is intensely grassy (and yes, that can be a compliment, although it isn't always).

In France, Sauvignon Blanc is the important grape of the Loire Valley wines from Sancerre to Pouilly-Fumé, and a major component in Sauternes from south of Bordeaux. The grape provides backbone and flavor to the luscious, sweet wines of Sauternes and Barsac.

White Graves and Pessac-Leognan wines of Bordeaux are primarily Sauvignon Blanc. They range in style from dry to semisweet and are usually mediocre quality, although some are of exceptional quality. As the Bordeaulais learn to make better white wines, you will see more and more good wines from this region.

Sauvignon Blanc is higher in acidity than Chardonnay. Some wine lovers savor its crispness; others prefer Chardonnay. Sauvignon Blanc wines are light- to medium-bodied and generally dry. The European varieties are largely unoaked. The California versions are usually oaked. Maybe Californians just like to experiment. California Sauvignon Blancs range from dry to slightly sweet. "Fumé Blanc" is a popular varietal label.

Grape Alert
Wines labeled White Riesling or Johannisberg Riesling may be made from the noble grapes of Germany—or they may not. When buying a Riesling wine, be sure to read the label thoroughly and pay careful attention to the fine print as to what country it was produced in.

Riesling

If Chardonnay is the king of white grape varieties, Riesling is its queen. Riesling is a white vinifera variety that gained its ranking among noble grapes through the great Riesling wines of Germany. Unfortunately, the name has suffered a lot of misuse on wine labels.

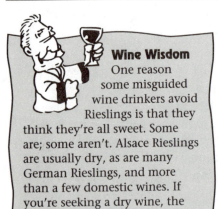

The noble grape is the Johannisberg Riesling; Gray Riesling and Silvaner Riesling wines are actually made from lesser grapes. To add additional insult, vast quantities of simple jug wines from South Africa and Australia are designated as "Rieslings," although they bear little resemblance to the fine wines of the Rhine.

Riesling does thrive in a few places outside of Germany, notably Alsace in northeastern France (near Germany), Washington state, and the Finger Lakes district of New York. Quality varies, so be sure to use caution here as well.

Riesling wines are currently off the popularity charts, but they are often good values and I urge you to try them. Oaky is in these days, but Rieslings refuse to be oaked. An oaked Riesling would taste awful. They're lighter in body than Chardonnay, but light can be refreshing and equally satisfying to the palate. Overall, Rieslings are high in acidity, low to medium in alcohol content, and have a fruity or flowery taste and scent that is distinctively Riesling.

German Rieslings come in a variety of styles, all with their own levels of dryness, aromas, and flavors. If you're looking for a top-quality dessert wine, a fine German late-harvest Riesling is the perfect choice.

Gewürztraminer

Gewürztraminer (ga-VERTZ-tra-mee-ner) wines are a lot easier to drink than pronounce. The grape is a clonal selection of the once widely planted traminer white vinifera. Its name literally means "spicy grape from Traminer."

Gewürztraminer wines have recently gained in stature, due to their distinctive appearance and taste. The wines are deep gold in color, with the spicy aroma of roses and lychee fruit. They're exotic and intriguing. The scent is spicy, floral, and fruity, the flavor surprisingly dry.

The Gewürztraminer grape tends to be high sugar, low acid. The result is a soft wine with a high alcohol content. However, Gewürztraminer wines also have high extract (essentially, the solid matter of the wine left after you boil off the water and alcohol), which counteracts the feeling of softness. In short, the high extract adds substance and verve and keeps the wine from being flabby.

The most distinctive examples of Gewürztraminer come from Alsace. U.S. styles tend to be lighter and sweeter than their Alsatian counterparts, but dry Gewürztraminers are produced in California and Oregon.

Chenin Blanc

This noble white grape originally hails from the Loire Valley in France, where it is used both for still wine and vin mousseux (sparkling wines). It's also popular in California, Australia, South Africa, and South America.

Chenin Blanc is a fruity wine ranging from bone dry to slightly and even very sweet. The best sweet versions come from the Côteaux du Layon and Vouvray in France, and occasionally rise to legendary quality. Wines of the highest quality have high acidity and an unusual oily texture, age to a beautiful deep gold color, and can last for 50 years or more. The aroma is typically reminiscent of fresh peaches; when harvested early, it's slightly grassy and herbaceous.

Müller-Thurgau

Müller-Thurgau is Germany's most often planted white vinifera, although its heritage is uncertain. It may be a cross between Riesling and Sylvaner or between two clones of Riesling. It ripens earlier than the Rieslings, which gives it an edge in cool climates. The wine is fragrant, soft, and round and may lack character.

Muscat

The Muscat family includes Muscat Blanc, Moscato, Muscadelle, and Muscat of Alexandria. All are white grape varieties with a unique, easily recognizable aroma—pungent, musky, piney, and spicy. The Muscat Blanc offers the best potential for winemakers, although all varieties have been made into table, sparkling, and fortified wines. Muscat is used for Italy's sparkling Asti, which tastes just like the ripe grape itself.

The Muscat character ranges from subtle to overpowering, depending on growing conditions and winemaking. The styles range from dry to very sweet. Alsatian Muscat is a light, dry, pleasant wine, and California produces some appealing semisweet table wines.

Unfortunately, the Muscat family name has gotten bad press from its association with Muscatel, a cheap fortified wine usually consumed specifically for its high alcohol content. Most of the styles you'll find in your wine shop bear little resemblance to this nefarious brew. Muscat wines are low in acidity and have a perfumed, floral aroma ranging from spicy to evergreen, and an inherent bitterness often countered by sweetness.

Pinot Blanc

Pinot Blanc, the white variant of the noble Pinot Noir, is grown in many regions. Its main production is in Burgundy, Alsace, Italy, Germany, Austria, and California. In Germany, it's called Weissburgunder, and in Italy it goes by Pinot Bianco or Pinot d'Alba.

The better versions present a spicy fruit, hard, high acid, almost tart profile that demands some cellaring. In California, it is used by many wineries as a sparkling wine blender. As an early ripener and very shy bearer, the grape has lost out in competition with Chardonnay.

Semillon

Semillon is the blending partner of Sauvignon Blanc in the sweet wines from Sauternes. Grown throughout the wine world, it is always the bridesmaid—its main role is as a blender. It is relatively low in acid and has appealing but subtle aromas. It can have the scent of lanolin or smell mildly herbaceous when young. It yields Sauternes-like wines in South Africa and pleasant, dry wines in South American countries. The Australian versions range from dry to semisweet and are often labeled "Rieslings." In California, the wines are finished sweet and are blended into generics.

Trebbiano

This white vinifera is widely grown in Central Italy. It ripens late, is very productive, and derives its importance from its role in making Soave, Orvieto, and other popular Italian white wines. In France it is called Ugni Blanc or St.-Emilion and is favored for Cognac production. Characteristics are high acidity, low sugar, light body, and neutral aromas.

Viognier

Native to the Rhône Valley of France, this grape is a shy bearer, which limits its production. The wines are marked by a spicy, floral aroma, similar to melons, apricots, and peaches. It is medium- to full-bodied with low acidity. Viognier grapes have recently interested California winemakers, but so far quantities have been limited.

The Most Popular Reds

As with white wines, there are hundreds of red wine grape varieties. Similarly, only a handful appear on wine labels as varietal names. The following section will introduce you to the most popular red grape varieties.

Cabernet Sauvignon

Cabernet Sauvignon is the red counterpart to the royal Chardonnay. It's the reigning monarch of the red vinifera. Ideally, Cabernet Sauvignon wines offer great depth of flavor and intensity of color, and develop finesse and breed with bottle aging.

Important Things to Know

HEY!

The red royal grows well in many wine regions, yielding wines that range from outstanding to mediocre in quality (after all, the grape is not solely responsible for the outcome). In France, Cabernet Sauvignon takes the credit for the grand reputation of Bordeaux red wines. It's the prime element in many of the finest bottlings. In northern Italy, it can yield reasonable facsimiles of Bordeaux. Cabernet also grows in many eastern European countries, where it is made into pleasant, light-style wines.

Cabernet is one émigré that thrives in the California sunshine. Some of its California bottlings are on par with Bordeaux, with a few attaining noble quality. Other California Cabernets run the entire quality spectrum. South American countries, particularly Chile and Argentina, produce Cabernet in vast quantities, but quality can be shaky.

Cabernet Sauvignon is a versatile vinifera that works well by itself and in the company of other grapes. It's at its best and longest-lived when made with close to 100 percent Cabernet grapes, but it has an affinity for blending with other wines. A few of its favored companions are Cabernet Franc, Merlot, Malbec, and Petit Verdot in the Médoc, Merlot and sometimes Zinfandel in California, and Shiraz in Australia.

Grape Alert

In the mind of many wine lovers, Cabernet Sauvignon may be synonymous with quality, but things can be different in the real world. The least expensive varieties can lack the firmness of the better-quality wines, and the fruitiness may be devoid of the true Cabernet pungency.

Cabernet Sauvignon wines are high in tannin and medium- to full-bodied. Their distinctive varietal character is a spicy, bell pepper aroma and flavor with high astringency. Deeply colored wines made from very ripe grapes are often minty and cedary, with a black currant or cassis character.

Merlot

This French variety red vinifera is grown in many wine regions. It is an early ripening, medium-colored red grape. As a varietal, it makes wines that are soft and subtle, yet substantial (say that very fast while swooshing the wine in your mouth). The finest Merlots possess great depth, complexity, and longevity.

Merlot has a distinctive, herbaceous aroma quite different from the bell pepper quality of the Cabernet. It is softer in tannins and usually lower in acidity, producing a rounder, fatter, and earlier maturing wine.

The very qualities that make Merlot less powerful than Cabernet Sauvignon make it more palatable for some wine drinkers. Don't be intimidated by wine snobs. Merlot is easier to drink by itself and it goes well with lighter foods.

Important Things to Know

HEY!

In the Médoc and other regions of Bordeaux, Merlot is used as an elegant and mellowing component in Cabernet Sauvignon. In the St.-Emilion and Pomerol regions of Bordeaux, Merlot is the star, usually comprising 60–80 percent of the blend, and produces complex, velvety, and sometimes frightfully expensive wines. In California, Italy, Chile, and elsewhere, an increasing number of wineries are producing varietal Merlots, but it is used primarily as a blending agent with the more powerful Cabernet. In California terminology, Merlot is the best supporting actor. Cabernet Sauvignon is still the big box office draw.

Pinot Noir

Pinot Noir is one of the noblest of all wine grapes. It is grown throughout the wine world, but success varies due to its sensitivity to soil, climate, and the clonal variant of the vine. This is one temperamental vinifera!

Important Things to Know

HEY!

In France, Pinot Noir is the principal red grape of the Côte d'Or region of Burgundy, where it produces some of the world's most celebrated and costly wines. With the exception of Blanc de Blanc, it is used as a base for all Champagnes and is admired for body and elegance.

Pinot Noir grows best in well-drained chalky or clay soils and cool climates. Happily ensconced in clay, it produces wines that often go on to a long aging process and are replete with complex fragrances resembling violets, roses, truffles, or other intricate scents. Under less ideal conditions, its wines have a distinctive grapiness, which is still appealing. Under poor conditions, it produces coarse, undistinguished, frequently thin and acidic wines unworthy of varietal bottling. (I said it was temperamental.)

Until fairly recently, winemakers believed that Pinot Noir would remain a true French patriot, giving its best only under the banner of the tricolor. However, a handful of wineries in the U.S. (California, Oregon, Washington, and New York), Australia, South Africa, and Italy have shown that with the proper selection of the vine's clones, exacting care in the vineyards, and appropriate winemaking techniques, the variety can be grown to rival its French counterparts.

In Switzerland, Pinot Noir is grown in Valais and produces a wine called Dole, which is full-bodied and rich and has some aging potential. In Germany, it is known as Spätburgunder or Rotclevner and yields only thin and acidic red wines of little distinction. Maybe it doesn't like its Germanic names. In northern Italy it produces wines with verve and aging potential. In Hungary, Romania, and South America, it yields medium- to full-bodied wines, simple and direct for jug wine consumption.

Zinfandel

Zinfandel is a red vinifera that is grown commercially only in California, an interesting sort of status. It is related to an Italian grape, but with no French heritage whatsoever, it is exempt from the unfair comparisons many fine California wines have to endure.

Although not as finicky as Pinot Noir, Zinfandel is sensitive to climate and location. It tends to raisin in hot climates and overproduce in others (quantity and quality go in inverse proportion). The wines range from thin jug wine quality to wines intensely rich in flavor, heavy-bodied with tannins and extract. The typical character is berrylike—blackberry or raspberry—with a hint of spiciness. Styles vary from light and young to heavy, syrupy, and late harvest. The current trend favors heady wines that are warm, tannic, and rich in flavor, and call out for some cellaring.

Even more popular than a full-bodied red Zinfandel in today's market is the blush wine known as White Zinfandel. Skin contact for white Zinfandels is very minimal; in contrast, Zinfandel reds have a rich, deep color.

Syrah/Shiraz

Syrah traces its origin back to the days of the Roman and Greek Empires. Its ancestral home is the northern part of the Rhône Valley, where it is used to make the full-bodied, deeply-colored, powerful, long-lived wines from the Côte Rôtie, Chateauneuf-du-Pape, and Hermitage regions. In Australia, where it's known as the Shiraz or Hermitage grape, it yields potent wines that are often blended with Cabernet. The Syrah is also responsible for South Africa's finest red wines. This is one grape variety where California is lagging behind. So far, it has had only small success with this shy-bearing, mid-season ripener.

Syrah's firm and full-bodied wines have aromas and flavors that suggest roasted peppers (á la Cabernet Sauvignon), smoked meat, tar, and even burnt rubber (as I mentioned before, some wine scents are just plain strange). Some of the Australian varieties are softer, less full-bodied, and more berrylike than the archetype Syrah.

Nebbiolo

Nebbiolo is the pride of Italy's Piedmont region. Their pride is well-earned; the red vinifera is sensitive to subtle changes in climate and soil and grows well in few places. It reaches its peak in the rich, aged wines of Barolo, Barbaresco, and Gattinara (in some districts it is known as Spanna).

Most Piedmont versions share a deep color and full body. They have a distinctive fragrance of violets, truffles, or earthiness, sometimes with a hint of tar. Some are herbaceous, and the young wines have a fruity aroma.

Sangiovese

Sangiovese is the principal grape variety used to make Chianti and several other red wines from Tuscany. A small-berry variant called Brunello is used in Brunello di Montalcino wines.

The wines have moderate to high acidity and are moderately tannic. They can be light- to full-bodied, depending on the exact location of origin and the winemaking style. The aromas and flavors are fruity, particularly cherry, with a subtle hint of violets. Sometimes they have a slight nuttiness. Basically, their style is direct and simple, but Chianti Riservas and Brunello di Montalcino can be complex and ageworthy.

Tempranillo

Tempranillo is a Spanish vinifera. Its wines have low acidity and moderate alcohol. The grape itself has a deep color, but this is often masked by long wood aging and blending with lighter varieties like Grenache as in many Rioja wines.

Aglianico

Indigenous to southern Italy, this little known grape is used to make Taurasi and other powerful red wines that demand cellaring.

Barbera

Barbera is grown primarily in Italy and California. In many Italian districts it is bottled as a varietal identified by a place name (for example, Barbera d'Asti). Depending on the growing conditions and the location, the Italian versions range from pleasantly fruity to slightly rich and tart in flavor. In California, the plantings are primarily in warm to hot regions, with the resulting wines fruity and soft. They are usually intended for blending into jug wines, but every now and then a robust, rough, rich wine emerges. The current trend is to age the wine in new oak to increase the tannin level and enhance crispness.

Gamay

Gamay reaches its peak in the Beaujolais district of France. It's also grown in California, where it is known as Napa Gamay. (There is a Gamay Beaujolais grown in California, but this is believed to be a clone of Pinot Noir.) Gamay has been traditionally banned in most of Burgundy by a royal edict from centuries ago, but it thrives in Beaujolais where it produces light, delightfully fresh and fruity wines for immediate consumption. In its nouveau style, it yields a fresh, fruity wine with strawberry or raspberry flavors. Check out the wine shops in late fall; you'll see signs announcing the arrival of Beaujolais Nouveau on November 15th.

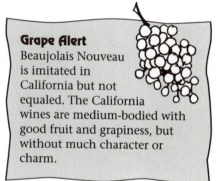

Grape Alert
Beaujolais Nouveau is imitated in California but not equaled. The California wines are medium-bodied with good fruit and grapiness, but without much character or charm.

Grenache

Grenache is Spanish by heritage, but most often identified with France's Rhône Valley, where it yields full-bodied rosés and fruity reds ranging from simple Côtes-du-Rhône to magnificent Châteauneuf-du-Pape. In Spain, it is known as Garnacha, and is one of the many varieties blended to make Rioja.

The grape has a distinctive orange color and a fruity, strawberry flavor that makes it ideal for rosés and blending. A prime example is Tavel, a rosé produced in the Rhône Valley. At its best, it is full-bodied, assertive, dry, and bronze-colored. Grenache is used as a blending variety in Châteauneuf-du-Pape, Gigondas, and Côtes du Rhône, the well-known reds of the Rhône. It also produces some full-bodied, fruity reds and stylish rosés in the Languedoc and Provence regions. It thrives in hot climates, and is found in many wine regions throughout the world, where it is blended into generic reds and rosés.

The Least You Need to Know

➤ The most popular white grape varieties are Chardonnay, Sauvignon Blanc, and Riesling.

➤ The most popular red grape varieties are Cabernet Sauvignon, Pinot Noir, Merlot, and Zinfandel.

Chapter 7

Stomp Your Feet—We're Making Wine Here

> **In This Chapter**
>
> ➤ How wine is made
>
> ➤ How winemakers adjust the taste
>
> ➤ Wine flaws you can taste in the glass

Unless you plan to be actively involved in reading wine magazines or advanced books on wine, you really don't need to know how wine is made. But aren't you just a bit curious? Things have progressed considerably since workers took off their shoes, rolled up their pant legs or hiked up their skirts, and climbed into a vat of grapes. The winemaking process today is less picturesque, but it's a lot more sterile and quality control has improved a great deal.

Once again, the three key factors that interact to determine the character of a wine are 1) the grape variety and how it is grown, 2) the climate and soil in which it is grown, and 3) the vintner's (winemaker's) intent and expertise in making the wine.

In this chapter, you'll see the tricky relationship between the grape, the climate and soil, and the humans trying to figure them out.

The Grape Calls the Shots

Each grape variety has its own exacting requirements. The key to it all is picking the grapes when they have developed the target level of sugar, acidity, and flavor for the type of wine being made.

As grapes begin heading toward maturity, the three components undergo relatively rapid changes. In warm winegrowing regions, the prime concern is the changing sugar/acidity ratio. Ideally, that means seeking good sugar without losing the necessary acidity. In the coolest winegrowing regions, the vintners are more preoccupied with achieving the desired sugar and flavor ripeness. Too often, grapes grown in cool climates ripen with inadequate sugar levels. Fortunately, this can be corrected; we'll get to that later.

Grapes signal their ripeness by changes in composition, with sugar levels increasing and acidity falling when the grape is ready. A few varieties, such as Gewürztraminer and Sauvignon Blanc, are flavor-mature within a narrow range of sugar development. When picked too late or too early, the grapes lack their distinctive character. This can occur within a matter of hours, so the winemaker has to be sharp.

HEY! Important Things to Know

Even within the same vineyard, grapes may vary in maturity due to differences in the direction of the slope of the vineyard in relation to the sun, soil type, depth, fertility, and water penetration. Therefore, it's crucial that the vintner test the grapes in every part of the vineyard. The instrument for this task is a refractometer. With this handy gadget, the vintner walks through the vineyard and measures the sugar content of the grapes on the vine. Today's sugar is tomorrow's alcohol. The sugar is expressed in terms of degrees Brix. Depending on the desired outcome, acceptable degrees of ripeness range from 17 to 25 degrees Brix.

The grape consists of various parts, each of which contribute to the final wine.

➤ Stems comprise two to six percent of the cluster's weight. They are rich in wood tannins, but they can also leave the wines with a bitter flavor. For most wines, the stems are removed prior to fermentation, but they are left in for some wines to augment the tannins and add complexity to the flavor.

➤ Skin represents about 5 to 16 percent of the grape's weight. When mature, the skin is covered with a bloom of wild yeasts that is sometimes used for fermentation. The skin and the layers just below it contain most of the aromatic and flavor constituents of the grape. They also contain the grape tannins. In this case, there's a distinction between tannins: The ones found in the skin tend to be softer and less bitter than the ones in the stems and pits. Grape tannins are the essential element of red wines intended for aging.

➤ Pulp, which contains the juice in a fibrous membrane, comprises most of the grape's weight. Think of a cocoon. The juice consists of the ever-changing proportions of water, sugar, and acid. Within the pulp, the membrane responds to the changing needs of the juice. It gets filled or depleted as the grape vine responds to its environment.

The sugar in the grape can drop drastically if it is needed to support the vine. It may end up being diluted if the vine receives too much moisture. This is where soil and climatic conditions are critical.

The pulp also contains a number of complex fruit acids that undergo chemical changes—along with glycerins, proteins, and other elements that may or may not be desired by the winemaker. In the end, the pulp presents the winemaker with a serious concern. All of it must be removed to get only clear, clean wine.

Thanks to advances in technology, grapes can be harvested and transported to the winery with a minimum of damage. Hand-picking is still practiced by the highest quality producers, but more and more frequently, giant machines resembling praying mantises work night and day in the vineyards to harvest grapes at their peak. (Not a bad idea for a sci-fi flick, actually—they really do look like giant insects.)

The machines sometimes work in tandem with portable crushers. The juice, crushed in the vineyard, is sent to the winery protected by a thick film of carbon dioxide to prevent premature fermentation and oxidation. However the grapes are harvested, the trick is to transport them to the winery as quickly as possible. Those quirky wine-bearers begin to deteriorate as soon as they leave the vine.

Wine Wisdom
Many high-quality white wines begin as unfermented juice left in contact with the skins for anywhere from a few hours to a day or two. Red wines—which ferment in contact with the skins—occasionally remain on the skins after fermentation is finished in order to leach out more tannins, color, and flavors. This is the celebrated skin contact, one of those strange-sounding wine terms.

The Winemaker (Vintner): Artist and Scientist

The winemakers begin working as soon as they have the grapes in their hands. In the simplest terms, the grapes are picked and then dumped into a crusher/stemmer where the stems are removed and, for white wine, put directly into a wine press where the juice is extracted and the skins separated. The juice, called must, is pumped into a tank or vat.

There it ferments on its wild yeasts—or more likely with modern winemaking, the winemaker inoculates it with a selected yeast strain because each yeast has particular characteristics of fermentation and the flavors it leaves behind. The yeast enzymes react with the sugar, producing alcohol and carbon dioxide. Often, there's an additional element—minute quantities of highly aromatic compounds that may or may not be pleasing. During fermentation, the liquid in the vats is called "must." After fermentation, the transformed juice is called wine. The wine is stored in either casks or tanks. Finally, it is clarified, stabilized, and ultimately, bottled.

All winemakers wish it was that simple.

Crushing and Stemming: Red, White, and Rosé

The juice of most grapes is white, which is why we can make white wine from red grapes. The red wine gets its color from the pigmentation lodged within the skins, but only during skin contact. For most white wines, the must is separated from the skins immediately after crushing. However, the skins can add bitterness (not necessarily a bad thing) and sometimes tannins to white wine. Depending on the type of wine being made, the winemaker may favor some skin contact prior to fermentation.

Dark-skinned grapes are used to make full-bodied Champagnes and the still white table wines called Blanc de Noirs. The vintner moderates the color by separating the must from the skins at first blush.

For red wines, the skins remain with the juice and go with it into the fermentation vessel. During the fermentation process, both color and tannins are leached from the skins. Sometimes the stems also remain with the must, and some winemakers will even add a percentage of stems back to the wine. The purpose of this act is to enhance the firmness and complexity of certain red wines.

Rosé wines remain with the skins just long enough to pick up the required tinge. Then they're vinified in much the same way as white wines.

Lights, Camera, Fermentation

During fermentation, winemakers perform both as scientists and creative artists. For most jug wines, the vintners are basically manufacturers. But for distinctive, quality wines, they get to be film directors, molding their characters and shooting their scenes until they have a full-scale artistic work.

Unfortunately, they don't get to re-take the bad scenes, which sadly often make it to market.

In essence, the winemaker directs a wine, molds its structure, flavors, nuances, and character to correspond to a personal vision, and produces a vinous work of art. The process of fermentation is like a fickle audience that determines its chances for success and failure.

Important Things to Know

Alcoholic fermentation is the reaction between yeast and sugar that creates alcohol and carbon dioxide. It's a complex chemical reaction involving numerous stages. In its simplest form, the chemical equation looks like this:

$$C_6H_{12}O_6 = 2C_2H_5OH + 2CO_2 + HEAT$$

| natural grape sugar | = ethyl alcohol | + carbon dioxide gas |

The vintner's greatest concern is healthy fermentation. Certain yeasts are good for wine, while others can turn a wine straight into vinegar or leave it with some very unpleasant flavors. The idea is to create a vigorous population of the appropriate yeast before an alien yeast can take over (yet another sci-fi inspiration).

The Bordeaux vintners pick some grapes early to develop a "starter vat" in which they begin fermentation when all the grapes have been picked. Once started, fermentation continues slowly, but soon picks up speed. As the yeast cells multiply, fermentation proceeds, usually until all the sugar is transformed into alcohol or until the vintner deliberately calls a halt. For most table wines, this occurs between 11 and 14 percent. Should the alcohol level reach 15 or 16 percent, fermentation normally stops automatically, since most yeasts cannot survive in a high alcohol environment.

The traditional fermentation vessel is a wooden vat or cement-lined tank. The trendy method, however, uses a temperature-controlled stainless steel tank. Stainless steel is neutral in flavor, easy to clean, and easily outfitted with cooling coils and a thermostatic temperature-controlled refrigeration unit.

Hold That Thermostat!

The temperature of fermentation is an essential consideration in the winemaking process. Each grape variety or strain of yeast reacts differently at various temperatures, affording a kaleidoscopic range of winemaking possibilities. The winemaker's ability to control temperature to produce individual flavors, nuances of character, and harmony of structure is like having a magic wand. Or at least a unique signature stamp.

In short, the essence of a wine as interpreted by the winemaker begins with the control of the wine's fermentation temperature. This seems like such a simple thing. But fermentations also produce heat as a by-product of transforming sugar into alcohol. In excess, heat is an enemy. For example, high temperatures can make fermentation proceed at an irregular rate, often too rapidly. It can oxidize or break down certain aromatic compounds, resulting in a baked flavor, or it can spur the growth of undesirable organisms.

Important Things to Know

HEY!

The rate and length of fermentation contribute to a greater fruity fragrance, or complexity, of a wine. At low or cool temperatures, fermentation proceeds slowly, frequently over weeks. For white wines, this leisurely process retains the aromatic flavors of the grape and provides flowery, pleasing wines. It even enhances the flavor of wines made from the lesser grape varieties. In fact, cold fermentation has been responsible for the vast improvement in most American jug wines.

The range of temperatures for most white wines is between 45 and 55 degrees F. Reds generally ferment in the 55–75 degree range. The character of many red wines is determined by the rate of fermentation at specific stages of the process. This is accomplished under the winemaker's meticulous control.

Since the reds are fermented with both skins and seeds, the mass of solids, called the cap, rises to the surface. To extract maximum flavors and tannins, as well as to allow for the release of heat, the cap must be broken from time to time. It can be done in a number of ways: 1) the must is pumped over the cap, 2) the cap is punched down several times a day, or 3) a false top is added to force the cap into the must.

Deciding how to accomplish this task is only one of many choices in the winemaking process. During the growing season, the winemaker—however skilled and experienced—is a gambler. During the fermentation process, science replaces chance. In contemporary winemaking, winemakers act rather than react.

Monitoring is an essential part of the winemaking task. The vintner monitors the fermentation frequently by checking the sugar, alcohol, acid, and balance, both through tasting and laboratory analysis. Tasting is critical; no matter how advanced and elaborate the machinery, there's nothing that equals knowledgeable human taste buds.

Many winemakers taste each of their wines at least once a day during crucial periods. That way, they can make any needed adjustments or corrections. Where needed, they can alter the process, applying new techniques in the quest for the balanced wine.

Yeasts and Bacteria: The Good and the Bad

Yeasts are minuscule one-celled organisms that act as the key players in the fermentation process. Without the presence of yeasts, you'd be drinking ordinary grape juice. Yeast enzymes work with sugar to produce alcohol and carbon dioxide, and voilà—vino! Assisted by the winemaker's expertise and technology, they're essentially user-friendly microbes.

A few types of bacteria are user-friendly; most are not. Certain microorganisms, which may come along with the grape itself or be present within the winery or casks, can survive both the fermentation process and the development of alcohol. As everyone knows, bacteria are hearty creatures. The two most common bacteria are Acetobacter xylinium and Lactobacillus.

Acetobacter xylinium is always present in small amounts in fermenting wines and produces small and acceptable levels of acetic acid (vinegar). It also produces ethyl acetate, which smells slightly of nail polish remover. As long as they exist in diminutive quantities, these compounds add to the complexity of a wine.

> **Wine Word**
> The term *yeasty* refers to the smell or taste of yeast in a wine. In young table wines, it refers to the smell of live yeast, an undesirable trait that dissipates as a wine ages. In sparkling wine—particularly French Champagne—it refers to the character imparted by the dead yeast cells through the process of autolysis, which is complex and pleasing, and therefore desirable. This type of yeastiness is a whole different story from the character of fresh yeast.

However, it's when oxygen appears as a partner that Acetobacter becomes a threat. The bacteria thrive on fermented wine, and in the presence of oxygen, quickly turn the wine into vinegar by converting alcohol into acetic acid. Winemakers have to be constantly on their toes to prevent air and Acetobacter from becoming an evil Batman and Robin and ruining their product.

Lactobacillus is the most common variety of lactic acid bacteria, and is essentially harmless. During fermentation, it produces by-products that add to the complexity of the wine. Occasionally, Lactobacilli run out of control, producing a peculiarly pungent and offensive odor of geraniums that can only be corrected by stripping a wine of all its flavors.

Certain bacteria cause the wine to undergo a second (or malolactic) fermentation. It may or may not be wanted, depending on the type of wine being made. If it's wanted, obviously the bacteria are good.

Adjusting Sweetness

There are many styles of wine that require that some of the grape's natural sugar not be entirely transformed into alcohol. Among these are the low alcohol, sweet, late harvest wines for which Germany is renowned. These wines are produced by arresting the action of the yeast once the desired level of alcohol or sweetness is achieved.

Chilling the fermenting must and removing the yeast cells by filtering to prevent the wine from refermenting is one way to accomplish this. For other styles—for example, fortified sweet wines—alcohol is added to the fermenting wine. The extra alcohol kills the yeast and the process is called to a halt.

Many styles of white wines retain a slight sweetness, usually around 2 percent. Chilling is not always enough to give the winemaker full control over the balance needed for these wines. The modern technique is to ferment the wine completely dry, then add an appropriate amount of grape juice, which has been set aside to sweeten the wine. The resulting wine can be adjusted with more precision, and makes it easy for the winemaker to stabilize the wine and prevent it from refermenting in the bottle.

This technique is known as sweet reserve or must. It's widely used in the U.S. and Germany, where fine, well-balanced, fragrant, slightly sweet table wines are a favored commodity.

Malolactic Fermentation

Called second fermentation, this is the bacterial fermentation. A malolactic fermentation transforms the wine's malic acid—which tastes hard or more acidic—into the softer, less acidic-tasting lactic acid. The transformation takes place with only a slight decrease in the actual measurable acidity of the wine.

The second fermentation also produces certain by-products that may or may not be desirable for a particular kind of wine. It's up to the winemaker to decide whether to encourage or prevent malolactic fermentation.

For most whites, the process is decidedly undesirable. It reduces the wine's sense of crisp freshness. One exception to this rule is Chardonnay. When Chardonnay undergoes a malolactic fermentation, it produces diacetyl, the major flavor component of butter. As a result, the wine gets a buttery complexity, which marries well with the flavors of the Chardonnay grape.

For noble reds like Cabernet Sauvignon and Pinot Noir, the malolactic fermentation is favored to soften the acid taste. It also enhances the wine by adding considerable complexity, flavor nuances, and suppleness.

appeal. The wine will simply smell and taste moldy. Until there is a better way to seal a bottle, even the most costly wines can succumb to this plight.

The "Old World" Winery—Old Fashion Winemaking

The traditional old-world winery lacks state-of-the-art equipment such as stainless steel fermentation tanks, filtration, centrifuge, and sterile bottling—all important innovations essential to modern viniculture (winemaking). Some of the world's finest wines are still produced the old-fashioned way. The trend, however, especially in California and increasingly in Bordeaux and elsewhere, is to utilize modern equipment and avoid the pitfalls of the traditional winery.

When white wine is made by the traditional old fashion method, the grapes, either white or red, are crushed and destemmed and pumped directly into the wine press. The wine is pressed quickly to prevent it from picking up color or tannins from the skins. Following pressing, the wine may settle or be pumped directly into fermentation tanks.

Some wines are aged in oak following fermentation; some are not. Most wines are clarified (solid particles removed) with egg white. Following clarification, the wine may be pumped into a "cold room" or into refrigeration tanks to precipitate tartrate crystals. This helps to stabilize the wine's acidity. It also allows for removal of crystals before the wine enters the bottle. However, some traditional wineries leave out this step, which explains why some wines' bottles have crystals in the bottle and on the cork. Bottling is the final step in the process.

For red wine, the grapes pass through the crusher/destemmer and are pumped into wooden or concrete vats (cuves). There, the wine ferments with its skins, pulp, pits, and possibly, stems. Following fermentation, the free-run juice is run off for the best wine and the remaining grapes are pressed in a basket press for "press wine." The wine that flows freely, without heavy pressure from the wine press, is called free-run juice. It is the cleanest and usually most distinctive wine.

The wine is aged in small oak barrels or in larger upright casks. The aged wine is clarified by "fining," usually with egg white. After clarification, the wine is bottled. Occasionally, bottling is still done by hand, although rarely in the U.S.

Once the first fermentation is complete, the wine is drawn off the lees (solids in the bottom of the barrel) and placed in tanks or large casks. This allows the remaining solids suspended in the wine to settle.

Wine Wisdom
Many traditional old fashion wineries now use stainless steel to some extent, but most use glass- or epoxy-lined concrete vats. Some use wood. Small wooden casks are sometimes used also, particularly in Burgundy and in California for Chardonnay.

For wines fermented on the skins, the remaining pulp containing juice is pressed, leaving behind a cake-like mass of solids called pomice. This wine is called press wine. It varies from light press to heavy press depending on the pressure exerted.

Frequently, the wine is separated into different vats as the pressing proceeds. The heavier the press, the darker the color, the fuller and coarser the flavor, and the more bitter and tannic the wine will be.

Often, each press batch is handled and aged separately. Later on, it may be combined with another wine in some proportion. Then again, it may not.

The Modern Winery—The Triumph of Technology

The modern winery uses state-of-the-art techniques that make for better control of the winemaking process. These techniques also give the winemaker more artistic control over the winemaking process and can help him achieve his vision of the wine he wants to make.

For white wine, the grapes are brought to the winery in gondolas or special tank trucks blanketed with inert carbon dioxide or nitrogen to prevent oxidation. State-of-the-art techniques include mechanical harvesting and field crushing. The grapes are gently crushed in a special horizontal press to eliminate harsh tannins.

Prior to fermentation, the grape juice is often centifuged. Or it may be centifuged after fermentation, or both before and after (more of that later). The wine is "cold-fermented" to capture the freshness and fruitiness of the grapes. If desired, the wine is aged in small or large wood casks. If the fermented wine has not been centrifuged, it will be filtered. Then it is cold-stabilized to precipitate tartrate crystals.

In the final step, the wine is bottled in a state-of-the-art sterile bottling line to prevent air and other contaminants from entering the bottle.

For red wine, the crushed grapes are pumped into concrete or stainless steel fermentation vats. Ordinary or "everyday" wines may be heated first to extract color and flavor rapidly without tannin. Next the wine is aged in small or large wooden casks. The desired quality of the wine determines the type of cask: new oak for most super-premium or noble wines, used oak or redwood for lesser wines, or little or no wood for everyday wines.

The Centrifuge

The centrifuge has been called "God's gift to the winemaker." Those who have one swear by it; those who don't, wish they had one although some winemakers feel that the wine is stripped of flavor by this process and will never touch one. The centrifuge is the vintner's equivalent of a Cuisinart. This nifty device has a vast and varied usefulness in the winemaking process. It simply swirls the wine at high speed, taking full advantage of the laws of gravity and the fact that certain components of wine weigh more than others. The spinning separates these components according to their molecular weight. Unwanted items like yeast cells, pulp, dirt, or dust are cast off, and the liquid is clarified as it passes through.

Important Things to Know

Many winemakers find that the centrifuged juice ferments more easily and produces a cleaner wine than batches fermented by the conventional method. That's why they use the centrifuge to clean white wine must before fermentation. Both white and simple reds may be centrifuged instead of racking or filtering.

Wines with certain off-flavors may receive a heavy centrifuging (sounds like a punishment, doesn't it), which will strip them of all character, but salvage an otherwise unusable wine. For jug wines, this isn't a problem. The centrifuge is widely used to clean jug-quality wines prior to bottling.

Chaptalization

Chaptalization is the process used to compensate for a grape's inadequate supply of natural sugar by adding commercially produced sugar in the appropriate amount in order to achieve a desired alcohol level. No, there is no Chaptal region of France where the practice originated—it was named after Jean Chaptal, the French Minister of Agriculture who invented the process.

Of course, the practice is governed by legal standards. There are limits to the amount of sugar that can be added (although few winemakers would choose to go sky-high on sweetness), in addition to national and regional regulations. Chaptalization is permitted in France and Germany, as well as in most European countries. It is allowed in the winemaking states of the U.S., except for California (where it isn't needed anyway).

When used to increase the alcohol level of a wine by a small amount, say one percent, and applied carefully, the process is virtually undetectable to even the most discerning wine expert. The amount of sugar needed is meticulously calculated—no guessing required.

Some purists decry the process, claiming it affects the quality of the wine, but chances are they've drunk chaptalized wine themselves, blissfully ignorant. Only when the process is ineptly applied or used to excess is the character of the wine adversely affected. Carelessly applied (although within acceptable and legal limits), the wine can become alcohol-imbalanced, tasting hot and harsh. When used to excess, the resulting wine will taste hot, thin, or diluted in flavor or character. However, these are worst-case scenarios. The vast majority of winemakers value their product and reputation too highly to abuse their technology.

> **HEY!**
>
> ### Important Things to Know
>
> Chaptalization entails the addition of beet or cane sugar to the fermenting wine. This type of "cheating" compensates for insufficiently ripe grapes in a cool vintage. It increases both body and alcohol level, enabling the wine to meet certain standards.

The Least You Need to Know

➤ Simple wine is not expensive to make.

➤ The grape and the winemaker play equally important roles in making fine wine.

➤ More expensive wine is more costly because the winemaker uses expensive grapes, oak barrels, and other costly techniques.

➤ A knowledge of winemaking will help you better appreciate a fine wine.

➤ Careless winemaking can result in bad-tasting wine.

Chapter 8

Wine Jargon and Other Gobbledegook

In This Chapter

➤ Wine terms to describe your taste sensation

➤ The role of oak in fine wine

➤ The complex flavors of wine

➤ Aroma, taste, and finish

Ever look at a wine taster's notes? "Subtle yet assertive, with just a hint of violets and a trace of truffles." Oh yes, and maybe "a touch of tar." Sounds pretty neat, doesn't it? Being able to say something that sounds like nonsense to most people and being hailed as an expert. Of course, tasting being a subjective experience, you might look at the notes of another taster and wonder if they were actually drinking the same wine.

Wine-tasting is one area where purple prose is accepted, if not encouraged. Wines have the scents of flowers, herbs, fruits, and a host of other evocative elements. They're described as robust or flabby, silky or coarse, with a fleeting or lingering finish. Not only can you expand your sensory experience and awareness, but your vocabulary as well. No longer will you think that "astringent" refers only to your mouthwash or facial cleanser.

Sounding Like a Pro

You've probably noticed by now that some words seem to crop up repeatedly. *Complex*, for example. Or *acidic*. Or *herbaceous*. Just like English, French, Italian, and German (four languages that are helpful for deciphering wine labels), have their nouns, verbs, adjectives, et al, wine jargon has its categories for classification. The preceding three adjectives all fit into the categories of wine-tasting. The possibilities are vast, but not unlimited. Someday some over-enthusiastic wine writer might say, "This wine has a triangular structure with a diminished fifth harmony, an elliptical balance, and a nose reminiscent of wild mushrooms, rosehips, and comfrey, with just a *soupçon* of mustard. And a brief but resolute aftertaste." Only he will understand what he means. You can be creative, but try to stick with the terms you see in this book and in the wine magazines and newsletters. Overall, it's better to learn the real stuff than make up your own. Try to evoke comparisons with scents and flavors that you already know such as violets, truffles, chocolate, berries of all sorts, and the like. Of course, it is perfectly acceptable to say that a wine tastes like a Bordeaux, a Cabernet Sauvignon, or Chardonnay as this communicates an identifiable style and taste.

Wine Wisdom
The vinification process is usually divided into two parts. The first is *fermentation*, when the grape juice becomes wine. The second is *maturation* or *finishing*, the period when the newly fermented wine hones its rough edges and goes from callow adolescent to mature adult. Some wines are fermented *and* finished in oak barrels, while others are oaked only during maturation.

Oaky Makes the Wine

In wine jargon, the term "oaky" makes no reference to a song by Merle Haggard or a novel by John Steinbeck. A wine is described as "oaky" if it has received oak flavors from being in contact with oak. The wine will have a woody/oaky scent and taste. These days, oaky wines are very much in favor. Chardonnay, for example, is at the peak of popularity while the non-oaked Riesling is considered by some to be slightly outré (remember, this is purely subjective; there's no reason why you can't prefer a non-oaky wine).

Important Things to Know
Oak barrels are typically 60-gallon containers (although exact size may vary) which house the wine during one or both stages of vinification. The most expensive wines reach maturity in brand-new barrels with full-power oakiness (barrels lose some of their oakiness over time). Contact with oak imparts special flavor and aroma to the wine. Oaking also acts as a catalyst for chemical changes in the wine, although most wine lovers would consider this secondary (or tertiary) to the distinctive quality of an oaked wine.

Some lesser wines are made by immersing the maturing liquid in oak chips or oak shavings or even by the addition of liquid essence of oak (illegal in some places; legal in others). The best wines, however, are allowed to sleep happily in those oak barrels.

The term barrel-fermented refers to those white wines that went into barrels (usually oak) as grape juice and emerged as vino. Barrel-aged refers to wine put in barrels after fermentation. Because they are fermented with their skins, red wines are fermented in stainless steel containers or large wooden vats and then aged in small oak barrels after the skins have been removed from the liquid. Some fruity wines (red or white) are not aged in oak at all.

Brix Are Not Bricks

Brix refers to a measure of potential alcohol based on the sugar content of the grape. The more sugar, the higher the potential level of alcohol. You will frequently see this term on the back labels of wines (California in particular) and in the wine literature.

Vanilla, Butter, and Other Good Things

No, this is not part of a recipe for cake or cookies. Actually, vanilla goes hand in hand with oaky. New oak barrels contain vanillin, and the wines aged in these barrels take on vanilla flavor as part of their oaky charm. As an ice cream flavor, vanilla may be simple; in a wine, it adds complexity and smoothness.

Important Things to Know

HEY!

Butter is the taste of diacetyl, which is a by-product of the malolactic fermentation. Some winemakers make a point of putting their wines through a malolactic fermentation to impart this taste to their wines.

Winetasters and Other Vinous Terms

There are many wine terms that you will find in advanced wine books and in the wine magazines and newsletters. Here are a few of them so that a wine magazine will not seem to be written in Greek on first reading.

Bouquet

Bouquet is the smell of a wine after it has lost its grapy fragrances (something like losing baby fat). The bouquet usually develops after years of aging and continues as the wine matures in the bottle. The result is a complexity of flavor nuances that did not previously exist. It's very much like smelling a floral arrangement with many different flowers.

Backbone

Backbone refers to the structural framework of the wine, built on the wine's alcohol, acids, and tannins. Think of the connotation: What do you think of when you hear that a person has "backbone?" A wine with a firm backbone will seem to be well-structured and will provide a pleasing mouthfeel. A wine that is flabby will seem to be lacking in acidity, tannins, or flavor.

Finish

As noted previously, the finish is the aftertaste when the wine has been swallowed. In essence, the quality of the wine determines the finish. Simple wines have a short finish or no finish at all. Premium wines generally have a finish that lingers on the palate for several seconds or more and mirrors the taste of the wine. With noble wines, the finish can linger and linger on the palate and go through a kaleidoscope of flavors. It's this kind of sensory experience that makes wine appreciation so fascinating.

Aged

An aged wine is one that has had a chance to mature in the bottle for a number of years to acquire complex scents and flavors different from what it displayed in its youth. A wine that has aged to maturity is said to be at its peak. And a wine that has become tired or lost its flavors from being aged too long is said to be over the hill. Something like people.

Bottle Sick

After a wine is bottled, it suffers from the shock of the process. For a period of several months or years, it may be lacking in aroma and taste. When this occurs, the wine is described as being bottle sick. It usually recovers after a few months.

Cru Classé

This term will be found frequently on French wine bottles and in the wine literature. It refers to the classification system in which French wines are specifically defined by French wine law. I will discuss this at great length in the chapters on Bordeaux and Burgundy.

Elegant

Like people, some wines show elegance and others do not. It's like being well dressed and perfectly coiffeurred. An elegant wine is one that provides a sense of grace, harmony, delicate balance, and beauty. It is a characteristic that is found only in the finest of wines.

Éleveur

You will find this French term or its equivalent in other languages on wine labels. It refers to a wine company that buys finished wines and cares for them in its barrel aging and refining procedures. Often, this firm is also a wine distributor or shipper.

Négociant

This is another French term you will find on wine labels. It refers to the wine broker or shipper responsible for the wine. Some negocians buy bottled wines from the wine producers and others buy finished wine and produce blends under their own name. A number of these firms have acquired a reputation for fine wines; their names are worth looking for.

Extract

Extract refers to the non-sugar solids in a wine that are frequently dissolved in alcohol. A wine with a lot of extract will feel fuller on the palate.

Goüt de Terroir

No, this does not relate to Ivan the Terrible. This French term is hard to define, but translates into the flavor that comes from the specific vineyard or wine area encompassing the soil, microclimate, drainage, and other characteristics of the vineyard.

Herbaceous

You will find this wine-tasting term used frequently in wine-tasting notes. It refers to an aroma and flavor evocative of herbs that are frequently found in wines made from Cabernet Sauvignon, Sauvignon Blanc, or Pinot Noir. This characteristic is sometimes desirable and sometimes not.

Legs

No, we are not referring to Marlene Dietrich. The legs of a wine are the "tears" or streams of wine that cling to the glass after a wine is swirled. It is a result of the differences of evaporation rates of alcohol and other liquids, such as glycerin, in the wine. It is usually a sign of a wine with body and quality and is something wine lovers look for. Besides being a sign of a good wine, they are pretty to look at as they develop, stream down the side of the glass, and then disappear.

Maître de Chai

A wine cellar in France is called a Chai and the cellarmaster is called the Maître de Chai. He is responsible for tending the maturing casks of wine. Frequently, he is also the winemaker. This is the position of highest importance in a French winery.

Mis en Bouteilles Sur Lie

The French term "Mis en Bouteilles sur lie," indicates wines that were bottled off the lees directly from the barrel without racking. Wine bottled this way retains a fresh, lively, zany quality, often with a slight effervescence (prickly sensation) due to carbon dioxide absorbed during fermentation that did not have the time to dissipate before being bottled.

Middle-Body

You will find this term in wine writers' tasting notes, which are frequently published in wine magazines and newsletters. It refers to that part of the taste sensation that is experienced after the initial taste impact on the palate. It provides the core of the taste on which assessments are usually based. The first, or "entry," taste and "finish" should be in harmony with the middle body in a well-structured wine.

Round

This is a wine-tasting term that describes the smooth, gentle feel of a wine with a particular alcohol/acid balance that smoothes the sharpness of the acidity and makes a wine feel "round" in the mouth rather than "sharp-cornered."

Unresolved

No, this is not a confused wine. It refers to the impression of a wine that has not yet harmonized its various components in order to create a smooth or harmonious impression, a result of aging.

Charm

Like people, a wine can display charm. Wines that have a lovely scent and taste and are generous with their attributes are frequently described as having "charm." This characteristic transcends quality categories, and is frequently found in young and fruity wines like those from Beaujolais or Provence.

Fighting Varietal

This is, in my opinion, a stupid term devised by some clever wine industry writer to describe how the less popular varietal wines fight to gain market share. Thus, wines such as Chenin Blanc and Johannisburg Riesling are described as "fighting varietals." You will see this term in wine magazines and newsletters—I wish they would stop using it because it does not describe the wine but only its marketing.

Off-Dry

A wine that contains a slight amount of residual sugar—from one-half to two percent—is said to be off-dry. When the residual sugar is low, it tempers the acidity of the wine and gives the impression of a wine that is softer and easier to drink. At the higher end, the wine is slightly and pleasingly sweet.

Blind Tasting

No, this is not a tasting where you are blindfolded when you taste the wine. It is the practice of hiding the identity of the wine from the wine taster so that his impression will not be influenced by the name on the label. You can do this by placing the open bottles of wine in brown bags when conducting a wine tasting. It's fun to do this at home, but it is de rigueur at wine judgings at wine competitions worldwide (wine judges do not want to rate a famous wine with a low score lest it be a reflection on their tasting ability). Some experienced professional tasters in the wine trade correctly point out that they do not need to taste blind when they have confidence in their palate—frequently, famous wines are flawed or not up to snuff in a particular vintage, and it's up to these professionals to determine this so that these wines do not reach the marketplace for you to buy.

The Least You Need to Know

➤ There are numerous wine terms you should know.

➤ A wine has a "bouquet, "middle-body," and "finish."

➤ Off-dry wines are soft, mellow, and easy to drink.

Part 3
The Kinds of Wine

This part will take you on a breathtaking tour of the wine world. The majority of the world's finest wines come from France, and this part will introduce them to you. You'll learn about the extraordinary wines of Bordeaux and Burgundy, and also about more affordable wines from France.

Next is on to Italy. You will learn about the great Barolos from Piedmont and Chianti from Tuscany. Then on to Spain, Portugal, Chile, and Argentina, whose wines are similar to each other in style and many offer true bargains.

German wines are low in alcohol with a delightful fruitiness and sometimes a pleasing sweetness balanced by refreshing acidity. American wines have come into their own, with California the leader of the pack. You will learn about the varietal wines from such famous districts as Napa and Sonoma counties. Australia is on a similar tack and produces varietal wines very much like those of California, however frequently in a different style.

Finally, this part tells you how to tell real Champagne from the cheap and very inferior imitators, and then concludes with a look at fortified wines, which pack quite a punch.

Vive La France

France was a wine country even before Joan of Arc heard her first voice. Records indicate that the Greeks may have introduced wine to Marseilles as early as 600 BC. Later, the Roman colonization of Gaul resulted in the wide dispersion of vines throughout France—no doubt because wine tasted good, could be kept for a long time, and could be easily traded.

The ancient wines actually bore little resemblance to the wines we enjoy today, but the ever-resourceful French perfected the art of winemaking to produce some of the finest wines on the market. This chapter introduces you to the culture of French winemaking.

Fathoming French Wine Law

The French like to regulate everything, even their chickens. This is good, because France produces the very best chickens. Similarly, the French regulate their wine to the nth degree, all for the better. The French regulations provide the most specific guidelines for interpreting the contents of a wine bottle from its label. In theory, the structure is simplistic and easy to understand. However, in the real world, theory and application do not always match. Especially when the label is attached to a bottle of one of France's best wines, interpreting the label requires some background knowledge.

What Are Appellations?

The French system of identifying and regulating wine regions is known as the Appellation Contrôlée (AOC or AC), translated as regulated place name. Most French wines are named for places, not grapes. Each wine district has its own organization for enforcing the Appellation Contrôlée regulations (which are specific to that region), and for determining and implementing criteria that can vary from vintage to vintage. The system works to guarantee a minimum quality level and provides a means of classification that differentiates the various quality levels.

French culture is said to be more hierarchical than American culture (in fact, even the French say so). This is certainly true in the wine world. According to French wine law, a wine can aspire to one of four status levels. One of the following French phrases will appear on the label:

➤ **Appellation d'Origin Contrôlée (or AOC).** The highest tier. On the label, the place name usually substitutes for the "d'Origin." For example: Appellation Bordeaux Contrôlée indicates a wine from the Bordeaux region. These wines range from mid-premium to noble in quality.

➤ **Vin Délimité de Qualité Supérieur (VDQS).** The second highest tier, translates as demarcated wine of superior quality. These wines range from simple-premium to premium in quality.

➤ **Vins de Pays.** Literally, country wines. On the label, the phrase is always followed by a place name; however, it's more of a generic place name, generally encompassing a much larger area than the places named in the two higher tiers. These resemble the jug and magnum wines you will find from California, Chile, and Italy—they are simple-premium wines.

➤ **Vin de Table.** This label indicates ordinary table wines. These wines have neither a region of origin nor a grape variety on the label. You will rarely find a wine of this quality in the United States—these are the wines sold in plastic bottles in France. At best, they are jug quality, sometimes not even that good.

Most of the wines in the two lower tiers were not marketed much in the U.S. until recently; however, wines labeled "Vins de Pays D'Oc" and other regions have become more and more available as these regions are able to make fine varietal and blended wines far above the traditional quality level of these regions. This is an example of the progress made in French winemaking. Many French winemakers provide good value and pleasing, flavorful wines at this level. VDQS wines are also relatively ordinary, although some with extra flavor and distinction are sold in American wine shops. The vast majority of the French wines consumed in the U.S. are AOC (Appellation Contrôlée) wines—this category is also tiered in a complex and sometimes confusing hierarchy (just when you were thinking it was really simple after all).

Many French wines are named for the places they come from in France.

The first or lowest tier within the AOC category refers to a very broad geographic region whose wines meet certain minimum standards. From here, the regions keep getting tighter and higher in quality. Some outstanding vineyards even have the honor of their own appellation. From the broadest to the most specific, the Appellation Contrôlée name refers to tiers—think of concentric circles with districts within districts:

➤ **First tier.** A region (Bordeaux, Burgundy). Simple-premium to premium quality. Wines are labled simply as Bordeaux, Bordeaux Supérieur, etc.

➤ **Second tier.** A district (Haut-Médoc and Côte de Beaune are examples). Somewhat higher in quality than the first tier but still range from to simple-premium to premium quality, with some wines occasionally better. Within this tier are sub-districts within an AOC area that produce somewhat better wines (Côte de Beaune Villages, Beaujolais Villages).

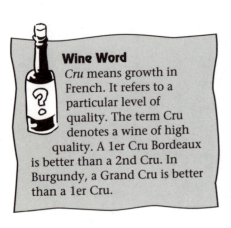

Wine Word

Cru means growth in French. It refers to a particular level of quality. The term Cru denotes a wine of high quality. A 1er Cru Bordeaux is better than a 2nd Cru. In Burgundy, a Grand Cru is better than a 1er Cru.

➤ **Third tier.** A village or commune (Pauillac or Meursault, for example). These wines are considerably better than the previous appellation depending on the producer. When wines are blended from several or more vineyards within the commune or district, they are known as Regional or Village wines depending on the custom of the locality. These wines range from mid- to super-premium quality and noble. Within such a district, some wines can be much better than others and the key is to know the château or vineyard names. In Bordeaux, a number of the commune wines are classified as "growths" or "Cru Classé," which are immediate indicators of higher (or highest) quality. Some of these wines are equal in rank to the Fourth tier.

➤ **Fourth tier.** A vineyard (such as Le Montrachet). In Burgundy and (rarely) other districts, a wine of extraordinary distinction and fame is honored with its own appellation. These wines are designated as a Grand Cru and are the equivalent of a First Growth (Premier Cru Classé) of Bordeaux.

Important Things to Know

HEY!

While the French regulations are strict for the winemakers, they require no more than that the designated appellation appear on the label. Therefore, judging the quality of the wine by the appellation alone requires doing some homework. Technically, the more specific the appellation, the costlier the contents. However, that does not necessarily mean that the wine will be higher quality—even French regulations have loopholes. You may also see the word Cru on the label. Within certain appellations, the wines are classified into Crus that have legal standing. The Cru is another factor affecting the quality of the wine.

There are specific regulations that specify the quantity of grapes that can be grown per acre and other quality factors within each AOC district, as well the "crus." As the wines go up the quality tier, these regulations become more and more stringent. In many AOC regions, the wine must also pass a government tasting test in order to earn its AOC designation for that vintage. A winemaker creating wine from a higher tier may declassify some of its wine to a lower tier if it is not up to snuff. Frequently, wine made from younger wines are declassified and sold under a second label or in bulk to a négociant or éleveur to be used in their blends.

In short, the French wine label looks fairly simple. Deciphering it for quality and value, however, is a lot harder than it appears at first glance. You have to know your French wines to decipher what's in the bottle from the label.

Are French Wines Better?

Before the 1960s, drinking French wines was considered de rigueur. They were the only wines to drink. As the home of those legendary vineyards that make the finest wines in the world, France developed a reputation for producing the best wine. Most people dismissed the California jug wines made by Gallo and others as mere plonk (cheap wine). Italy's reputation was damaged by a barrage of cheap, thin, and acidic Chiantis that were imported in squat bottles shrouded in straw.

The 1960s changed our attitude about a lot of things, including wine. Modern winemaking techniques have since migrated to most winemaking countries, and wines no longer have to wave the tricolor to gain respect. Many countries are capable of producing wines that rival the finest wines of France. On the other hand, many wines from the lesser regions of France are ordinary to mediocre—no better than the inexpensive wines of other countries.

When thinking of France, think of a wide range of variety and quality. Think of wines that are unique in style and frequently wines that present good value. Just remember that thinking of good wine does not mean thinking only of France. As you gain confidence in your skills as a wine connoisseur, you can conduct your own comparison tests to determine whether a French wine is really the best of its kind, or just good to indifferent wine.

The Least You Need to Know

➤ There are four quality tiers in the French appellation system: Appellation d'Origine Contrôlée (or AOC), Vin Délimité de Qualité Supérieur (VDQS), Vins de Pays, and Vin de Table.

➤ AOC wines are the best quality. Within this category there are subcategories of increasing quality.

➤ French wines are the role model for most other wines but they are not necessarily better just because they come from France.

Bordeaux—The King of Wine

The name Bordeaux refers to a large industrial city and the wine regions surrounding it in the southwest corner of France. It is by far the largest quality wine region in the world, and the most prolific producer of famous and high-quality wines. The city of Bordeaux is a major commercial port, and the top wine brokers and shippers maintain their offices along the port's *Quai de Chartrons*.

In this chapter, we'll tour the renowned wine region of Bordeaux. Bordeaux is the stuff that legends are made of—home of such famous names as Château Lafite-Rothschild, Château Latour and Châteaux Margaux. Not all of the region's exports are in this rarefied category (fortunately for most of us), but Bordeaux winemakers are also known for producing high-quality, highly enjoyable, and generally affordable wines.

With its appellations, communes and *crus* (growths), it's easy to get a bit lost in Bordeaux. This chapter will unravel the mysteries of the region known for the King of Wine. We'll cover the inner appellations and vineyards that make up Bordeaux, and the different wines, grapes (no, they're not all Cabernet Sauvignon), and price tags.

The wine regions of Bordeaux have districts within districts as the wines get better.

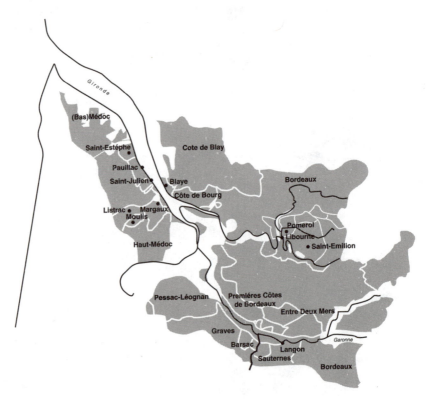

Bordeaux, Vive Bordeaux

Providing the Bordeaux brokers and shippers with their liquid gold are the several hundred *châteaux* (vineyards) which produce the outstanding quality wines that have made Bordeaux a legend. A few names—Château Lafite-Rothschild, Château Mouton-Rothschild, Château Latour, and Château Margaux—have become symbols of superlative wine. Names like these have imbued Bordeaux with a sort of *je ne sais quoi* mystique. Before we get carried away, we must note that the region also makes gallons of ordinary wines for local consumption. Since most of these do not appear on our shelves or tables, the legend remains.

Important Things to Know

Bordeaux produces 10 percent of all French wine and 26 percent of all AOC wine. Most Bordeaux wines are dry reds. Fifteen percent are dry white wines, and two percent are sweet white wines, most notably Sauternes.

Bordeaux wines come in all price ranges. Some noble wines from great vintages have price tags in the mid-three figure range, but you don't have to splurge to enjoy a fine Bordeaux. Most fine-quality Bordeaux, both red and white, begin selling at about $15 a bottle when they are young.

Many of the Bordeaux you will read about are super-premium and noble quality. They are the wines many winemakers aspire to imitate. When they are young, the typical Bordeaux classified growth will have a deep ruby hue with aromas of black currants, spice, cedar, fine leather (like fine leather gloves), chocolate, and cassis.

For the first five to ten years, they can be very vinous and austere with puckering tannins. As they age, their color changes to garnet, frequently with a gem-like brilliance. They are capable of developing an extraordinarily complex bouquet and flavor with more agreeable tannins. On rare occasions, the best will develop an unusual scent that is almost devoid of flavor, like the air after a rainstorm, with subtle nuances of bouquet that are delicate and beautiful. I call this quality "vaporous."

Important Things to Know

The greatest Bordeaux châteaux wines develop power, yet display delicate nuances of flavor, like the piccolo coming through a full orchestral crescendo in a Beethoven symphony. The finest also develop an extraordinary refinement that we have already described as finesse and breed. The greatest classified red Bordeaux wines will frequently take 20 years or more before reaching their maturity and some continue to improve after 50 years in the bottle. As you may expect, the greatest of these wines in extraordinary vintages command a king's ransom—recently a 12-bottle case of 1945 Château Mouton-Rothschild sold at auction for more than $160,000!

The Médoc Maze

The Médoc is a district—our second tier of wine quality within the larger AOC of Bordeaux. The most famous—and definitely the best—red wine vineyards of the Bordeaux

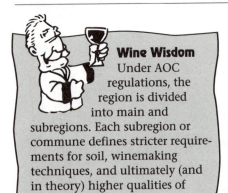

Wine Wisdom
Under AOC regulations, the region is divided into main and subregions. Each subregion or commune defines stricter requirements for soil, winemaking techniques, and ultimately (and in theory) higher qualities of wine.

district lie within the Médoc, north of the city along the Gironde River. The best vineyards are situated along a narrow strip of gravely soil, about 10 miles long and seven miles wide, sometimes less. In this small area, the ideal conditions of climate and soil combine with centuries of winemaking tradition and dedication. Here, the noble Cabernet Sauvignon grape happily thrives.

The wines of the four major communes of Médoc each have distinct characteristics and subtle nuances, described in Table 10.1, as do the red wines of Graves, a district to the south known for its high-quality wines.

Table 10.1 The Four Major Communes of Médoc and Graves

Commune	Example	Distinct Characteristics
Margaux	Château Lascombes	Moderately tannic; medium-bodied; fragrant, perfumed aromas; complex, generous, elegant, and finesse; long-lived.
St.-Julien	Château Léoville-Poyferré	Softer tannins; rich, flavorful; medium/full-bodied; sometimes fruity; elegance and finesse; earlier maturing.
Pauillac	Château Lafite-Rothschild	Firm tannins; rich, powerful, yet with delicate nuances of flavor; firm backbone; full-bodied; extraordinary finesse and elegance (First Growths) black currants and cedar aromas; extremely long-lived.
St.-Estèphe	Château Cos d'Estournel	Tannic hard, firm; full-bodied earthy and vinous; rarely elegant but pleasingly masculine; slow to mature.
Graves	Château Haut-Brion	Moderately tannic; vinous with (ironically) a gravely mouthfeel; earthy; early to mature.

The 1855 Classification

If you're still pondering the *Cru* on the label, this should straighten it out. First we have to go back to 1855, when the organizers of a Paris Exposition asked the Bordeaux Chamber of Commerce to create a classification of Bordeaux wines for the exposition. They delegated the job to the Bordeaux wine brokers, who named 61 superior red wines, dividing them into five categories or crus (the cru or growth refers to the wine estate) based on price; in those days, price was indeed an indication of quality and fame. While the classification was supposed to be limited to the district of the Médoc, one wine of the Graves, Château Haut-Brion, was also listed because of its excellence and fame.

Wine Words

First Growth is the English translation of Premier Cru—the highest quality level in Bordeaux. A Growth is known as a Cru in France. In the Médoc, the Crus range from First to Fifth Growths.

Important Things to Know

If you are confused about our four tiers and crus, you are not alone. A cru is a separate classification within an appellation or district in our tier system. Some appellations have classifications; others not so worthy do not. Some appellations that are not so worthy have classifications too. It's very political and confusing. In any event, for the purposes of this chapter, you need to know that a cru or growth is a classification within a district in Bordeaux. Thus a classified wine has both an appellation and a classification designation reflecting that within a particular district some wines are much better than others.

The listing made by those wine merchants remains today, still known as the classification of 1855 of the Médoc. The châteaux listed in Table 10.2 comprise the first and second crus.

Table 10.2   The First Two Growths of Bordeaux

Château	Commune
First Growths	
Château Lafite-Rothschild	Paulliac
Château Latour	Paulliac
Château Margaux	Margaux

continues

Table 10.2 Continued

Château	Commune
First Growths	
Château Haut-Brion	Graves (Pessac)
Château Mouton-Rothschild*	Paulliac
Second Growths	
Château Rausan-Ségla	Margaux
Château Rauzan-Gassies	Margaux
Château Léoville-Las Cases	St.-Julien
Château Léoville-Poyferré	St.-Julien
Château Léoville-Barton	St.-Julien
Château Durfort-Vivens	Margaux
Château Lascombes	Margaux
Château Gruaud-Larose	St.-Julien
Château Brane-Cantenac	Margaux
Château Pichon-Longueville Baron	Paulliac
Château Pichon-Lalande	Paulliac
Château Ducru-Beaucaillou	St.-Julien
Château Cos d'Estournel	St.-Estèphe
Château Montrose	St.-Estèphe

* Elevated from Second Growth in 1973

For a listing of the 3rd, 4th, and 5th crus, see Appendix A.

The 61 ranked wines are also known as *Grands Crus Classés*. While some vineyards have deteriorated or been incorporated into others, the rankings have been firmly set in stone with only one second growth, Château Mouton-Rothschild, ever changing its status—it has been elevated to first growth. Today there are rumblings about this rigidity as several château have been improved by multimillion-dollar renovations to winery and vineyard and are politicking to be elevated to a higher status. As you may expect, there is considerable controversy over this issue of the 1855 classification as many lesser classified growths feel worthy of elevation to a higher rank. To fully understand the honor of being one of the 61 Grands Crus Classés, remember, even in 1855, there were thousands of wine producers in Bordeaux.

You've probably noticed that with the exception of Château Haut-Brion, all of the wines listed are from the Médoc. Château Haut-Brion was included because it was considered one of the finest wines of Bordeaux as well as one of the most expensive—it could not be ignored. Only two regions were classified in 1855: the Médoc and Sauternes (a sweet wine area in southern Graves). Over the years, other regions such as St.-Emilion and Pomerol have been classified; however, with the exception of Château Pétrus and a handful of others, none of these wines compare with the First Growths of the 1855 Médoc classification.

Saint-Emilion and Pomerol

The districts of Saint-Emilion and Pomerol lie to the east of the city of Bordeaux. Picturesque Saint-Emilion has many cafés that look out over the vineyards. You can sip your wine and watch it grow at the same time. Thousands of small châteaux cover the district, although only a handful can claim the best soil and microclimate for producing great wines. St. Emilion produces many fine wines from a variety of soils and microclimates that are different from that of the Médoc and Graves. It is classified with first growths; however, with rare exception its first growths do not compare with the first growths of the 1855 Médoc classification. There are at least 40 excellent estates in this district.

Smaller and lesser known, Pomerol has gained recognition from wine connoisseurs over the past two decades as its best wine, Chateau Pétrus commands the highest price in Bordeaux. There are several estates that rival those of the 1855 Médoc classification and many others that produce some very fine wine. The soil here contains large amounts of clay in which Merlot grapes merrily grow. This gives the wines of Pomerol a distinct character from their Cabernet Sauvignon-producing neighbors.

Graves

The district of Graves, located along the southern limits of the city of Bordeaux, gets its name from its gravely soil. Interestingly, the wines of Graves also seem to have a gravely sense on the palate. Graves produces both red and white wine, but it is most famous for its fine white wines. Dry and sweet wines

Wine Wisdom
You may find the less tannic taste of Merlot preferable to the haughtier Cabernet Sauvignon. Merlot wines are also more enjoyable younger, which makes them a better value as well.

Wine Wisdom
Dry white Bordeaux are well-matched with shellfish, delicately flavored fish like sole, and fresh fruit and berries. The lush, sweet Sauternes go with pâtée de foie gras, rich consommés, full-flavored fish, mild cheeses, and of course, sweet desserts. They're also wonderful all by themselves!

are divided pretty much by north and south lines respectively. Northern Graves, specifically the district of Pessac-Léognan, is home to some of the world's most prestigious dry white wines. The best dry white Graves are refreshing, crisp, and delightful when young. With age they become mellow, developing complexity and richness. However as I mentioned before, there is still a vast sea of mediocre, overly sulphured white wine coming from this district. You have to be careful when buying white wines from this district to choose the modern producers who make good wine.

> ### Important Things to Know
> The main grape varieties of the white wines of Graves are Sauvignon Blanc and Semillon. This blend is well-chosen because the Sauvignon Blanc grape offers immediate flavor and charm, while the Semillon adds body and depth to the wine.

Sauternes—Where Noble Rot Reigns Supreme

Within the larger Graves district south of Bordeaux are the Sauternes and Barsac districts (there are districts within districts), which produce mostly sweet wines. This is where noble rot is at its most noble and prolific. The best Sauternes wines have a unique and luscious flavor thanks to the work of *Botrytis*—and the labor of vineyard workers who hand-pick the grapes. Each berry is picked by hand, and only the fully mature berries are selected. The vineyard is harvested over and over, frequently 10 times or more at the best château to select each grape as it matures. This is one reason why the best Sauternes—like its most famous, Château d'Yquem—are so expensive. This is where it pays to know your vineyards—some properties are more meticulous and obsessive with these procedures than others. The most outstanding (and expensive) Sauternes are produced by only a few vineyards in the district.

Wine Wisdom
Red Bordeaux wines are a hearty and robust lot that go well with foods that stand up to them. If red meat is your meal of choice, you've met your match. Red Bordeaux are excellent with steak, rib roasts, venison, and lamb. They also go well with game birds, full-flavored, firm fish like salmon, and cheeses like brie, goat cheese, Swiss cheese, and Parmesan.

Where Are the Values?

If you're looking for a good buy in a Bordeaux wine, the rule is to avoid the classified *crus*. They are much in demand, and are expensive to extremely expensive. A wine doesn't have to be in the 1855 classification to be enjoyable; in fact, the ones that aren't are drinkable long before their classified cousins and frequently are almost as good.

Roughly 400 red wines make up the classification *Cru Bourgeois,* a classification of Bordeaux just below the 1855 classification. They generally sell for less than $20 (sometimes under $10), and several can be comparable to or better than the lower-end classified growths. In addition, there are many red and white Bordeaux referred to as *petits châteaux* that have no formal classification. Selling for $10 or less, these are light-bodied wines that are made to be enjoyed young. They're fine for an informal dinner at home.

When to Drink or Not to Drink

You might have to wait a lifetime to drink a Premier Cru unless you pay a fortune for a mature bottle, but many fine Bordeaux mature much sooner. Many of the lesser 1855 Cru Classé wines will be drinkable in five or ten years, while others can take longer. Most petit châteaux, commune wines, and négociant blends are made for early consumption. You can generally tell by the price of your wine and its classification (or lack of classification) whether it is made for early consumption or yearns for solitude in a cellar. A wine that needs cellaring will taste unpleasantly tannic if you try to drink it too soon. Drinking such a wine before its time is more than infanticide—it's a waste of good wine because a wine that requires long cellaring does not display its extraordinary qualities when too young. In fact, it can be rather unpleasant.

Wine Wisdom

If someone gives you a First Growth like Château Lafite-Rothschild or Château Mouton-Rothschild as a gift, you might consider trading it in for a case or two of more accessible wines for current consumption. Any of the wine auction houses listed in Chapter 21 will be pleased to sell your wine and provide you with the opportunity to purchase wines that will be almost as enjoyable. Think of it as two or three to one.

The Least You Need to Know

➤ Bordeaux wines come in varying qualities, from average to exceptional.

➤ You can tell the quality of a Bordeaux wine from its appellation.

➤ The best Bordeaux wines are classified in "growths" or "crus."

➤ Sauternes is a sweet white wine that is revered for its unique flavors.

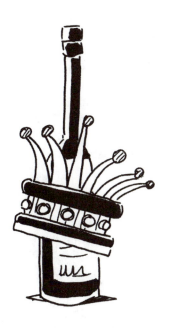

Burgundy—The Queen of Wine

Many Burgundy wines available in the U.S. are good, although not necessarily exceptional. Some expensive Burgundies can be downright awful when produced by low-quality négociants and careless estates. The best wines from Burgundy, however, are truly *vins extraordinaires*. They stand among the most fascinating and interesting of all wines. Unfortunately for the consumer, they also bear price tags displaying their stratospheric status, and many importers and wine merchants refuse to handle such expensive wares in such tiny amounts. So, unless you happen to be touring Burgundy or you've hit that lottery number, the ultimate Burgundies may be beyond your grasp. But be assured that you can enjoy some very pleasant red and white Burgundy wines without putting a severe dent in your wallet.

In this chapter we'll cover Burgundy's five unique wine districts, each home to a number of small estates. You'll find out how the *terroir* effects the grapes grown on each estate, producing distinctively different wines, and learn the characteristics of fine red and white Burgundies. You'll also find out about the refreshing Burgundy bargain—Beaujolais, the inexpensive, refreshing, light-bodied red wine that is served chilled like a white. Part of the problem with importing fine Burgundy lies in the fact that compared to Bordeaux, the Burgundy region produces a lot less quality wine and considerably smaller quantities of wine. Once Beaujolais is excluded (the Beaujolais district is technically part of Burgundy, but it produces a different type of wine), Burgundy accounts for only 25 percent as much wine as Bordeaux, and only a small portion of that are your better wines.

Burgundy Is Organized Like This...

Vineyards in Burgundy are much smaller than those in Bordeaux. An estate of 50 or 60 acres represents a very large holding, and a vineyard owned by only one proprietor is the exception. For example, Clos de Vougeot consists of 165 acres, but is owned by more than 80 different individuals. This can make it somewhat complicated to judge the quality of a wine by reading its label, but more on that later.

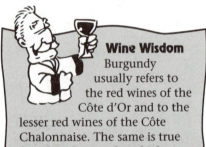

Wine Wisdom
Burgundy usually refers to the red wines of the Côte d'Or and to the lesser red wines of the Côte Chalonnaise. The same is true for white Burgundy, which usually refers to the white wines of the Côte d'Or and Côte Chalonnaise. Chablis and Beaujolais are generally referred to by name. However, there are exceptions to this rule. The name Burgundy can take on different meanings in different contexts. Once you become experienced in wine jargon, you'll be able to pinpoint your Burgundy exactly.

The *citoyens* of the French Revolution had a hand in the fragmenting of Burgundy vineyards. Before the Revolution, the majority of vineyards were owned by the nobility and the Catholic church. After the revolution, the vineyards were distributed among the French citizenry. With the institution of the Napoleonic Code, which required that land be divided equally among all heirs, vineyard ownership was divided even further.

As a reflection of the size difference between vineyard holdings in Bordeaux and in Burgundy, an estate in Burgundy is usually called a domaine, in comparison with the more majestic château in Bordeaux.

Burgundy is composed of five districts, all of which make distinctive wines. The five districts include the Mâconnais, Beaujolais, Chablis, the Côte Chalonnaise, and the Côte d'Or. The Côte d'Or (literally golden slope) is again divided into two parts: the Côte de Nuits and the Côte de Beaune.

Burgundy's climate is marked by hot summers and cold winters and is subject to hailstorms that can result in damaged grapes. Limestone and clay are the prevalent soil types.

The prime varietals of this region are Pinot Noir for red Burgundy and Chardonnay for white Burgundy. This is where that fussy vinifera, Pinot Noir, is on its best behavior and shows its most regal and charming character.

As you head south into the Beaujolais district, the soil becomes granite. This is the home of the red Gamay grape.

The *terroir* of Burgundy is a tricky item. Soils vary from one site to the next. Within one vineyard, two plots of the same varietal growing only a short distance from each other can yield two distinctively different wines. This is where it becomes important to fully understand how to read a Burgundy label. Two owners of the same vineyard do not necessarily produce the same quality or style of wines.

The AOC structure for Burgundy takes this factor into consideration. In addition to the AOC tiers of Bordeaux, Burgundy tiers include AOC appellations for individual vineyard sites that are of exceptional quality. In Burgundy, the terms *Premier cru* (first growth) and *Grand cru* (great growth—the highest quality) are official designations under AOC law. This is in contrast to Bordeaux, where the same terms designate status imparted outside of AOC legislation.

Table 11.1 provides examples of AOC names in Burgundy from the most general to the most specific—individual vineyard site. The two broadest categories—regional and district—represent approximately two-thirds of all Burgundy wines. These wines range from $7 to $15 per bottle. Commune or Village wines, such as Gevrey-Chambertin, comprise one-quarter of Burgundy, and retail for $15 to $30 per bottle. There are 53 communes in the Burgundy region with their own appellation.

Premier crus, such as Chassagne-Montrachet Les Pucelles, make up approximately 11 percent of Burgundy wines. Five hundred sixty-one vineyards have been given the Premier cru appellation. These wines sell for $25 to $80 per bottle. The 32 Grand crus, such as Corton-Charlemagne or Le Montrachet, represent a mere one percent of Burgundy wines. Grand cru prices begin in the $40 to $50 price range and can soar to upwards of $500 a bottle for Romanée-Conti (and upwards of $3,000 a bottle in a mature great vintage—Romanée-Conti is the most expensive Burgundy wine).

> **Grape Alert**
> You've probably seen California wines labeled chablis and burgundy (note: no capital letters). These domestic wannabees are simple, mass-produced jug wines which bear no resemblance to their Gallic namesakes: the 100 percent Pinot Noir Burgundy from Burgundy, France and the 100 percent Chardonnay Chablis from Chablis, France.

Table 11.1 The Structure of Burgundy AOC Names

Specificity of Site	Examples
Region	Bourgogne Rouge
District	Côte de Nuits Villages; Mâcon-Villages
Village or Commune	Nuits St. Georges; Gevrey-Chambertin; Fixin Premier Cru; Puligny-Montrachet Les Pucelles; Beaune Clos-des-Ursules; Nuits St. Georges—Les Perriéres
Grand Cru	Le Chambertin; La Romanée; Le Montrachet

The last two classifications refer to specific vineyards.

HEY! Important Things to Know

You may have read in another wine book that the labels for Premier cru wines bear the name of the commune plus the name of the vineyard in the same size type, and that if the vineyard name appears in smaller lettering than the commune name, the wine is not a Premier cru. *This is misinformation.* In practice, most Premier cru labels display the vineyard name in smaller type than the commune name; however, the vineyard name may appear in the same size or even larger type. Generally, if there is a vineyard name on the label of a Burgundy wine, it is either a Premier or Grand cru.

The classification of the wine may appear on the label, but it doesn't always. Grand cru Burgundies with their own appellation may display only the vineyard name on the label with the term "appellation controlée" below, or they might also state Grand cru. This can be quite confusing as wines with brand names can also use only their name with an appellation. The way to tell the difference between brand name wines and Grand Cru Burgandies is to look for quotation marks around a brand name and the name of a specific appellation between the words *appellation* and *controlée*, appellation Meursault cômtrolée for example. When in doubt, check a good wine encyclopedia or a book on Burgundy.

Wines can be made by blending the grapes of two or more Premier cru vineyards in the same commune. These wines are still called Premier crus, but the label will not have the name of a specific Premier cru vineyard. Instead, the label will have a commune name with the words *Premier cru* or *1er cru*. These wines generally come from négociants (wine brokers who buy wine and sell it under their own name); however some growers with several tiny, lesser-known vineyards may blend them together and sell them simply as Premier cru for marketing reasons.

A Fine White Burgundy Is Like This

White Burgundy combines a silky mouthfeel with a fullness of flavor and lively acidity. The better appellations have a touch of oak. They develop complexity and finesse with age. Grand crus may require up to ten years in the bottle, but most white Burgundy is ready to drink after two or three years. The aftertaste is frequently a lingering kaleidoscope of flavors—both those of the taste of the wine and some which are new. Chardonnay wines from elsewhere can achieve greatness, but there's nothing that can compare to a great white Burgundy, except a great red Burgundy.

A Fine Red Burgundy Is Like This

A fine red Burgundy is as different from its Bordeaux counterpart as night and day. Since it is made from the Pinot Noir grape, it is lighter in color. It is medium-bodied to full-bodied, and is relatively low in tannin and often silky or velvety on the palate. The aroma is unique to Burgundy, with flavors that frequently defy description; however, flavors often resemble cherries and ripe berries or moss and woodsy mushroom scents. With age, a great Burgundy develops great complexity with subtle nuances of flavor and finesse that can be memorable. A red Burgundy requires from seven to ten years to mature, and great Burgundies can continue to improve for decades.

The Wines of Burgundy

This section covers the principle wine districts of Burgundy. The wines from these districts are the ones that you will be most likely to find in the United States.

Mâcon-Villages

The Mâconnais district lies directly south of the Chalonnaise and north of Beaujolais. The overall climate is sunny and mild, and the winemaking center is the city of Mâcon. The hills surrounding this area are replete with the chalky limestone beloved of Chardonnay grapes.

Mâcon-Villages wines are white wines with excellent value. Selling for $5 to $10 a bottle, they lack the complexity and distinction of the more expensive Pouilly-Fuissé wines, but they are lively and crisp and meant to be enjoyed young. Most are soft, round, and fruity. Made from 100 percent Chardonnay grapes, their unoaked freshness contrasts with the oaky majority of Chardonnay wines.

The label will read Mâcon or Mâcon-Villages. Mâcon-Villages is a cut above mere Mâcon, and the best wines are those that come from a specific village. You can tell by the name of the village added to the appellation (for example, Mâcon-Viré, Mâcon-Lugny).

Pouilly-Fuissé

Pouilly-Fuissé became the darling of wine importers during the 1960s. This skyrocket to fame was matched by a skyrocket in prices. In this case, the fleeting nature of fame worked to the consumer's benefit: Priced way over its worth during its 15 minutes in the limelight, Pouilly-Fuissé has returned to being a pleasant, unpretentious, and reasonably priced white wine.

Pouilly-Fuissé and Saint-Véran are two inner appellations within the Mâcon district made from Chardonnay grapes grown on rolling hills with a soil that imbues them with a unique quality. Both wines are similar to Chablis, but softer and less steely.

Pouilly-Fuissé wines are mid-premium quality, usually selling for $15 to $25 a bottle. They are distinctly Chardonnay and have a crisp apple aroma, with a smooth texture and slight depth of flavor. Unlike the simple Mâcon wines, they are often oaked and are richer and fuller in body. The best quality wines come from the villages of Solutré-Pouilly, Davayé, and Fuisse. They possess more fruitiness and depth than Chablis, and the finish reveals a clean, earthy flavor. Within three or four years of aging, Pouilly-Fuissés develop a subtle degree of finesse. Saint-Véran wines are an excellent value at $7 to $14 a bottle.

Wine Wisdom
A young Beaujolais makes a good introductory red wine. If the very thought of Cabernet Sauvignon makes you pucker, try a Beaujolais first. Not all Beaujolais wines are that light-hearted. Wines carrying the appellation Beaujolais-Villages fall within the mid-premium range. Like their simpler cousins, they are fruity wines, but possess more depth, body, and better structure. Light in tannins, they can improve in bottle for two years or so.

Beaujolais

You've probably seen the signs in the wine shops and restaurants every year around Thanksgiving proclaiming, "Beaujolais Nouveau is here!" Actually, it has nothing to do with our American holiday, other than fortuitous good timing.

Beaujolais wine, nouveau or not, is made from the red Gamay vinifera, not Pinot Noir. While the Gamay thrives in Beaujolais, it performs so badly elsewhere that it was once banned by royal decree. Beaujolais and Beaujolais Supérieur (which has one more percent alcohol) are district-wide AOC appellations; the wines come from the southern area of Beaujolais. The primarily clay soil in this district produces simple, light-bodied fruity wines that sell for under $8 a bottle and are best served no more than a year or two after their vintage. Unlike most red wines, they go well with light foods and are great to drink in warm weather.

Beaujolais nouveau is only six weeks old when it begins to appear on Thanksgiving tables. Its vinous and fruity quality (very low in tannins) makes it a refreshing beverage on its own or with your favorite snacks. Don't even think of storing it—it is meant to be enjoyed within six months of the vintage.

Several communes in the north of Beaujolais produce wines with potential mid-premium quality. These are the crus Beaujolais which are distinctly better than Beaujolais-Villages. Only the name of the cru appears on the label, so you have to know the names of crus to know that they are Beaujolais wines.

The crus are: Brouilly, Chénas, Chiroubles, Côte-de-Brouilly, Fleurie, Juliénas, Morgon, Moulin-a-Vent, Regnié, and Saint-Amour. Wines from Brouilly and Fleurie tend to be elegant in style and very fragrant. Those from Moulin-a-Vent and Morgon offer rich flavor and style and are capable of longer aging. Over time, the best may resemble a village red Burgundy. Table 11.2 reviews the cru of Beaujolais.

Table 11.2 The Cru of Beaujolais

Cru	Description
Brouilly	The lightest and fruitiest of the cru. Drink within two years.
Côte de Brouilly	A step better than Brouilly, fuller with more concentration; drink within three years.
Regnié	This is the newest addition to the Beaujolais cru. It is very similar to Brouilly in style and flavor.
Morgon	This cru resembles a red Burgundy more than a Beaujolais. It is full, rich, and earthy. Can age up to five to eight years.
Chiroubles	Very delicate, flavorful, and perfumed. They are often super-premium wines. Drink within four years.
Fleurie	Rich and flavorful with a medium body and velvety mouthfeel. Drink within four years.
Moulin-a-Vent	This is the richest and most concentrated of the cru. Powerful with the capacity to age up to ten years or more.
Chénas	Rich and flavorful. Similar to a Moulin-a-Vent. Drink within four years.
Juliénas	Rich, full-bodied and full-flavored. One of the best of the cru. Drink within four years.
Saint-Amour	Light to medium body, soft and delicate. Drink within two years.

Beaujolais are sold primarily by large négociants—companies that buy grapes and wines from growers to blend, bottle, and sell under their own labels. Two of the premier négociants are Georges Duboeuf and Louis Jadot. These names on the label are reliable indicators of quality as they do more than just buy finished wine. They work with the growers and set high standards for what they will buy. There are also higher quality estate-bottled Beaujolais available, primarily imported by Kemit Lynch, Alain Junguenet, and Louis/Dresner Selections.

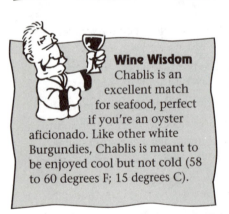

Wine Wisdom
Young and simple Beaujolais are closer to light white wines or rosés than to their more tannic red counterparts. They are best served chilled at about 55 degrees F (13 degrees C) to bring out their youthful vinous vitality. The fuller and more complex cru Beaujolais should be served at the same temperature as any red Burgundy, 60 to 62 degrees F (17 degrees C).

Wine Wisdom
Chablis is an excellent match for seafood, perfect if you're an oyster aficionado. Like other white Burgundies, Chablis is meant to be enjoyed cool but not cold (58 to 60 degrees F; 15 degrees C).

Chablis

The village of Chablis, unfortunately and unjustly, shares its name with the best-known generic wine name from the U.S. This is where wine knowledge comes in very handy. The vineyards of Chablis are the northernmost in Burgundy, situated on the hills of the Serein River valley. There, the limestone soil imparts a special character to the Chardonnay grape and combines with the cooler climate to give Chablis Chardonnay a distinctive quality.

Chablis wines are also fermented differently from other Burgundy whites. Where the white wines of the Côte d'Or are generally fermented and aged in oak barrels, most Chablis winemakers have switched to stainless steel.

The best Chablis wines come from a relatively small vineyard area. Chablis wines are light, austere, and crisp wines with a characteristic bouquet and a steely taste resembling gunflint. The finest Chablis, ranked as Grand Crus, develop a degree of elegance and style, although they are no match for their cousins of the Côte d'Or.

The Côte Chalonnaise

The Côte Chalonnaise is a Burgundy lover's dream—wines that are enjoyable and reasonably priced. They lack the refinement of the Côte d'Or wines, being somewhat coarser and earthier and with less perfume, but they make perfectly drinkable wines and you don't have to skimp on a meal to pay for them.

The district lies to the south of the Côte d'Or and has five appellations that produce quality wines for $8 to $20 per bottle.

➤ **Mercurey.** Wines are mostly reds, some white. This is the home of the best Chalonnaise wines ($15 to $20).

➤ **Rully.** About evenly divided between reds and whites. The earthy white wines are far superior to the reds.

➤ **Givry.** Mostly red, some white. Here the reds are superior, although quite earthy.

➤ **Montagny.** All white wines, which are pleasant and enjoyable.

➤ **Bouzeron.** Wines from this district are frequently labeled as Bourgogne Rouge, Bourgogne Blanc, or Bourgogne Aligote (the other white grape permitted in Burgundy that does well here).

The Great Wines of the Côte d'Or

Wines from the Côte d'Or are unquestionably the most costly. Alas, this fact is often the result of overpricing rather than outstanding quality. When they are on target, Côte d'Or wines are superb. When they miss, they can be very bad to dreadful, suffering from poor winemaking or an overly ambitious quest for big production. They should be subtle, replete with nuances, supple in texture, and unique in style.

The ultimate quality depends on the skill and integrity of the grower. The temperamental Pinot Noir grape does not leave any margin for error—one mistake and you're out, according to this sensitive grape. The result can be a very disappointing batch of wine. The way to avoid disappointment is to become familiar with small growers and producers. For a list of the best and most reliable producers and négociants, see Appendix A.

The Côte d'Or, where wine legends are made, is a narrow 40-mile strip consisting of two main subdivisions. The northern part is the Côte de Nuits, named for its commercial center, the city of Nuits-Saint-Georges. This is the home of some of the finest red Burgundies. The southern part is the Côte de Beaune, named for its most important city, Beaune. The Côte de Beaune is famous for both red and white wines, but its white Burgundies are especially celebrated.

You'll find mid-premium Burgundies from the Côte d'Or have two general appellations. Those from the larger place names will either be called Côte de Nuits or Côte de Nuits-Villages, or Côte de Beaune or Côte de Beaune-Villages. Wines with village names are usually slightly higher quality, although all fall within the same general range.

The red wines have a recognizably fruity, vinous aroma of Pinot Noir with the regional character of red Burgundies. With experience, you'll come to recognize this distinctive flair and aroma. The wines are straightforward, simple, and reasonably well-balanced, with soft tannins and a lingering finish. Though sometimes coarse and lacking in finesse, they exhibit the character of the Burgundy region.

Côte de Nuits

The red wines from the Côte de Nuits tend to be fuller-bodied, firmer and more sharply defined than their southern counterparts from the Côte de Beaune.

Each wine district of the Côte de Nuits produces a unique wine.

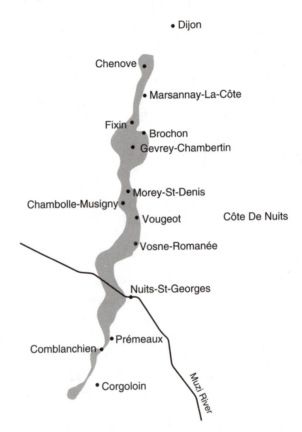

Wines of the Côte de Nuits:

➤ Gevrey-Chambertin in the Côte de Nuits is a rightfully-famous wine village. Its Premier cru wines are super-premium quality and offer great intensity of flavor and balance. The Grand crus (of which there are eight) are labeled "Chambertin" or Chambertin hyphenated as part of a vineyard name. Chambertin and Chambertin-Clos de Beze, its neighbor, are outstanding examples. Complex, rich, harmonious, and beautifully structured, they combine power with finesse as they age. The other Grand crus vineyards of Chambertin don't have quite so much complexity, but they still rank up there in quality.

➤ Chambolle-Musigny lies further south. Its wines tend to be delicate, feminine, soft, and elegant, and possess great finesse. This area is typified by the Grand cru vineyard, Le Musigny, a noble wine of uncommon breed. Unlike most of the vineyards of the Côte de Nuits, Le Musigny is noted for its superb white as well as red Burgundy.

➤ Vougeot is the home of the immense Grand cru vineyard (by Burgundy standards) Clos de Vougeot. Although quality varies (remember, this domaine has beaucoup multiple owners), Clos de Vougeot wines are enormously aromatic, sturdy, and complex. They are medium-bodied, not as muscular as those of Chambertin. The finest offerings of the vineyard have unquestionably noble bearing.

➤ Flagey-Echézeaux is the name of a commune, but is not used as an appellation. It contains two Grand cru wines, Grand Echézeaux and Echézeaux, each of which has several owners. These are super-premium quality wines, aromatic, with a slightly more refined style than their Vougeot cousins.

➤ Vosne-Romanée is a village associated with many of Burgundy's most famous and revered wines. Its Grand crus—La Romanée-Conti, La Romanée, La Tache, Richebourg, and Romanée-Saint-Vivant—are the stuff legends are made of. These rich, velvety wines combine a depth and complexity of flavor from truffles, herbs, and berries, in a style that epitomizes finesse and rare breed. All of the Grand crus—with the exception of Saint-Vivant, which is slightly lighter—usually achieve noble quality status. The aging potential is tremendous. Bottle aging accentuates the wines' harmonious character and finish.

➤ Nuits-Saint-Georges contains no Grand cru vineyards but has many Premier crus. Stylistically, these wines are strongly aromatic, earthy, and often more tannic than the wines of other communes. They possess a sturdy, full-bodied, very vinous flavor that comes into full harmony with long aging. If they are not noble wines, they are not far off the mark.

➤ Fixin is the northernmost district in the Côte de Nuits. It produces sturdy, earthy red wines which do not develop finesse.

➤ Morey-Saint-Denis produces full-bodied, sturdy, rich red wines. Grand crus include part of Bonnes Mares, Clos des Lambrays, Clos de la Roche, Clos Saint-Denis, and Clos de Tart. These wines provide good value for the high quality they offer.

Côte de Beaune

The Côte de Beaune produces fewer Grand cru wines, but there are numerous Premier crus and super-premium red wines. The red wines from the northern part of the Côte de Beaune, around Aloxe-Corton, are softer, fuller-bodied, and richer in flavor than the wines from the Côte de Nuits.

Like the Côte de Nuits, each wine district of the Côte de Beaune produces a unique wine.

Pernand-Vergelesses •

• Ladoix-Serrigny

Savigny-lès-Beaune •   • Aloxe-Corton

• Chorey-lès-Beaune

• Beaune

• Pommard

Volnay •

St-Romain •   • Monthélie   **CÔTES DE BEAUNE**

Auxey-Duresses •

• Meursault

• Puligny-Montrachet

St-Aubin •

• Chassagne-Montrachet

Dheu River

Dezize-lès-Maranges •   • Santenay

Sampigny-lès-Maranges •   • Chagny

• Cheilly-les-Maranges

The following is a list of the wines of the Côte de Beaune:

➤ Aloxe-Corton produces full bodied, sturdy mid-premium wines labeled under the simple "Corton" appellation. The better, Premier cru Le Corton, Corton-Clos du Roi, and Corton-Bressandes are super-premium wines. Aloxe-Corton also has two superlative white Grand cru vineyards—Corton-Charlemagne and Charlemagne. These two Chardonnay wines are of noble quality. Stylistically, they offer a rich, perfumed aroma of complex fruit and butter with classical proportion. The texture is oily, like butterscotch, but with fine acid balance for structure and longevity.

➤ Savigny-les-Beaunes wines offer good value. Five of the wines are Premier cru appellations. The wines labeled under the Savigny-les-Beaunes appellation are mid-premium quality. The Premier crus possess superior delicacy and finesse.

➤ Beaune, Côte de Beaune, and Côte de Beaune Villages are wines from the village of Beaune, which is entitled to use one of three appellations. Beaune wines are medium-bodied, gentle reds and whites. Côte de Beaune Villages wines are generally mid-premium quality with some finesse and moderate aging potential. The Premier crus are complex wines, capable of combining great depth with a distinctive aroma, and lightness of body with a firm structure.

➤ Chorey-les-Beaune has red wines, similar to the Côte de Beaune wines, which offer good value.

➤ Pommard is a village that produces many mid-premium wines under its appellation. Wines can be village bottlings or from specific vineyard sites. These are full-bodied masculine reds. The Premier crus are fairly rich in aroma and body, with a typical earthy characteristic finish. They age reasonably well and can aspire to super-premium status. Three recommended Grand crus are Les Grands Epenots, Clos Blanc, and Les Rugiens.

➤ Volnay are the lightest in style of all the Côte de Beaune wines, almost to the point of being fragile. Delicate and early maturing, the Volnay Premier crus are soft and elegant red wines with delicacy and finesse that place them in the super-premium division.

➤ Auxey-Duresses, Monthelie, Saint-Romain, and Saint-Aubin are little-known villages producing mostly red with some good white wines; they provide good value as they are not in much demand.

➤ Pernand-Vergelesses is another little-known district that provides good value in red and white wines.

➤ Santenay, in the south of the Côte de Beaune, are lighter and more delicate wines and have less aging potential in bottle.

➤ As a place name, Meursault offers some red wine; however, it is most famous for its white wines, which range from mid- to super-premium. The general rule is that those labeled simply "A.C. Meursault" are the mid-premiums—floral in character and streamlined in body with high, crisp acidity. The Premier crus of Meursault are the super-premiums, which display a silky texture, full body, assertive aroma, and complex flavors.

➤ Puligny-Montrachet white Burgundies are created to perfection. The Grand crus—Le Montrachet, Bâtard-Montrachet, Chevalier-Montrachet, and Bienvenue-Bâtard-Montrachet are legendary single vineyard appellations which are capable of achieving noble quality. Some of the vineyards, namely Le Montrachet and Bâtard-Montrachet, cross over into Chassagne-Montrachet. The wines have a rich, complex fruity aroma, often buttery in character, and combine depth of flavor with a hard veneer that is intense yet austere. They achieve unusual power and finesse for white wines, and require upwards of ten years of cellaring before they reach their peak.

➤ Chassagne-Montrachet offers some red wines, but is most famed for its stylish white wines, particularly the Premier crus which are full and firm in structure, with a distinct earthy flavor and character. They are often super-premium wines. Chassagne-Montrachet are somewhat sturdier than Puligny, but with less finesse.

The Premier crus of both Puligny and Chassagne tend to be super-premium wines. Some, such as Les Combettes and Les Pucelles have, on occasion, rivaled the Grand crus in noble quality. However, as the vineyards are owned by so many different proprietors and these appellations are used by so many shippers, the names of owners and shippers become crucial quality determinants.

Where Are the Values?

In Burgundy, value is a relative term—value priced wines such as the village and lesser-known appellations offer good value, but these wines do not display the qualities and subtleties which make Burgundian wines so revered. When it comes to the Premier crus and Grand crus, the values are to be found in the vineyards and growers that are less in fashion as collectors drive the price of the most desired wines up to the stratosphere. Wines from the best growers, as well as most revered vineyard sites, command such a high price that they offer little value considering their cost. Finding the best values requires a familiarity with the numerous growers, their properties and reputation. Did I ever say learning about wine would be easy? Burgundy presents the greatest challenge for the wine lover.

When to Open the Bottle

While there are guidelines for aging Burgundy, there are exceptions for every rule as the techniques of the different growers in any quality tier can make for early or late maturing wines. Generally, red or white wines labeled as being from the Bourgogne or village appellations can be consumed from three to five years from the vintage. Red wines from Premier cru vineyards are mature from five to ten years from the vintage, with notable exceptions that can age for decades. The Premier cru whites should be consumed from three to seven years from the vintage. Grand cru reds should not be drunk before seven years because it takes time for them to develop their noble qualities. They generally peak in 10 to 15 years, with some having aging potential of decades. The Grand cru whites should have a minimum of three years aging, preferably five years, and many improve for upwards of 10 or more years.

The Least You Need to Know

➤ Burgundy is the most complex and confusing wine region in the world.

➤ Burgundy produces both red and white wines, many of which are the finest wines in the world.

➤ Good values can be found in the village appellations and in wines from the lesser-known producers.

·Sip·

Chapter 12

Other Regions of France

In This Chapter

➤ The Loire Valley: fresh and fruity wines

➤ The Rhône Valley: wines of substance

➤ Alsace: the German wines of France

➤ Provence: land of sunshine

➤ Champagne: where the bubbles sparkle

➤ D'Oc: simple wines for everyday

Bordeaux and Burgundy may be the chart-toppers for French wines (still wines, that is; we'll get to the Champagne region later in the book), but virtually all of France is replete with grape-growing terrain. In this chapter, we'll begin with the Loire River Valley, the longest winegrowing region in the world. The grapes, flavors, and styles vary along with the scenery, providing us with a number of distinctive, enjoyable, and best of all, affordable wines.

After departing the Loire, we'll explore the Rhône Valley with its characteristically hearty, full-bodied wines. Then on to Alsace where three centuries of contention between France and Germany have resulted in a French wine region with a decidedly German flair, and where the noble Riesling varietal shares its fame with the spicy Gewürtraminer. South near the Riviera is sunny Provence, which gives us large quantities of straightforward, refreshing wines, and finally, you'll learn how modern technology has transformed the once inferior wines of D'Oc in central France into good-value table wines.

The Loire River Valley

Extending nearly 650 miles, the Loire River nurtures the world's longest viticultural region. The area is rich in vineyards, pleasant and agreeable wines, and magnificent castles and châteaux. If you want to savor your wine in its homeland, this is a fascinating region to visit. The cool climate produces light-bodied, refreshing white wines. The rest of this section covers the districts within the Loire region.

The Loire River nurtures the world's longest viticultural region.

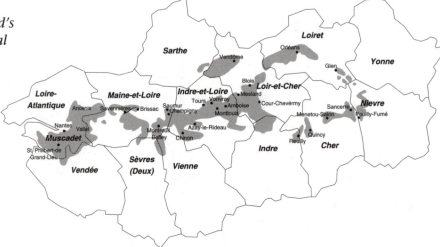

Muscadet

Near the city of Nantes in the western part of the Loire Valley are vineyards producing the Muscadet or Melon grape. Muscadet wines are light-bodied, pleasant, slightly fruity wines. The best Muscadets are crisp and bone dry. Muscadet is an excellent companion to oysters, clams, and delicate fish. It's also a great summer drink.

Not only are Muscadet wines refreshing, their prices are too; you can easily find a good Muscadet for $5 to $8 a bottle. Buy it while it's still young—at its best, it retains a zesty effervescence and piquant vinosity for about one year from its vintage date. The best Muscadet wines will bear the name of the Sèvre-et-Maine region on the label. Also look for the term *sur lie*, which are wines bottled right out of the cask. This procedure of bottling off the lees gives the wine freshess, and sometimes a lively slight prickle of carbon dioxide on the tongue. The most refreshing and flavorful Muscadet is bottled sur lie and is best drunk as early as possible.

Pouilly-Fumé

Pouilly-Fumé is a Sauvignon Blanc wine made in the vicinity of the town of Pouilly-sur-Loire. It is somewhat fuller than Sancerre and can have aromas of gun flint and spicy flavors. Pouilly-Fumés range from slightly thin and ordinary wines to more aromatic and slightly complex premium wines. Pouilly-Fumé can be quite a fine wine when made by a good producer like Ladoucette. Richer than Sancerre, Pouilly-Fumé complements poached salmon, veal, or chicken.

The price range for Pouilly-Fumé is from $10 to $25 per bottle. It is best enjoyed young, within three or four years of the vintage.

Grape Alert
It's easy to mix up the names Pouilly-Fuissé and Pouilly-Fumé, but they are two very distinct wines. The Pouilly-Fuissé is made from Chardonnay from the Mâcon in Burgundy and is a more full-bodied wine. The Pouilly-Fumé is made from Sauvignon Blanc and is lighter and more refreshing.

Sancerre

In the eastern end of the Valley, just south of Paris, are the towns of Sancerre and Pouilly-sur-Loire, located on opposite banks of the Loire River. Here, the Sauvignon Blanc grape thrives, making lively, dry wines that have spicy, green-grass flavors which can range from ordinary to outstanding and can be very distinctive. Compared to Pouilly-Fumé, Sancerre is somewhat lighter in body and more refreshing. It makes a good match for shellfish and delicate fish like rainbow trout and is an enjoyable summer beverage. Sancerre wines fall into the same price range as Pouilly-Fumés. They are also best enjoyed within three or four years of their vintage.

Vouvray

The home of Vouvray wines is central Loire Valley near Tours, also home to palatial châteaux. Most Vouvray wines are white, made from the Chenin Blanc grape, which thrives on the formerly royal terrain. The wines of Vouvray are produced in three distinct styles—dry, medium-dry, or sweet (called

Wine Wisdom
You can find reasonably priced Vouvrays for $6 to $10 a bottle. When young, they are very pleasant. While some Vouvrays are dry (usually marked "sec" on the label), a typical Vouvray will be slightly off-dry. They go well with white meats or fowl in a rich butter or cream sauce. After dinner, try them with semi-firm cheese, grapes, apples, pears, or other fruit (you can pick your own favorite).

moelleux) which are luscious and are super-premium wines at their best. The sweet wines can only be made in vintages of unusual ripeness, which occur infrequently; thus, they are rare and costly. Vouvray also produces sparkling wines that are pleasant and inexpensive.

The best quality Vouvray wines are agers, and require several years to develop. With their high acidity, they can last years without risk of becoming salad dressing. These bottle agers begin in the $12 to $17 price range.

Rosés of the Loire

The Loire Valley produces huge quantities of rosé wines. Most hail from an area around Anjou. The popular Anjou rosés are a lovely pink-orange color. They are low in acidity, appealingly fruity, and sometimes slightly spritzy. They range from slightly to very sweet in finish.

The Rhône River Valley

In southeastern France, south of Beaujolais and between the city of Lyon and the area of Provence, is the warm, sunny, and wine-rich Rhône Valley. The region consists of a northern and southern division, ironically separated by an area unsuitable for wine production. The regional reds are full, robust, and hearty with good color and a ripe, fruity character—not much complexity here, but there's nothing wrong with simple, straightforward red wine. The whites age well and are light- to medium-bodied, rich, and earthy.

Northern and southern Rhône produce distinctively different wines. The greatest distinction, however, may be in amount of wine produced: 95 percent of the wine comes from southern Rhône. The prime varietal in southern Rhône is the Grenache, which produces wines high in alcohol content. Most Rhône wines are simple, inexpensive, and enjoyable—great for an informal evening at home. The section that follows describes the different districts of the Rhône.

Côtes du Rhône

The Côtes du Rhône and Côte du Rhône-Villages appellations encompass a wide range of highly drinkable red and white wines. Reds are more available in the U.S., ranging from $5 to $12 per bottle. Wines from the higher appellation—the 17 villages that make up Côtes du Rhône-Villages—are fuller and occupy the higher end of the price spectrum.

The reds are generally fruity and light-bodied, similar to inexpensive Beaujolais. Uncomplicated by nature, they can withstand a slight chilling to bring out their fruity vinosity, low acidity, and light tannins. The result is thoroughly pleasant drinking. The less-frequently found white Côtes du Rhône bottlings are mildly fruity, somewhat coarse and rough—but that's earthy wine at its best.

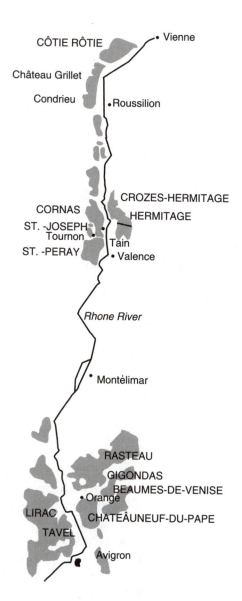

The Rhône River Valley produces some superb wines.

Gigondas and Vacqueyras

Gigondas and Vacqueyras are two former members of Côtes du Rhône-Village who now merit their own appellations. Gigondas, especially, is robust, rich, and a good ager. A quality vintage (1989 and 1990 are two prime choices) can thrive for ten years or more in bottle. At $10 to $15 a bottle, it's an excellent buy.

Chateâuneuf-du-Pape

Chateâuneuf-du-Pape is the pride of the southern Rhône Valley. Its intriguing name evokes the 14th century, when the Popes resided on French soil in Avignon, and the vineyards with this regal appellation extend over 8,000 acres, producing over a million cases of wine.

Chateâuneuf-du-Pape is a robust red wine made from a blend of up to 13 grape varieties. The primary ones are Grenache, Mourvedre, and Syrah. Quality ranges from mid-premium to an occasional super-premium. At the upper levels are slow-maturing, hard, sturdy, tannic wines. The best have a full body and are rich, complex, and high in alcohol. Some more accessible wines are fruitier, less complex, and rounder.

The best vintages age well in bottle for 15 to 20 years. One of the finest Chateâuneuf-du-Papes is Château Râyas, which differs from type by being 100 percent Grenache, made from very old vines. Château Beaucastel is a notable wine which can mature for 20 years or longer.

Tavel and Lirac

A close neighbor of Chateâuneuf-du-Pape, Tavel excels in producing the world's best—and most expensive—rosés. Less celebrated than Tavel, Lirac produces both reds and rosés. Lirac rosés are not equal in quality to their Tavel cousins, but they offer tasty, refreshing wines, and they are reasonably priced. The wines of both areas are made primarily from the Grenache and Cinsault grapes.

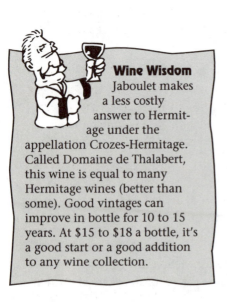

Wine Wisdom
Jaboulet makes a less costly answer to Hermitage under the appellation Crozes-Hermitage. Called Domaine de Thalabert, this wine is equal to many Hermitage wines (better than some). Good vintages can improve in bottle for 10 to 15 years. At $15 to $18 a bottle, it's a good start or a good addition to any wine collection.

Hermitage

Hermitage reds are mid- to super-premium wines, rich and full-bodied with great aging potential. They are made from the noble Syrah grape. They are not quite up to Côte-Rotie wines in finesse, but are high in tannins and alcohol and they develop complexity and vigor when fully aged. The best vintages will mature in bottle for 30 years or more (1988, 1989, 1990, and 1991 were stellar years for the northern Rhône; 1989 was the finest for Hermitage). The three best producers of Hermitage are Chapoutier, Jean-Louis Chave, and Paul Jaboulet Aîné. The best Hermitages range from $35 to $60 but Hermitages from lesser producers are as low as $15 to $25 a bottle.

Hermitage also produces a small quantity of white wine, made from the Marsanne and Rousanne grape varieties. White Hermitage is a full, rich, earthy wine that needs six to ten years to really develop.

Condrieu

Condrieu is made from 100 percent of the Viognier grape variety and is another excellent white wine from the northern Rhône. This wine is one of the most fragrant and floral wines you can find. It has flavors that are delicate yet lush, with fragrant fresh apricot and peach nuances. It is a wine to drink young. Condrieu sells for about $18 to $25 a bottle.

Côte-Rotie

Côte-Rôtie wines are almost uniformly high in quality with many reaching super-premium quality. They are more subtle than Hermitage wines; firm and long-lasting, they develop a berry and truffle flavor with aging, and their smooth texture gives them finesse as they mature.

Peak vintages of Côte-Rôtie possess aging potential of 20 years or more (1991 was a prime year). The most celebrated producer of Côte-Rôtie is Guigal. La Mouline, La Landonne, and La Turque, Guigal's single-vineyard wines, are superb (although quite expensive). The range for most Côte-Rôties is $20 to $45 a bottle.

Alsace—the German Wines of France

Located in the northeast corner of France near Germany, Alsace is set apart from the rest of France by the Vosges Mountains. Alsace became part of France in the 17th century, to be reclaimed by Germany in 1871, then lost to France once again after World War II. Less than 50 years of German rule over a span of three centuries may seem like a short time, but the style and character of Alsatian wines is closer to German wines than to their French counterparts. Like Germany, Alsace produces primarily white wines.

Wines from Alsace are different from other French wines in several ways. First, they are of a completely different character and style than other French wines and they bear a closer affinity with the wines of Germany. Almost all Alsatian wines carry a grape variety name and bear an appellation, which is simply "Alsace." Also, Alsatian wines come in a tall, thin, tapered bottle, called a flute, which is different from any other bottles in France.

The vineyards are situated on the lower slopes of the Vosges Mountains, west of the Rhine River. They are among the most beautiful in the world, dotted with picturesque villages and impressive cathedrals. Despite the northern latitude of the Alsatian region, the climate is temperate, sunny and dry, the kind of climate grapes (and grape growers) love.

Alsatian vineyards are largely populated by German grapes—Riesling, Sylvaner, Gewürtztraminer—along with some Pinot Blanc, Pinot Gris, Pinot Noir, and Muscat varieties. The small quantity of light-bodied Pinot Noir is vastly outnumbered by the 93 percent of Alsatian wines that are white. The climate and vinification endow the Alsatian whites with a fuller body, stronger alcohol content, and greater austerity and dryness than their German counterparts. The Alsatian whites, Gewürztraminer especially, have a spicy character unique to the region.

Riesling

Riesling is the king of wines in Alsace (as it is in Germany); however, it is produced in a relatively dry style. Alsace Riesling has a flowery bouquet, but has a firmness which belies its flavors. Most Alsatian Rieslings are made to be consumed young; however wines from outstanding vintages are made in a late-harvest style and can be aged for a decade or more. Rieslings are in the $10 to $20 a bottle price range with late-harvest bottlings going for upwards of $50 a bottle or more.

Gewürztraminer

For dry, spicy Gewürztraminers, Alsace has no equal. The Gewürztraminer grape has a personality all its own—pungent and intense with a unique spicy flavor. You either like it or you don't! High in alcohol and low in acidity, its impression is rich and mellow. Gewürztraminer goes well with strong cheeses, spicy Asian cuisine, and your favorite fruit, or is fine all by itself before or after a meal. It sells in the same price range as Riesling, but is not as much of an ager.

Pinot Blanc

Alsace Pinot Blanc is the lightest of the Alsatian wines and has a mellow, fruity character. While it is generally dry, some producers make their Pinot Blanc medium-dry to appeal to wine drinkers who do not like an austere style. You cannot tell from the label which style is which and, therefore, you should ask your wine merchant as to the taste of a particular brand. In either style, these wines are best drunk young. Pinot Blanc range from $5 to $15 a bottle.

Other Varieties

The Sylvaner grapes make slightly fruity, highly acidic table wines. Only a small quantity is sold in the U.S. Similarly, Muscat d'Alsace, a slightly bitter, usually dry white wine is found here only in small quantities. Tokay d'Alsace, made from Pinot Gris, is a full-bodied, rich, and spicy wine with a lot to offer. Like Gewürztraminer, it is low in acidity and high in alcohol. It sells in the $8 to $15 category, and makes a good complement for spicy meat dishes.

Les Autres

Les Autres translates simply as "the others." The two areas in this section—Côtes de Provence and D'Oc, each of which is described next—produce simple, affordable wines.

Côtes de Provence—Land of Sunshine

Côtes de Provence is located in the south of France, bordering the French Riviera in the hilly region between Marseilles and Nice. It produces vast quantities of refreshing, simple red, white, and rosé wines, along with tiny amounts of sparkling wine.

The white wines are labeled either "Côtes de Provence" or "Cassis." When well-made, these relatively dry wines are fruity and pleasingly refreshing, with some amount of distinction. White wines from the Appellation Controlée Cassis tend to be more austere and richer in flavor. The numerous rosés from this region are uncomplicated and dry to slightly off-dry. The red wine from Bandol, made primarily from the Mourvedre Franc varietal, is tasty and pleasant, although it tends to be overpriced.

Vin de Pays D'Oc—Simple Wines for Everyday

This is one of many districts in the large Languedoc-Roussillon region of central France that was formerly known only for very cheap *vin ordinnaire*. However, thanks to innovation and technology (and maybe some strong motivation on the part of the region's winemakers), the wines have been upgraded in quality. They are straightforward, simple wines, reasonably priced and fine for everyday drinking. They range in price from $4 to $10 a bottle and frequently offer fine value. Other wines similar in quality are Faugeres, St. Chinon, Fitou, Corbieres, Minervois, Côtes du Roussillon, Côteaux du Languedoc, Pic-St.-Loup, and Vin de Pays de L'Heroult.

The Least You Need to Know

➤ There are many fine wine regions in France.

➤ The wines of the Loire are mostly white and are young and refreshing.

➤ Côte de Rhône wines are simple, delightful, and fine for everyday drinking.

➤ The wines of Alsace are more in the German style than French.

Chapter 13

O Solo Mio

In This Chapter

➤ Italian wine laws

➤ The major wine regions of Italy

➤ Deciphering the Italian wine label

With grapevines growing virtually everywhere, Italy boasts of producing more wine than any other country in the world. No Italian meal is complete without the clinking of wine glasses.

Yet perhaps surprisingly, Italy is a relative newcomer to the world wine market. Italian winemaking tradition goes back three millennia to the Etruscans; its formal system of classification goes back only three decades. Today there is still no equivalent to the French *cru* system of vineyard classification. For generations, Italians kept the best premium wines for their own consumption. Yes, its possible to find great Italian wines with breed and finesse—it just requires some homework, and you'll learn the basics in this chapter.

The grapevines of Italy proliferate over a vast array of soils and climates. There's Alpine soil in the northern climes and the sunny shores of the Mediterranean to the south. As we go south of Rome, the wines tend to become more ordinary, but there are some notable exceptions. High-altitude cultivation protects the vines from grape-withering heat. The white wines of Mount Etna are the only wines in the world made on the slopes of an active volcano.

If Italian winemakers seem to reflect a provincial attitude, Italian grapes are not only provincial, they're excessively patriotic! Even the finicky Pinot Noir grudgingly concedes to perform outside of France. In contrast, the Italian grape varieties, such as Sangiovese, Nebbiolo, and Barbera, are outstanding performers only in their native soil; they either don't grow well or don't grow at all anywhere else.

Italy has 20 wine regions, corresponding to its political sectors. Wine regions here are called *zones* (as in Twilight), to avoid political connotation.

The best wine districts of Italy.

Getting a Basic Handle on Italian Wines

Italy's wines for our purposes fall into three categories:

1. Inexpensive red and white wines often sold in magnums for everyday drinking.

2. The better wines, which range from simple to mid-premium quality.

3. A small, select number of world-class wines that are of super-premium quality and on occasion noble quality.

In the first category is one of the best-known Italian wines for casual drinking, Lambrusco, an effervescent, slightly sweet red wine that rose to popularity in the United States in the 1970s and continues to please drinkers who want a pleasant, undemanding wine. In the second category are most of the Italian wines described in this chapter, and many other wines that space does not permit us to discuss. The third category includes wines that have been created to emulate the finest wines of Bordeaux and California as well as the best homegrown wines of Italy—Barolo, Barbesco, Gattinara, and Brunello. In particular, the new kids on the block have been receiving acclaim worldwide and have brought a new respect for the Italian wine-producing community.

Italian Wine Laws

For many years, all Italian wines were equated with a cheap and largely undrinkable product sold in straw flasks under the blanket label "Chianti." While some of these wines were actually from Chianti, many were not. Not surprisingly, a great number of Italian winemakers who took pride in their wares considered themselves unfairly stigmatized. To correct the unfortunate impression, as well as provide a viable structure for the Italian wine industry, the Italian government enacted a body of laws called the *Denominazione di Origine Controllata* (DOC). First introduced in 1963, DOC laws were implemented in 1967.

DOC laws control the quality of Italian wines by legally defining viticultural districts, controlling the principal yield per acre, grape varieties, and alcohol content, and by setting minimum requirements for cask aging. The terms "Superiore," "Riserva," and "Classico," which appear on wine labels, were endowed with legal significance.

Important Things to Know

There are three categories of Italian wines. The first category is simple table wine—non-DOC wines that for the most part do not come to the United States. Most Italian wines that you will see imported into the United States are DOC, which is a large category spanning quality from simple everyday wines to super-premium. There are currently more than 250 DOC-designated districts. You'll see the phrase Denominazione di Origine Controllata on the labels of these wines. As with French regulations, specific requirements for each DOC vary. An appellation of a Classico region, which has more stringent standards than the broader DOC, provides a two-tiered rank order—Chianti Classico for example.

Above the basic DOC classification is a designation given to only 13 wines: Denominazione di Origine Controllata e Garantita (DOCG). These elite wines, mostly in the super-premium quality category, must pass all the requirements of the DOC, with additional specifications concerning winemaking practices and taste-testing of the wine itself. DOCG wines that fail to pass the taste test are declassified as ordinary table wine rather than DOC wine. Obviously, this motivates winemakers to produce a superior product. However, tasting requirements do not guarantee superior quality; too much is dependent on the qualifications of the taster, the tasting methods, and the taste standards employed—all the more reason to be informed about your wine.

Italy's Major Wine Regions

Italy has hundreds of wine districts, too many to cover in this book. Instead, this chapter covers the most well-known districts that produce wines which are readily available in the United States.

Italy's Main Wine Regions

Red Wine	White Wine	Grape Variety
Piedmont		
Barbaresco		Nebbiolo
Barbera d'Alba and similar DOCs		Barbera

Red Wine	White Wine	Grape Variety
	Gavi (Cortese di Gavi)	Cortese
	Roero Arneis	Arneis
Barolo		Nebbiolo
Gattinara		Nebbiolo, Bonarda[1]
	Tuscany	
Brunello di Montalcino		Sangiovese Grosso
Chianti, Chianti Classico		Sangiovese, Canaiolo, and others[1]
	Vernaccia di San Gimignano	Vernaccia
Vino Nobile di Montepulciano		Sangiovese, Canaiolo, and others[1]
Carmignano		Sangiovese, Cabernet Sauvignon[1]
Super-Tuscans[2]		Carbernet Sauvignon, Sangiovese
	Veneto	
Amarone della Valpolicella		Corvina, Rondinella, Molinara[1]; semi-dried
Bardolino		Corvina, Rondinella, Molinara[1]
	Bianco di Custoza	Trebbiano, Garganega, Tocai[1]
	Lugana	Trebbiano
	Soave	Garganega, Trebbiano, and others[1]
Valpolicella		Corvina, Rondinella, Molinara[1]
	Trentino-Alto Adige	
	Chardonnay (various DOCs)	Chardonnay

continues

continued

Red Wine	White Wine	Grape Variety
	Pinot Grigio (various DOCs)	Pinot Gris
	Pinot Bianco (various DOCs)	Pinot Blanc
	Sauvignon (various DOCs)	Sauvignon Blanc
Fruili-Venezia Giulia		
	Chardonnay (various DOCs)	Chardonnay
	Pinot Blanco (various DOCs)	Pinot Blanc
	Pinot Grigio (various DOCs)	Pinot Gris
	Sauvignon (various DOCs)	Sauvignon Blanc
	Tocai Friulano (various DOCs)	Tocai Friulano
Umbria		
	Orvieto	Trebbiano

1 *Blended wines, made from two or more grapes*

2 *Non-traditional wines produced mainly in the Chianti district (see Tuscany)*

Tuscany—Art, Antiquity, and Chianti

The history of winemaking in Tuscany started with the Etruscans some 3,000 years ago. Now that's quite a tradition! The name of its most famous wine, Chianti, was recorded as early as 1260 BC, only then it referred to a white wine. In an interesting twist of fate, white wine from Tuscany today cannot be called Chianti.

The best wines of Tuscany come not far from Florence, a city known for its works of art. The vineyards of Chianti, the largest DOC zone, are situated among olive groves, stone farmhouses, and an occasional castle. It's only a short hop from bucolic, picturesque vineyards to some of the world's most impressive art and architecture.

Important Things to Know

HEY!

Chianti is divided into seven sub-districts: Classico, Colli Fiorentini, Montalbano, Rufina, Colli Aretini, Colli Senesi, and Colli Pisani. All of them turn out good wine (in fact, all hold DOCG status), but Chianti Classico is the undisputed Numero Uno. Second in quality is Chianti Rufina.

Chianti wines may carry the name of the district, or may appear simply as "Chianti." The name Chianti by itself can mean the wine was made from the blended grapes of two districts. The cépage (blending of grape varieties) in Chianti is carried out to a certain degree at the producer's discretion, but only certain grape varieties are permitted, and certain ones are required by DOC law. Sangiovese is the dominant grape, with a requirement of 50 to 80 percent, and the other red—Canaiolo—at 10 to 30 percent. The blend also requires from 10 to 30 percent of the white grapes Trebbiano or Malvasia. Many producers make their Chiantis almost entirely from the Sangiovese grape, which is not consistent with the DOC regulations but makes for a better wine.

Chianti wines vary according to sub-district and, to a lesser degree, grape blending. They also vary in style and quality. Ordinary Chianti, at the lower end of the price range, is a prickly, fruity wine, made to be drunk young. The middle range is covered by simple to mid-premium wines, Classico or otherwise, which age well in the bottle for several years, but can also be enjoyed when you buy them. The highest quality is the Riserva, the product of a special selection of vines or harvest, greater TLC in winemaking, and longer aging before release (at least three years). Riservas are frequently aged in French oak, and are aged for a minimum of 10 years. Many will age well for 20 or 30 years.

Chianti is a very dry red wine that goes well with food. It is a vinous wine that frequently has an aroma of cherries and sometimes hints of violets. Its taste is sometimes similar to that of tart cherries, but for the most part Chianti is best described as tasting like Chianti. The best Chiantis are high in acidity and do not reach their peak until four to eight years after the vintage. Some of the better Chiantis, particularly the single-vineyard examples, can age for 10 years or more in great vintages.

Chianti is not the only red wine of Italy—it just seems like it is. One important Tuscan red wine, currently basking in glory, hails from the town of

Wine Wisdom
At any price, Chianti is a great value. A simple Chianti sells for about $6 a bottle. Chianti Classico is usually in the $8 to $15 price category, and well worth it. From there it's only a brief step to Chianti Classico Riservas, only $2 over the price of the regular Chianti Classico.

Montalcino, south of Florence in the Sienna hills. This relative newcomer emerged from a clone or variant of the Sangiovese, known as the Brunello or large Sangiovese. The resulting wine, Brunello di Montalcino, brings the highest prices of any Italian wine.

Important Things to Know

Brunello di Montalcino is one of those overnight successes that's been around for ages—literally. In 1970, the Biondi-Santi family (the leading producer in Montalcino) decided their wines could use some publicity. They invited some leading wine writers to a tasting of rare vintages. Needless to say, the 1888 and 1891 vintages were a smash! Brunello immediately became one of the most sought-after wines in Italy. Twelve years after its harvest, the 1971 reserve bottling retailed in the U.S. for $130 a bottle. Even by the extravagant standards of the '80s, that was pretty pricey for a young wine in no way ready to drink.

There's been some mixed publicity for this DOCG wine. Not all bottlings were up to the prices they demanded. Now that the rage has died down, however, there is general agreement that Brunello di Montalcino has the potential to be one of the world's most superb and long-lived red wines. Prices begin at $25 to $40 a bottle and scale upward.

This variant on Chianti is a huge, full-bodied, and intense wine with concentration and astringent tannins that require aging of up to 20 years when traditionally made. The wine should be opened several hours before serving to receive adequate aeration. Some producers in Montalcino are now making a more approachable version of Brunello that is ready to drink in about five years.

Wine Wisdom

Rosso di Montalcino is a less expensive wine made from the same grapes, and the same production area as Brunello di Montalcino. Rosso di Montalcino from a good Brunello producer is a superb value at $10 to $15, providing you with a hint of what Brunello tastes like at an affordable price.

From vineyards surrounding the hill town of Montepulciano comes another red wine, Vino Nobile di Montepulciano. Vino Nobile is close to a Chianti Classico, and responds better to aging. Its minimum age is two years; a Riserva must have three years, and with four it can be designated Riserva Speciale. Just as there is a younger and lighter version of Brunello, there's a Vino Nobile version as well: Rosso di Montepulciano.

The Carmignano district west of Florence produces a red wine that owes a good part of its high quality to the incongruous but welcome presence of Cabernet Sauvignon. Essentially a Chianti with a French flair, Carmignano can be made with up to 10 percent of the noble Bordeaux grape.

Possibly a descendant of the white wine of the Etruscans, Vernaccia di San Gimignano bears the name of a medieval walled village west of the Chianti Classico zone. Vernaccia is vinified to be drunk young. It is a refreshing white wine with a slightly viscous texture with hints of almonds and nuts. Most Vernaccias are in the $6 to $8 price range.

Super-Tuscans

During the 1970s, certain visionary winemakers decided to transcend the limits of traditional winemaking and experiment with unorthodox blendings in a quest to make wine of Bordeaux classified growth stature. Producers like Piero Antinori gained world-wide attention by creating new wines (for example, Tignanello and Solaia) that became known collectively as super-Tuscans. Like Carmignano, these blends were usually Sangiovese and Cabernet Sauvignon.

Important Things to Know

Today, there's considerable variance in the blend of the super-Tuscans. Some producers use Cabernet Sauvignon; others use Merlot or Syrah, while others stick to native Tuscan varieties. There's considerable variance in price, too: from $30 or $40 up to $75 or $100 per bottle. No doubt about it, these wines are not cheap. The common denominator is that they are all of superb quality—super-premium and sometimes better. The most famous super-Tuscan wines, Sassicaia and Solaia, are much sought after by wine aficionados and can cost up-wards of $200 in great vintages.

Piedmont—Home of Barolo, Barbaresco, and Gattinara

Situated in northwest Italy, bordering France and Switzerland in an area that combines agriculture, industry, and mountaineering, Piedmont is the site of two very important wine zones: Alba, which is known for its red wines; and Asti, famous for its sparkling wines (see Chapter 18).

Piedmont produces some of the very best Italian red wines. Some wine lovers call it the noble wine region of Italy, a reputation it owes to the noble Nebbiolo varietal. This sensitive grape is the pride of the Piedmont—nowhere else does it really strut its stuff.

Barolo and Barbaresco both come from the central part of the Piedmont region. Made entirely from Nebbiolo grapes, they hail from the Langhe hills near Alba. Both Barbaresco and Barolo are full-bodied, robust wines—high in tannin, acidity, and alcohol. Their

Wine Wisdom
To fully enjoy the finesse of Barolo and Barbaresco, you must find a good producer (see Appendix A). If not made well, these wines can suffer from overly high acidity or other unpleasant defects (even mercaptans or other serious flaws). The rule here is choose wisely. Three excellent vintages for the Piedmont are 1988, 1989, and 1990.

aromas evoke hints of tar, violets, strawberries, and black truffles. Barbaresco tends to be less austere than Barolo and slightly lower in alcoholic content. It is softer and more delicate, and can be consumed earlier.

Traditionally made Barolo and Barbaresco are agers—some (Barolo especially) need 10 years of aging or more before they are ready to drink. They should be opened a few hours before drinking to receive adequate aeration. Some producers are making these wines in a Bordeaux style so that they are enjoyable sooner and are using French oak barrels for aging to give the wine an oaked character.

Barolo, Barbaresco, and Gattinara are all excellent complements to a meal. Fine Barolo and Barbaresco are a bit pricey: $25 to $45 a bottle, although from a good producer and a good vintage, they are worth the price tag. You might want to start with Gattinara. It offers Nebbiolo style and verve at a more palatable price: $12 to $18 a bottle.

Important Things to Know

HEY! The red Nebbiolo grape is the heart of three of Italy's best DOCG wines: Barolo, Barbaresco, and Gattinara (in Gattinara, Nebbiolo is known by its local name, Spanna). A decade ago, Barolo was the undisputed king of the mountain, followed by Gattinara. These days, Barbaresco seems to have gained in popularity, but Gattinara remains a superb (if underrated in the 1990s) wine.

Important Things to Know

HEY! Roughly half of Piedmont's wine production comes from the Barbera grape. This is the everyday table wine of the Piedmont. Barbera is usually consumed young, although a good vintage can age well and attain mid-premium status. It is a rich, fruity wine with high acidity but little tannin. Barbera d'Alba is somewhat more rich than the more austere Barbera d'Asti.

Dolcetto is another favorite everyday red wine. If you know some Italian and you think "Dolcetto" refers to a sweet wine—it doesn't. Actually, it's the grape that's sweet; the wine is uniquely dry. It's vinous in quality, low in acidity, and rich in soft tannins. It's an easy-to-drink wine, even with its slight bitter undertone.

Important Things to Know

Barbera has recently soared in popularity in the U.S. That means it's widely available and in a reasonable price range. You can get two types of Barbera. The traditional style is aged in large oak casks that impart only a minimum of oak flavor. These wines retail in the $8 to $15 range. The newer method is aging in barriques (French oak barrels). The smaller containers endow the wine with more oaky flavor and a higher price tag: $20 to $40 per bottle. Although oaky is "in" in some circles, don't be afraid to go for tradition. You and your wallet may both prefer the old style.

Nebbiolo d'Alba is another Piedmont red to try. Lighter in body than Barolo or Barbaresco, it often has a sort of fruity, sweet undertone. It retails in the $10 to $15 range.

The Red Queen in *Through the Looking-Glass* would be happy in Piedmont; no doubt about it, reds dominate. There are, however, two white wines worth trying. Gavi is a very dry, refreshing wine with high acidity, named for a town in southern Piedmont. Most Gavis sell for $10 to $15 a bottle; however, some of the best examples go for as much as $35 a bottle and are worth the price.

The second white wine is Arneis, from the Roero zone near Alba. Arneis is named for its grape variety—Arneis. Arneis is a medium-dry to dry wine with a rich flavor and texture. It reveals its best qualities when consumed within a year of the vintage. It sells for $12 to $18 a bottle.

Wine Wisdom
Some wine enthusiasts like to compare Dolcetto to Beaujolais. Dolcetto, however, is usually drier and makes a better complement to a meal. Dolcetto sells for about $10 to $12 a bottle. The best Dolcetto wines are Dolcetto d'Alba. Most good Barolo producers have a good Dolcetto d'Alba.

Friuli—Venezia Giulia

Nestled up against Austria and Slovenia, this prolific winemaking zone has been letting the world know that Italy's wines come in two colors. Roughly four times as many white wines are produced here as reds. Over the last 20 years white wines from Friuli—Venezia Giulia (better known in our country as simply Friuli)—have been making their way to New World shores and stores.

> **Important Things to Know**
>
> The districts of Collio and Colli Orientali del Friuli are the top winemaking districts in Friuli. The cool climate produces wines that are crisp and clean. The grapes of Friuli include Riesling (both Rhein and Italico), Müller-Thurgau, Chardonnay, Sauvignon Blanc, Pinot Bianco, and Pinot Grigio. Add to this impressive area of white varietals two local winners, Tocai Friulano and Ribolla Gialla.

And now for something really different: One Friuli wine that falls into no category is Picolit, an unusual (and expensive) white dessert wine. It makes a good conversation piece when wine lovers gather.

Umbria—Home of Orvieto

To the south of Tuscany, almost in the center of Italy lies Umbria. According to legend, its best-known wine, the white Orvieto, has been planted since Etruscan times. The vineyards are made of volcanic rock, which gives the wine a distinctive, earthy character. Made from the Trebbiano grape, Orvieto also has a Classico zone, and is produced as both a dry and a semi-dry wine. You can find a good Orvieto for less than $10.

Sicily and Sardinia

Although Sardinian wines have achieved some popularity in the U.S., most of them are no more than ordinary. Sicily does produce some interesting wines, notably from Regaleali's vineyards, intriguingly situated on the slopes of Mount Etna. The white DOC wines of Etna have a volcanic character that makes them particularly attractive.

Regaleali produces red, white, and rosé wines; these range from mediocre to extraordinary reds that are among Italy's finest wines. As one producer of note in Sicily, Count Regaleali's best red wine is called Rosso del Conte. He makes a Chardonnay that rivals those of the Cote D'Or. Regaleali also makes a dry rosato (rosé) that sells for about $8.

Some good sparkling wines hail from Sicily, ranging from the brut to the sweet, muscat-flavored spumantes from the Island of Pantellaria (see Chapter 18).

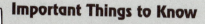

Important Things to Know

Sicily also produces a fortified wine known as Marsala, which ranges in style from dry to very sweet and in quality from average to very refined. Marsala is used either as an apéritif or in cooking, and is covered in Chapter 19.

We Next Play Veneto

The best wines from the Veneto zone come from vineyards surrounding the beautiful city of Verona. Verona's three leading wines are among the most well-known and widely available in our country: the reds, Valpolicella and Bardolino, and the white, Soave. Too bad the Montagues and the Capulets didn't raise a glass to settle their differences.

Important Things to Know

Valpolicella and Bardolino are both made primarily from the Corvina grape variety. Bardolino is named for the charming village situated on Lake Garda. It also has a Classico zone where the better wines are made. Bardolino is a light, fruity wine, pleasant when young. It's closer in style to Beaujolais than to its Corvina cousin, Valpolicella. Try a chilled Bardolino on a hot summer evening (and imagine you're on the beautiful lake in the Italian countryside). The Valpolicella district resides on a series of hills, some of which overlook Verona.

Valpolicella is fuller in body than Bardolino, with more color, alcohol, durability, depth, and complexity. Those labeled Classico come from the best growing area; the exception is Valpantena, made from a valley to the east. It doesn't have the Classico label, but its quality is as good as Classico—and sometimes better. If you see Superiore on the label, it means a minimum of a year's aging. Some Valpolicellas improve in the bottle for several years.

Another classification of Valpolicella is called Recioto. It's made from grapes grown high up on the hillside and dried on straw mats in lofts or attics to concentrate their sugars and fruits before vinification. Recioto contains from 14 to 16 percent alcohol and is made in three different styles: The first is a sparkling wine, which is rarely seen in the U.S.; the second—labeled simply Recioto—is sweet because fermentation stopped or "stuck" before all the sugar was fermented; lastly, there is Amarone Recioto (or Amarone della Valpolicella, or just Amarone), which has fermented completely. Amarone is one of the special wines of Italy that deserves super-premium classification. Amarone is velvety, round, soft, well-balanced, and full of character. Ten to 15 years are possible for a good Amarone, although most are delightful after five years.

Soave is an easy-to-drink white wine that comes from an area near Valpolicella. Made predominantly from the Garganega grape along with some Trebbiano, Soave is available as both Classico and non-Classico wine. Most of the better Soaves come from the Classico zone, an area to the northeast of the picturesque town of Soave itself.

No doubt Americans not only love the pleasant flavor of Valpolicella, Bardolino, and Soave, but the price as well: Most retail in the $5 to $8 range. Two other white wines of the region, Bianco di Custoza and Lugana, fall into the same range.

The Northern Climes—Trentino-Alto Adige

Trentino-Alto Adige, located at the northerly top of the "boot," is actually two very distinct zones: the Italian-speaking Trentino to the south, and the primarily German-speaking Alto Adige (or South Tyrol) to the north. Not surprisingly, the wines of both zones are as distinctly different as the languages.

Most of the red wine made in this border region goes to Austria. Its white wines rival those of Friuli. Pinot Grigio, Chardonnay, and Pinot Bianco from Alto Adige retail in the $6 to $15 range.

Lombardy

Once famous for its expert craftsmen, Lombardy is less well-known for its wine, although some delightful red and white wines come from this region. The best white wine is Lugana, produced from the slopes bordering Lake Garda. Four mid-premium reds come from the Valltellina region, high up in the pre-Alps, just below the Swiss border. The predominant grape is Nebbiolo, known here as Chiavennasca. The four light-bodied red wines are Sassella, Inferno, Grumello, and Valgella. All are highly drinkable and affordable too: usually under $10. They can be consumed young.

Latium

Latium (or Lazio) is the area around Rome. The best-known wine is Frascati, made from the Trebbiano grape and produced on the volcanic slopes of the Colli Romani southwest of Rome. Named for the town Frascati, the wine should be light, fresh, charming, and fragrant. It is usually dry (labeled asciutto or secco), although sweeter versions are made too (cannellino, dolci, or amabile). It's meant to be enjoyed young. Vast quantities of Frascati are produced and quality can be variable.

Emilia-Romagna

This region is famous for the city of Bologna and the ocean of soft, effervescent Lambrusco wine it produces each year.

Abruzzo

Abruzzo is best known in the U.S. for the red Montepulciano d'Abruzzo. It is a very inexpensive wine frequently sold in magnums for $4 to $6. It is easy to drink with low tannins and low acidity.

Marche (The Marches)

Out of the usual travel routes and without any great historical attractions, its white wine, Verdicchio, put Marche on the map. The most famous is the Verdicchio dei Castelli di Jesi, a large wine zone. The grapes are the Verdicchio with up to 20 percent of Trebbiano Toscano and Malvasio Toscano permitted. It's a dry, simple wine to be enjoyed young, within two years at most.

Campania

This is the area around Naples, the land of Mount Vesuvius. From the northeast of the city come some outstanding wines, ranging from mid-premium to, at times, noble quality. These are the work of Antonio Mastroberardino—if his name is difficult to pronounce, the wines are worth it.

Greco du Tufo and Fiano di Avellino are Mastroberardino's unique whites. Greco is viscous and quite strong in bouquet and flavor; sometimes it is also strong in alcohol, but it's always well balanced. Its flavors have a bitter almond edge that increases with bottle age. It retails in the $12 to $18 range. Fiano has greater elegance of body and texture and a sort of toasty bouquet.

Despite the excellence of the two whites, Mastroberardino's ultimate work of art is the rich, full-bodied, and tannic Taurasi. This DOCG wine is made from the Aglianico grape grown at 1,000 feet or higher. Great vintages of Taurasi age well for 10 or 20 years and can attain near noble status. The single-vineyard Taurasi, Radici, is especially recommended.

Apulia and Basilicata—The Southern Tip

Along with Calabria, these regions in the south of Italy are mainly responsible for Italy's famous resemblance to a boot (they are the shoe part) and for producing a sea of wine. Apulia is essentially a gigantic vineyard, although only in the past two decades have modern winemaking techniques resulted in wines of note. Formerly heavy in alcohol and often sunbaked, the trend in Apulia has been toward fruitier, fresher, lighter wines. The Aleatico di Puglia grape is used to make a red DOC dessert wine.

Basilicata is distinguished by the production of Aglianico del Vulture, a superb DOC red wine that improves with age. This is a mid-premium wine that is quite smooth and has a caramel background and lots of fruit.

The Least You Need to Know

➤ DOC (Denominazione di Origine Controllata) and DOCG (Denominazione di Origine Controllata e Garantita) are indicators of Italian wine quality.

➤ There are many regions of Italy that produce fine wine.

➤ Italian wines provide good value.

Olé!—Wines in the Spanish Style

Table wines from Spain, Portugal, Chile, and Argentina all share attributes in common—their taste, flavors, and styles are relatively similar and they all offer excellent value for what is in the bottle. You should look for these wines for everyday drinking.

The wines in this chapter range from the traditional wines of Spain and Portugal, like the regional red Riojas and Daos from Spain and Portugal respectively, to the eclectic wines of Chile and Argentina, where viticulture introduced by Spanish settlers has been transformed over the centuries by successive generations of immigrants. All of the countries covered in this chapter produce substantial quantities of agreeable wine of good value, and all deserve greater visibility worldwide.

Spain Olé!

Colorful Spain conjures up images of bright sunlight over mountains, vibrant Flamenco dancers, costumed toreadors, and if you're up on your architecture, that strange-looking Gaudi hotel in Barcelona. Wine? The color is red, and the quality ranges from ordinary to superb.

Despite the fact that Spain ranks third in world wine production, after Italy and France, few Americans are familiar with Spanish wines beyond the fortified Sherry and the red Rioja. In today's market, Spain offers a wide variety of wine styles and with good, careful selection, you'll find an impressive array of wines at bargain value.

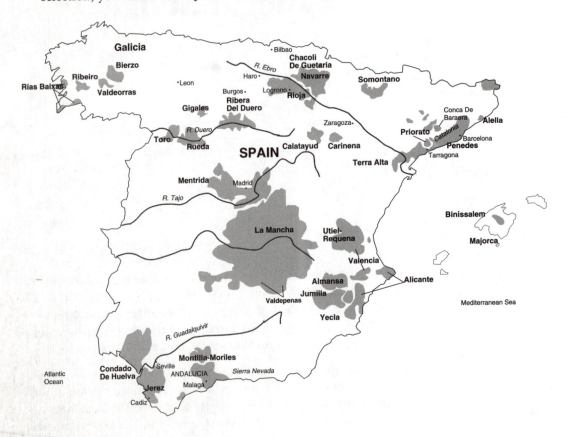

The regions of Spain's finest wines.

> ### Important Things to Know
>
> One obstacle to the recognition of Spain by the wine world has been the lack of a uniform regulation system, coupled with laxity of enforcement where laws existed. This has been in the process of changing considerably. Spain's wine laws, like Italy's, have a dual-level classification: *Denominaciones de Origen* (DO) and the higher classification *Denominaciones de Origen Calificada* (DOCa). The higher tier was recently added in 1991, and its only occupant to date is Rioja, the popular red wine from the Rioja region. Wines with no DO classification fall into the category of table wines, *Vino de la Tierra*, which is comparable to the French *Vins de Pays*.

Rioja

Located in north-central Spain, Rioja is the one region that virtually all wine lovers have heard of. Rioja is divided into three districts, Rioja Alavesa and Rioja Alta which have a cool climate, and Rioja Baja, which has the warm climate usually associated with Spain. The predominant grape is Tempranillo, although Rioja wine is typically a blend. The fruity Grenache (known in Spain as Garnacha) is one of the better-known varieties used in blending. The best Riojas are usually made using grapes from the two cooler districts, but Riojas may contain grapes from all three.

Rioja has recently seen the transition from traditional to modern winemaking, with impressive results. Using the traditional method for making red Rioja meant years of aging in small oak barrels (interestingly, American oak); the resulting wine was too often mediocre and flat, suffering the combined effects of overaging and poor winemaking. The modern trend is to replace cask aging with stainless steel and bottle aging, resulting in fresher, crisper, fruitier wines. While American oak is still traditional, there is a movement toward French oak, which imparts more character to the wine.

Before modernization and DOCa classification, the term "Reserva" on a red wine label was a statement of aging only, not quality. Not anymore. The term "Reserva," used exclusively for red wines, now denotes a minimum level of quality as well as aging. There are several types of red Riojas. Some Riojas are young wines with no oak aging. Others, labeled *crianza*, are aged by the vintner in oak and in bottle for two years; *reservas* are aged for three years (and now, quality is demanded). The finest Riojas are aged five years or longer and bestowed with the status *gran reserva*.

Red wines make up 75 percent of Rioja's total output. Rosé wines comprise 15 percent of Rioja wines, with the Garnacha grape used to make full-bodied rosés. Prices are generally reasonable: Crianza reds begin at about $6–7 per bottle. Gran reservas may go up to $25. The top recent vintages for Rioja are (in order): 1982, 1989, 1981, and 1990.

Penedes

The Penedes region in Catalonia, south of Barcelona, is less famous than Rioja, but it is easily Spain's region for table wines. Its two leading producers, Torres and Jean Leon, are both known for their outstanding red wines, which start in the $6 to $8 range with the better wines going for up to $30 a bottle. These wines are made in both varietal renditions as well as blends.

Important Things to Know

HEY!

A sizable percentage of Spain's sparkling wine emanates (or effervesces) from the Penedes. In the town of San Sadurni do Noya, located in the El Penedes Central, are the leading producers, including Cordorniu, the world's largest producer of sparkling wines by the *Méthode Champenoise* (champagne method) and Freixenet, which is growing in production and popularity. For more on sparkling wines see Chapter 18.

Ribera del Duero

Ribera del Duero, located north of Madrid, is Spain's new, upcoming wine region. Until recently, the legendary Vega Sicilia winery dominated the region and its acclaim by producing Spain's singular most renowned wine, Unico (mainly Tempranillo, with some Cabernet Sauvignon). Unico is an intense, tannic, and concentrated red wine that requires long aging after its 10 years in cask and several more years in bottle at the winery. It sells for more than $100 a bottle.

Rueda—Home of Verdejo

Located west of Ribera del Duero, the Rueda region is known for one of Spain's best white wines. Made from the Verdejo grape, which is slightly sweet and round on the palate, the wine is stylish with a fruity character. The price is attractive, from $6 to $8 a bottle.

Galicia

Galicia, on the Atlantic Ocean in northwest Spain, has one specific district, Rias Baixas, that boasts an exhilarating new wine: the white Albarino, which displays an intense acidity, flowery, scents, and delicate flavors reminiscent of a Condrieu (from the Rhône Valley, see Chapter 12). Albarinos range in price from about $8 to $17 a bottle.

Jerez de la Frontera—Sherry Anyone?

Jerez is a large wine region in southern Spain and is famous for the production of Sherry. The wines from Jerez are subject to the country's highest regulatory standards. The predominant grape here is the Palomino, a delicious variety that undergoes a unique process to produce the fortified Sherry.

The making of Sherry bears a definitive statement on the importance of soil as well as climate. As a viticultural area, Jerez is divided into three sections, all based on soil type. The most prized, and least productive, regions have soils characterized by *albariza*, a soil that is predominately chalk, with limestone and magnesium. These areas, easy to recognize by their white topsoils, bear the best Sherry grapes. By law, at least 40 percent of the grapes used in Sherry must come from the famed albariza soils. *Barro*, another soil division (literally "clay"), is more productive; árena, the third region (sand), bears vines that are immensely productive but weak in character.

Sherry is made in large volume by modern, efficient methods of crushing and vinification. As a fortified wine, Sherry will be discussed further in Chapter 19.

Deciphering the Spanish Wine Label

These are the important terms you will find on a Spanish wine label.

➤ **Crianza.** For red wines, the wine has been aged for at least two years, including a period of oak aging; for white and rosé wines, Crianza means that the wines are a minimum of one year old.

➤ **Reserva.** Red reservas must be aged in oak and bottle for a minimum of three years; white and rosé reservas must be aged for a minimum of two years, including six months in oak. Reservas are produced only in good vintages.

➤ **Gran Reserva.** Red wines must be aged in oak and bottle for a minimum of five years; white and rosé gran reservas must be aged a minimum of four years with a minimum of six months in oak. Gran Reservas are made only in exceptional vintages.

> ➤ **Cosecha or Vendimia.** The vintage year.

> ➤ **Bodega.** Winery.

> ➤ **Tinto.** Red.

> ➤ **Blanco.** White.

> ➤ **Viejo.** Old.

> ➤ **Viña.** Vineyard.

Portugal

If you grew up in the 1970s, there's a good chance your first wine was either Mateus or Lancer's. These two medium-dry and somewhat effervescent rosés in the interesting-looking bottles are two of Portugal's most familiar wines. Perhaps its most famous wine is the dark dessert wine, Port, although more Americans have probably heard of it than experienced an authentic one.

Ironically, most Portuguese drink red and white table wines, which are less well-known outside of their own country. However, the current trend of modernization and stronger quality control should ensure Portugal higher status and visibility in the expanding world wine market.

Within the Portuguese classification system, the highest tier is the *Denominação de Origem Controlada* (DOC), awarded to only 11 wine regions. The next tier, the *Indicação de Proveniencia Regulamentad* (IPR) has been awarded to 32 regions, many of which are waiting for elevation to DOC status. IPR corresponds roughly to the VDQS status of France. In the table wine category, *Vinho de Mesa Regional* corresponds to the Spanish *Vino de la Tierra* and the French *Vins de Pays*. All remaining wines are known simply as *Vinho de Mesa*.

Port has its own system of classification, implemented and enforced by the rigid Instituto do Vinho do Porto. The appellation system for Port is called the *Denominação de Origem*, and follows stringent standards.

Wines of Portugal.

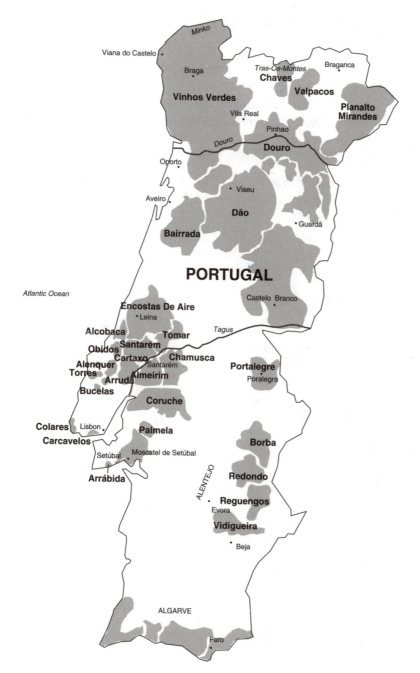

Vinho Verde—Do You Like Your Wine "Green"?

The color refers to the grapes, not the wine. This DOC region, between the Minhos and Douros Rivers, is the country's largest wine producing region. Vinho Verde wines are made for early consumption as fresh, fruity wines. Their tart, bracing, refreshing character is enhanced by a distinct degree of effervescence. As the name suggests, the wines are acidic and have a pleasantly underripe character. White Vino Verde wines can add a unique flair to your favorite seafood dish. Yes, there are red Vinho Verdes, but the description "acidic" is an understatement—definitely an acquired taste.

The most widely available Vinho Verdes are the brands Aveleda and Casal Garcia, which sell for $6 to $7 a bottle. These are medium-dry wines, meant to be served chilled, and are usually no more than ordinary. More expensive Vinho Verdes are made from the Alvarhino grape from the sub-region of Monção (as in the Spanish Albarino) and retail for $12 to $20 a bottle. The higher quality Vinho Verdes are more complex, with some potential for aging. They may be hard to find but are worth the effort.

Dao—Affordable Table Wines

Dao is the country's finest table wine region. The best Dao wines are the reds, although there are some quality whites as well. Most wines are blends from within the region, and some are vintage-dated. Those that are aged in wood casks are entitled to Reserva status; cask-aging makes them soft and mellow. Dao reds are typically smooth and full-bodied, while the whites are light and simple. Few stand out as distinctive, but they offer pleasant drinking at equally pleasant prices.

Douro—Home of Port

Located in northeastern Portugal, the Douro River region produces Portugal's most renowned wine, Port, along with sturdy red table wines. The steep and hilly terrain, with hot summers moderated by cool evenings, are ideal for growing the deep-colored, full-flavored grape varieties needed for Port. For more on Port, see Chapter 19.

Some interesting table wines made from the local grapes used to make port also come from the Douro. These wines are intense and robust and require years of aging.

Moscatel de Setubal

The excellent fortified sweet wines of this region still suffer the stigma of an erroneous and unfortunate association with the inferior, American-made Muscatel. They are both fortified wines—the resemblance ends there! Setubal wines are deeply colored with a strong, complex Muscat character; they improve with long aging. Interestingly, the producers usually offer a six-year-old and a twenty-five-year-old bottling. They are available here in fine wine stores, often at an attractive price for a wine of this high quality.

Deciphering the Language of Portuguese Wine

These are the important terms you will need to know to be familiar with Portuguese wine:

➤ **Reserva.** A vintage wine of superior quality.

➤ **Garrafeira.** A reserva that has been aged a minimum of two years in cask and one year in bottle for a red wine; six months in cask and six months in bottle for a white wine.

➤ **Quinta.** Estate or vineyard.

➤ **Colheita.** Vintage year.

➤ **Seco.** Dry.

➤ **Adega.** Winery.

➤ **Tinto.** Red.

➤ **Vinho.** Wine.

Chile—Spanish Roots, New World Flavor

Chilean winemaking enjoys something of a hybrid tradition. The first vineyards were planted in Chile by Spanish settlers in the mid-16th century. Then, in the 19th century, a wave of immigrants, mostly Italian, brought with them their own winemaking legacy. To add even more international flair, much of Chile's climate is suited to the Bordeaux grape varieties, like Cabernet Sauvignon, Chardonnay, and Merlot, while a few regions are ideal for the Riesling, which emerges delightfully fresh and dry, austere, and similar in style to the German Steinwein (see Chapter 15 for more about German wines).

In short, Chilean winemaking is a cosmopolitan affair; particularly interesting for a country that's relatively isolated—bordered on one side by the lofty peaks of the Andes and on the other by the Pacific Ocean. High coastal ranges protect much of the growing land from excess humidity, and the soothing Pacific protects it from excess heat.

> ## Important Things to Know
>
> The Central Valley, located between the coastal mountains and the Andes, is the main grape-growing area. Here, vineyards are categorized according to latitude. The best winemaking grapes are grown in the middle region, which spans an area from roughly 50 miles north of Santiago to 150 miles south of this major city. The land to the north of the middle area where it's warmer (remember, this is the Southern Hemisphere) is used mainly for growing table grapes, along with the grapes used in *Pisco*, the Chilean brandy. The land to the south is the home of Pais and Moscatel—popular grapes for the domestic wine market, although little of the wine is exported.

From south to north within the Central Valley, the wine regions are

➤ **Maule.** This is where the Curico district is located. It is cooler and less dry than Rapel; parts of this region grow Pail.

➤ **Rapel.** This is where the Colchagua district is located. It is a cooler region than Maipo.

➤ **Maipo.** This is where many of the major wineries are located. It is a relatively small region.

➤ **Aconcagua.** This region is north of Santiago and is the warmest area for quality grapes.

➤ **Bio Bio.** This region is planted mainly with Pais and Moscatel.

➤ **Casablanca.** Another of Chile's wine regions, Casablanca, is near Santiago to the north and is known for its new plantings of white grapes.

Chile is a relative newcomer to the export market. In fact, if you mention that you're buying a Chilean wine to a lot of people, you're likely to get a blank stare. The Pais grape, which locals have enjoyed for centuries, is hardly a household word outside of its native land. Chilean Merlot and Cabernet Sauvignon were hailed internationally two decades ago, but export efforts were minor and inconsistent. Only since the mid-1980s has winemaking for export become a serious industry. The number of vines bearing Cabernet Sauvignon, Merlot, and Chardonnay grapes has multiplied, and so has the number of bottlings designated for global consumption.

Foreign investment has had a great influence. The Miguel Torres winery in Curico has a Spanish owner. Even a California winemaker, Augustin Huneeus of Franciscan Vineyards, has become a developer of the new Casablanca wine region.

It was inevitable that the acclaim received by Chile's French-style reds would inspire the interest of Bordeaux's best. Château Lafite-Rothschild is an owner of the Los Vascos winery, and the Vina Aquitania is the collaboration of the noted Bordeaux châteaux, Château Cos d'Estournel, and Château Margaux. In Chile the byword is "the French are coming!"

Important Things to Know

> Like California wines, Chilean wines carry varietal names, usually in conjunction with the region and sometimes the district. Many of Chile's white wines resemble inexpensive magnum wines from California. The reds are better and offer excellent value, ranging in price from $4 to $12 a bottle. Chilean reds are not yet contenders in making world-class wines; however, Chile has the potential, as exemplified by the outstanding Don Melchor made from Cabernet Sauvignon by Concha y Toro, a winery known for its excellent, inexpensive varietal wines. The Chilean wine industry is moving toward producing better varietal wines, and in a decade or so, should be a factor in world-class wines.

Argentina—Good Beef, Good Wine

Argentina produces roughly about the same amount of wine as the U.S. It is the fifth largest wine-producing country in the world, with a per capita annual consumption of more than 22 gallons—one of the world's highest. Maybe this explains why so little is exported!

Historically, the pattern of grape-growing and vinification is similar to Chile's: Vineyards were introduced by Spaniards in the 16th century, and the industry was influenced and expanded by the (mainly) Italian immigrants of the 19th century. Today, Argentinian winemaking is under strict control of the government.

Important Things to Know

> Most of the vineyards are concentrated in the hot, arid Mendoza region, shielded from the ocean by the Andes. The next largest wine producing area is San Juan, north of Mendoza and even hotter and drier. La Rioja is north of San Juan.

Most grapes grow in the flatlands, though the better vineyards are situated at higher elevations where the climate is tempered. Temperature during the maturation period can exceed 110 degrees F, which encourages high sugar content, but can give the wines a peculiar sunbaked flavor.

The predominant red grape has historically been the Malbec, which adds body and substance to many French wines. Recently, it seems to have been displaced by the Italian Bonarda. Other red varietals that manage to thrive in the *caliente* environment include Tempranillo, Barbera, Syrah, Lambrusco, Cabernet Sauvignon, and amazingly, Pinot Noir. Among the whites grown here are the Pedro Jiminez, Moscatel, Torrontes, Chardonnay, Riesling, Chenin Blanc, and Semillion. The red varietals remain better than the whites.

With the exception of a few superior reds, Argentinian wines are typically rough on the palate, ordinary in quality and ranging from powerful and hot to powerful and volatile (that is, bordering on vinegar). With the trend toward modernization, this should all soon be in the past. At the helm of the modernization movement is the vast Penaflor winery—one of the world's largest. Argentina offers many good-value reds between $4 and $7 a bottle.

The Least You Need to Know

➤ Spain, Portugal, Chile, and Argentina all offer excellent values in simple, inexpensive table wines.

➤ The best reds of Spain come from Rioja.

Chapter 15

Germany— and Wines from Other Interesting Countries

In This Chapter

➤ The many wines of Germany

➤ Austrian wine

➤ The wines of Switzerland

➤ Greek wine

➤ Wines from Hungary

The wines of Germany offer a wide range of delightful wine experiences. However, you must memorize, memorize, and memorize to be fully knowledgeable on the topic. The wines of Switzerland offer a unique style and taste. The wines of Austria are similar in style to German wines, but do not achieve the quality of the best German examples. The wines of Greece and Hungary offer simple, inexpensive wines that are delightful for everyday drinking. In this chapter we will explore these wine regions.

Germany—Zum Wohl! (Cheers!)

If you've ever tasted a German red, chances are you were not too far from the banks of the Rhine. Virtually no German red wines are exported. All the German wines you'll see in your favorite wine shop are white, although contrary to legend, not all are sweet. Some carry the word *"Tröcken"* on the label, which means dry. They do tend to be medium-dry to sweet, floral and fragrant, refreshing, and characteristically un-oaked.

The finest wine regions of Germany.

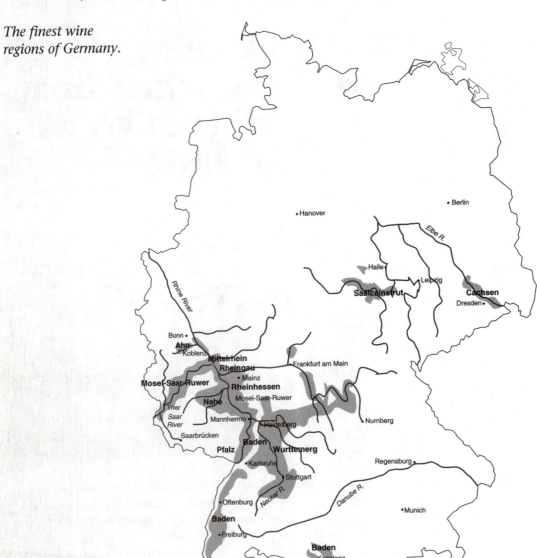

When reading a German wine label, always look for a varietal name along with the place. And don't be too complacent about how well you've gotten to understand the French

AOC classification system. German wines require even more memorization. Since 1971 when German wine regulations were revised, they are even stricter than the French.

For a wine-producing country, Germany is pretty far north. There's little of that bright golden sunshine needed for red grapes to flourish. As a result, at least 85 percent of German wine produced is white.

Microclimates and More

Instead of having one generalized climate like most winegrowing districts, German wine districts have a series of microclimates that vary with every turn of the winding rivers, like the Rhine and the Mosel, on which the choicest vineyard sites are located. The rivers temper the harsh extremes of weather and help protect the vulnerable grapes.

The best vineyard sections face south rather than east or west. Every element of topography affects the wine: the steepness of the hill on which the vines are planted; the amount of sun reflected from the adjoining rivers; the nearness of a sheltering forest (and its density) or a mountain peak, both of which can protect the site from strong, cold winds; the altitude; and, as in other winegrowing areas, the soil variation. The climate not only varies from place to place, but is easily subject to change from year to year. This is one country where vintages do count.

Where Riesling Reigns

Germany is the first home of the noble Riesling, which unlike many vinifera, is not a sun worshipper. It is, however, something of a snob. Only in Germany's best vineyards does it ripen consistently; as a result, it represents only 21 percent of all viticultural plantings.

The most prolific grape variety is Müller-Thurgau, which is reputedly either a cross between Riesling and Sylvaner or two clones of Riesling. It ripens earlier than Riesling, and yields a soft, round, fragrant wine, but is not in the same class as Riesling. Müller-Thurgau loves the cool German climate; not surprisingly, it's loved in return by the winegrowers. Other important white varietals include Sylvaner, Kerner, Scheurebe, and Ruländer (Pinot Gris). The red varietal Spatburgunder (Pinot Noir) is grown in the warmer parts of the country.

German Wine Laws Simplified

German words or place names are often formed by adding one word to another to another, until the result is a pretty lengthy appellation (pun not intended). Well, German wine labels evolve along similar lines. German wines, like many other European wines, are named for their place of origin, which is usually a village name and a vineyard such as

Bernkasteler (town) Graben (vineyard). Add to this the principle of naming the wine for the varietal (as in Bernkasteler Graben *Riesling*). And finally, there is one more qualification that is unique to Germany—the ripeness of the grapes, or *prädikat* (as in Bernkasteler Graben Riesling *Spätlese*). Wines that are given a *prädikat* form the highest tier in the German classification system representing the highest qualities. Germany is the only country where you can judge a wine's quality by how long it takes you to read the label.

The system of assigning rank to ripeness is not so unusual when we consider the cool German climate in which ripeness is the desired, but sometimes elusive, goal. There are five *prädikat* levels, the higher usually indicating a higher quality. From the lowest to the highest (ripest), these are

➤ Kabinett

➤ Spätlese

➤ Auslese

➤ Beerenauslese

➤ Tröckenbeerenauslese

Important Things to Know

The wine's classification is assigned according to the Oechle scale, which measures the quantity of sugar in the grape juice prior to fermentation. It does not necessarily mean that the finished product—the wine—is sweet. At the three highest levels, the wine *is* sweet; the amount of sugar in the ripe grapes inevitably results in a sweet wine. At the lower *prädikat* levels, the grape juice may be fully fermented to dryness.

The finest wines at each level are made from the Riesling grape, although the quality of wines made from other grape varieties improves as riper grapes are used. Kabinett wines are generally relatively dry, fruity, and well-balanced. Wines labeled from Spätlese on indicate some special degree of selection. Spätlese wines are made from grapes ranging from fairly ripe to greatly mature, and can span the spectrum from fairly dry to slightly sweet. For Auslese, Beerenauslese, Eiswein, and Tröckenbeerenauslese, see the section on "Sweet and Late-Harvest Wines."

Wines with a ripeness rating fall into the category of *Qualitätswein mit Prädikat* (QmP) (which translates as quality wines with a special attribute), the highest tier. Below QmP is *Qualitätswein* (QbA), the short form of *Qualitätswein bestimmter Anbaugebiet* (literally, quality wines from a special region). The lowest tier is the table wine category, either marked *Tafelwien* or *Landwein* (table wines with a regional indicator). Less than 10 percent of Germany's wines are in the table wine category.

Wine regulations also define viticultural areas as follows:

➤ *Bereich* is an enormous region, and may be subdivided into one or more *Grosslage*.

➤ *Grosslage* means large site. It's essentially a large vineyard that contains smaller vineyards (*Einzellagen*)—sometimes several hundred acres and thousands of vineyards, all of which produce wines of similar quality and character. A wine from a Grosslage is identified on the label with a generic name that reads like a vineyard name. The way to tell the difference is to memorize the Grosslagen names.

➤ *Einzellage* is the smallest defined region, an individual vineyard which is at least twelve acres. The Einzellage is indicated on the label after the village name.

Wine Wisdom
In addition to region, place, varietal, and sometimes ripeness, each bottle of German wine carries a control number that specifies the year of production, the year of registration, and a code number identifying the producer and the individual lot of wine. Each wine is scientifically analyzed to determine if it meets its requirements, and is also tasted.

What Is Liebfraumilch?

Liebfraumilch, which translates as *milk of the Virgin,* is a delightful, refreshing, enjoyable wine. Who can dislike a wine with a name like that? Actually, the name comes from its origin in a vineyard surrounding a church dedicated to Our Lady, in Worms in the Rheinhessen region. Liebfraumilch is probably the best-known German wine in the U.S., and for many people, their first taste of *vitis vinifera*.

Yellow in color, with a slight greenish hue, Liebfraumilch is a blend of several grape varieties, primarily Müller-Thurgau with Riesling, Silvaner, and/or Kerner. Along with the Rheinhessen, it is produced in the Pfalz region (the two main regions); with lesser quantities produced in the Nahe, and the Rheingau. Liebfraumilch is ranked QbA; typically low in alcohol, it is medium-dry, with a refreshing acidity, and a pleasant fruity flavor. It is definitely meant to be enjoyed young. Liebfraumilch sells from $5 to $7 a bottle.

> ## Important Things to Know
>
> Liebfraumilch and many other inexpensive German wines are produced using a method called *süss reserve*, which helps maintain a desired level of sweetness. The wine is fully fermented to create a dry wine with low alcohol and high acidity. But here's the trick: Before fermentation, a small quantity of grape juice is withheld, to be blended later with the fermented wine. The unfermented grape juice, or süss reserve, adds its natural, sweet, fruity flavor to the finished wine. Wines produced in this style are called *lieblich*, which means gentle. They are fruity, light-bodied wines with a pleasing sweetness and are perfect to drink on their own.

Tröcken Wines

Outside of Germany, many people are familiar only with lieblich style wines. But there are other styles, less sweet, which have become trendy in their homeland. The driest category is *tröcken* (dry). Trocken wines have virtually no residual sugar and range in taste from austere to tart. *Halbtröcken* (half-dry) wines are midway between tröcken and lieblich. More mellow than Tröcken wines, they have a certain amount of residual sugar and a fairly dry taste. They are somewhat higher in alcohol than Kabinett or Spätlese wines.

Sweet and Late-Harvest Wines

These are the wines from the Auslese category on up. They're made from grapes that are over-ripened, rot-infected, or frozen—but look, who's to argue with success? These are some of the world's finest and most unique wines.

Auslese wines are made from over-ripe grapes that endow the wine with a fuller body and a higher concentration of flavor. Their sweetness is usually balanced by sufficient acidity. Beerenauslese wines are made from grapes that have over-ripened and have usually been attacked by the noble rot, Botrytis, which gives them a honeyed and luscious opulence. Winemakers choosing to make a Beerenauslese are gamblers: They risk losing their crop to frost as the grapes are left on the vine to ripen. As a result, only a small quantity of Beerenauslese is produced each year; needless to say, it's suitably expensive.

Tröckenbeerenausleses are the most exotic wines in the hierarchy. The berries are individually selected, and are usually attacked by Botrytis (although it's not a legal requirement). These wines possess a concentrated lusciousness like nectar—no doubt this is the beverage the gods enjoy in Valhalla. The intense lusciousness is the combined effect of the grape's essence, the flavor of noble rot, and the high level of residual sugar (which may approach 20 percent). This wine is a killer to make. It's not only risky, it's a difficult wine to vinify and requires superior skill, dedication, and TLC throughout the winemaking process. Prices can easily be in the three-figure range.

Maybe it is the cool climate, or maybe it's the same spirit that produced Mozart, Beethoven, and Wagner, but the German winemaking industry has some truly unique aspects. Perhaps the strangest is Eiswein (literally, ice wine), made from grapes left on the vine to freeze (talk about turning a liability into an asset!). Once harvested, the grapes are crushed gently to retain the grape juice but not the ice. The juice left to undergo fermentation is richly concentrated in sugar, flavor, and acidity. Depending on the skill of the winemaker, this opulent wine can equal the finest Auslese, Beerenauslese, or Tröckenbeerenauslese.

> **Wine Wisdom**
> With the unification of Germany, the number of wine regions changed from 11 to 13. The two eastern regions are even further north than their western counterparts and are something of an unknown quantity in the world market. Even among the 11 regions in the west, only a few have made inroads into the U.S. wine market.

The Home of the Rhine Maidens

In the opera, *Das Rheingold*, the gold refers to the treasured precious metal that can be fashioned into a ring that grants the bearer ultimate power, and the rest is too long to explain. Some of the Rhine's golden treasures come in bottles, and you don't have to embark on an endless quest to find them (although admittedly, they're not as easy to find in wine shops as their French or Italian counterparts).

Four of Germany's wine regions bear the name of the renowned river: The Rheingau, Rheinhessen, Pfalz (formerly called the Rheinphalz), and the Mittelrhein.

Rheingau

The Rheingau is a tiny wine region (only one-quarter the size of the Mosel, which we'll get to in a moment), but along with the Mosel-Saar-Ruwer, it is the most important in Germany. It's divided into 10 Grosslagen and 120 einzellagen (vineyards) over 28 communities jutting steeply along the Rhine's banks. Riesling grapes account for more than 80 percent of the vineyard planting and produce the finest wines of the region. The Rieslings tend to be round, soft, and deep in color.

The following are the leading Grosslagen:

➤ Hochheim produces full-bodied and fruity wines, often with a trace of earthiness. The best vineyards include Domdechaney, Hölle, and Sommerheil, whose wines fall within the mid-premium quality range and are comparable in quality to wines from Johannisberg (see below). The finest estate is Schloss Eltz, followed by the vineyards of Taubenberg and Sonnenberg.

➤ Erbach's sturdy wines are noted for their fine, full-bodied flavors and long life. Erbach gained its stature primarily on the reputation of the wines produced by the Marcobrunn estate; in the best vintages, these noble wines rank with the world's best.

➤ In Hattenheim, the Steinberg estate produces superlative wines. The wines of other Hattenheim vineyards are somewhat more delicate and less firm than the noble class Steinbergers.

➤ In Winkle, the Schloss Vollrads vineyard eclipses all others. Its wines are characterized by their ripeness and great fruit—unquestionably noble quality material. Their Kabinett and Spätlese rank in the mid- to super-premium range.

➤ Rauenthaler wines are characterized by a distinctive sense of fruit and an almost spicy flair. Most of the wines fall into the mid-premium range, but some of the better *lagen*—Baiken, Wülfen, Langenstrück, and Nonnenburg—are capable of producing wines of noble stature.

➤ Eltville produces wines that are pleasing, fine, soft, and have good bouquet. Although less distinguished than the wines of the Rauenthal, they are highly drinkable, simple to mid-premium quality wines.

➤ Johannisberg, the village, is the most famous name of the Rheingau. The wines made here range from simple to super-premium in quality, with the Schloss Johannisberg standing out for its noble wines from great vintages. Johannisberger wines are distinguished for their finesse and fine bouquet. Schloss Johannisberg wines have an extra dimension of breed, placing them with the world's great wines.

Rheinhessen

The large Rheinhessen region produces a greater variety of wines—ranging from small table wines to *spritzenwein*—than any other German wine district. Its most famous export is Liebfraumilch, which is made by nearly 99 percent of the region's 167 villages. The Rheinhessen accounts for 50 percent of all German wine exports.

Important Things to Know

Rheinhessen wines tend to be soft, with a pronounced character that makes them the easiest to identify of all German wines. But due to the temperate climate, the wines lack the character they might have had if they had to fight for their lives. The popularity of the Rheinhessen wines is probably based on their intense bouquet and straightforward sweetness. Most Rheinhessen wines are made from the Müller-Thurgau grape, which produces juicy, soft, fruity wines. The next mostly widely used vine is the Sylvaner, which produces full, round wines.

The Rheinhessen is composed of three *Bereich*: Bingen, Nierstein, and Wonnegau. The highest quality wines come from Nierstein (and its towns, Oppenheim and Nierstein). Its long-lived Rieslings are unquestionably the best Rheinhessen wines. They are soft, full-bodied, and elegant, with a unique, easily identified, marvelous bouquet. On the whole, wines from the town of Nierstein have more elegance than those from Oppenheim, although in some vintages (particularly hot, dry years), Oppenheim wines reign superior. Remember, in Germany, vintages count.

In the Bereich of Bingen, the village of Bingen produces wines similar to the Nahe (see "Other Districts") which are fuller, heavier, and more concentrated than the average Rhine wine. The wines here profit from a warm microclimate that gives them a special fullness and ripeness. With time, Riesling wines develop elegance and style, and Sylvaner wines gain in distinction.

Wines from the finest vineyards of Nachenheim have great bouquet and are remarkable for their elegance, finesse and class. The best wines combine depth, fire, spiciness, and delicacy in marvelous and noble harmony.

Wonnegau is where the city of Worms is located. Alzey, the center of the inland area, and its surrounding towns, produce good, clean-tasting *lieblich* wines.

The Pfalz

The Pfalz region is close in size to the Rheinhessen. Situated along the main wine road of the Rhine, known as the Weinstrasse, its enchanting and scenic vineyards grow on the high plateau along the river's western bank. In the finer vineyards, the soil contains large amounts of schist (slate), which retains the heat during the cool evening hours. A long, warm fall fosters grape maturity, which enables the area to produce intense, sweet wines ranging from Spätlese to Tröckenbeerenauslese. Some of these high-ranked prädikat achieve super-premium or noble status.

As in other areas, the finest wines come from the noble Riesling, although Riesling accounts for only 14 percent of all vineyard plantings. Pfalz Rieslings offer an attractive and remarkable balance. They're fuller than those of the Mosel, less mild and soft than those of the Rheinhessen, and less overwhelming in bouquet than those of the Rheingau. This region produces some of the world's finest Auslese and Beerenauslese wines.

> **Wine Wisdom**
> Wines of the Pfalz tend to have more body and an earthier character when compared to wines of the Rheingau. Forst, Diedesheim, Ruppertsberg, and Wachenheim produce the region's best wine.

The predominant grape is Müller-Thurgau, which yields pale, fresh wines. The Sylvaner accounts for 20 percent of the vineyard production, ranging in quality from simple premium to mid-premium. A small amount of spicy wine is produced from the Gewürztraminer. Recently, Kerner, Scheurebe, and Blauburgunder (Pinot Noir) have gained in importance.

Mittelrhein

Mittelrhein, along the banks of the northern Rhein, is one of Germany's smallest wine regions. It is noted mainly for its Rieslings.

The Mosel

The region composed of the vineyards dotting the slopes of the serpentine Mosel and its tributaries, the Saar and Ruwer, has come to be known as the Mosel-Saar-Ruwer. Divided in two, the area is comprised of the Mittelmosel (Central Mosel), which produces the greatest wines of the region, and the Saar-Ruwer, which produces good, although not necessarily distinctive, wines.

More than half (55 percent) of the plantings are Riesling. Mosel Rieslings are light in body, delicate, and refined. They are often described as floral wines, evoking images of flowers in spring meadows. They have a lively and refreshing taste; low in alcohol, they often contain a slight effervescence. These are wines that are meant to be drunk young.

> **Wine Wisdom**
> You can easily tell that a wine comes from the Mosel by the color of its bottle. It's green—the rest of Germany uses brown bottles.

Bereich Bernkastel is the best known in the Mittelmosel, and premium and noble wines are produced by four of its six Grosslagen: Michelsberg, Kurfürstlay, Münzlay, and Schwarzlay. The two others, Probstberg and St. Michael, produce simple-premium wines.

➤ The villages of the Grosslage Michelsberg produce some of the most distinctive wines in the Mosel. There are the fresh, light wines of Trittenheim and the more intense wines of Neumagen. The best and most famous village in this Grosslage is

Piesport. Piesporter Michaelberg is the name of the district's Grosslage wines—do not confuse it with an individual vineyard wine. The Kabinett wines are usually mid-premium quality, with typical Mosel delicacy. Those of Auslese and above, from the better vineyards, can achieve super-premium quality—richly sweet, complex, and flavorful.

➤ In the Grosslage Kurfürstlay, the two best wine-producing villages are Brauneberg and Bernkastle. Brauneberg wines are very full-bodied, rich in flavor and long-lived. If from the best vineyards, such as Juffer, they can reach super-premium class.

Wine Wisdom
Bernkastle wines are noted for their elegance. The most famous vineyard is the celebrated Dokter (or Doctor) property, whose wines aspire to noble status. In great vintages, these are outstanding noble wines with extraordinary breed and finesse.

➤ In the Grosslage of Munzlay, the three villages of Graach, Wehlen, and Zeltingen yield wines capable of achieving super-premium or noble status. These wines are well-balanced and fragrant, although the style can vary from vineyard to vineyard and range from fine, fragrant, and delicate to full-bodied and big. Wehlen is the home of some of the finest Mosel wines, many of which come from the renowned Prums estate. The fuller-bodied wines of Zeltingen range from ordinary quality wines to super-premiums, ranking alongside Graach and Wehlen.

➤ The Grosslage of Scharzberg is the Saar of this hyphenated region. Depending upon Mother Nature's inclination, the wine quality varies greatly. Scharzhofberger is the noble wine of the Saar.

The tiny Ruwer valley gives us the lightest and most delicate of the Mosel wines. The top-quality names are Maximin Grunhaus and Eitelsbach.

Wine Wisdom
Saar wines are often described as having a steely character and a hardness and austerity that can contribute to great character and breed. (Yes, Saar grapes do have to fight for their lives.) The best wines come from the towns of Ockfen, Oberemmel, and Ayl. Those from Ockfen are somewhat more full-bodied, while those from Ayl are softer and fruitier.

Other Districts

The Nahe River region, west of the Rheinhessen, produces agreeable, pleasant wines which are somewhat fuller, heavier, and more intense than most German wines. Baden, the southernmost, and consequently the warmest, region, produces fairly full-bodied, pleasant, straightforward wines. The wines of Franconia are unlike other German wines;

they are fuller in body, higher in alcohol, and have an earthy and steely character that replaces the typical flowery, fruity wine profile.

Austria—From the Vienna Woods

Austria produces three times as much wine as Switzerland, and like Switzerland, it enjoys its own beverage: Annual per capita consumption is roughly ten gallons. Ironically, none of the wine comes from the regions that border Germany, Italy, or Switzerland. The best wines of Austria come from Langenlois, Krems, and Wachau, all in the eastern provinces. Baden, near Vienna, produces light, fruity-style wines.

Most of Austria's red wine is produced in Burgenland, one of the country's warmer regions bordering Hungary. The red wines are medium- to full-bodied, with a fruity character and moderate tannins.

Austrian wine laws follow the German model. Better wines are divided into Qualitätswein and Prädikatswein classifications. The only difference from the German laws is that, in Austria, prädikat begins with spätlese. The minimum ripeness required for each level is higher in Austria than in Germany, and Austrian wines are typically higher in alcohol.

The German system of labeling applies to Austrian wines, including linking the varietal name with the place-name. There are some exceptions—for example, in Burgenland, the wines generally carry varietal names followed by the region.

HEY!

Important Things to Know

Eighty percent of Austrian wines are white. The most popular wines are made from the indigenous white Gruner Veltliner. Its wines are full-bodied and refreshing, with herbal and, occasionally, vegetable flavors. Müller-Thurgau is widely planted, along with Welschriesling, a grape frequently used to make ordinary table wines in Eastern Europe. It excels in quality in Austria and tends to be light, soft, and aromatic. Sylvaner, noble Riesling, and Rulander (Pinot Gris) are also planted here. The wines made from these grapes are similar in style to German wines. They rarely reach the same heights, but Austria's sweet late-picked, berry-selected, and dessert style wines have received international acclaim. Austria's crisp, dry whites, which range from light- to full-bodied, are just beginning to gain recognition.

Switzerland—Keeping the Good Things for Themselves

Switzerland is a country that enjoys its wines; its unusually high wine consumption is close to 12 gallons per capita. Unfortunately for the rest of the wine world, the Swiss enjoy their wines so much that they keep most of them at home.

Important Things to Know

HEY!

The country is in an ideal position for winemaking—situated between Germany, France, and Italy—and vineyards dot the German-speaking, French-speaking, and Italian-speaking areas of Switzerland alike. The canton of Vaud is the largest winegrowing region; to the south of Vaud is the next major grape region, the Valais. Similar to Germany, roughly two-thirds of Switzerland's wines are white. Swiss wines tend to be expensive for their quality and, therefore, do not represent good value. They do, however, offer interesting wines with a character all their own.

Vaud

Most of the vineyards here are located on slopes surrounding beautiful Lake Geneva. The two major sub-regions are Lavaux and La Côte (guess which language they speak here). With its southern exposure, Lavaux enjoys the tempering effect of Lake Geneva. The predominant grape variety is the Chasselas, which yields a grapy, if neutral, white wine. Chasselas wines tend to be fairly full-bodied, with dry and straightforward earthy flavors. La Côte, on the northern shore, produces similar wines to Laveaux.

Valais

The Valais has a few warmer growing sites, particularly on the slopes near the Rhône River. Chasselas is known here by its local name, Fendant; in the temperate (for Switzerland) Valais, it develops full body and offers good balance. Dôle is the local name for red wine, made from either Gamay or Pinot Noir. Petit-Dôle is another name for Pinot Noir.

In Valais, wines from the Müller-Thurgau grape are called "Johannisberg." Malvoisie is a soft, sweet dessert-style wine made from the Pinot Gris grape. The area still cultivates several local wines such as Arvine, Amirgne, Humagne, and Rèze. Rèze has some historical—or mythical—importance: It was once used to produce a wine, *vin d glacier*, made by mountain peasants and was reputed to live for decades when kept at high elevation.

171

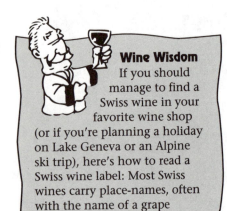

Neuchâtel

The region of Neuchâtel in the northwest corner is equally adept at producing quality in both red and white table wines—something a bit unusual this far north. Remarkably, the fussy Pinot Noir yields a delicate, fruity style of wine. The village of Cortaillod offers some of the better, light Pinot Noirs.

Ticino

Ticino is located in the southern corner, known as Italian Switzerland. Most of the vineyards here are planted in red varieties. Nostrano is the name for a light, blended red. Viti · is the name for fuller-bodied reds made from the Merlot variety.

Greece—Where the Bacchae Reveled

Greece is one of the oldest winegrowing regions in the world—this is the birthplace of the wine god, Dionysus. The Greek palate for wine is very different from ours, going back to the days of red and black Attic vessels. To prevent the wine from spoiling, the Greeks added preservatives such as herbs and spices—even goat cheese. A few vestiges of this practice remain. I don't know of any wines with goat cheese, but resin flavorings are still added to the white Retsina and the rosé Kokkineli.

Retsina is a favorite wine for most Greeks. If you're planning a trip to Greece, you may be curious to try it in its home territory. A word of caution: Many similarly inclined wine lovers have been so unnerved by their first taste of Retsina, they forget their desire to sample a native Greek wine. There are some pleasant and fruity wines produced in Greece. Most are not distinguished, but they don't taste like Retsina. (Incidentally, Retsina is flavored with resin, a substance used in the manufacture of varnish.) But then, they say Greek olives are an acquired taste, too.

Attica, the home of the Parthenon, is one of the principle wine-producing areas of Greece, and is where most of the Retsina is made. The Peloponnese, the area of Sparta, is the largest wine district, producing predominately sweet wines. Wine is made on many of the Greek islands, including Crete, Samos, Santorini, Rhodes, and Corfu. Little of it is exported to the U.S., but if you're planning a trip to Greece, there's plenty of it waiting.

Fortified dessert wines are the second most important Greek wine type. First in prestige is the dark red Mavrodaphne, similar to California Port, although lower in alcohol.

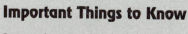

Important Things to Know

Some pleasant fruity red and white table wines are exported to the U.S. They're very drinkable and relatively inexpensive. The largest producers are Achaia-Clauss and Andrew Cambas. Boutari is a name linked with quality.

Hungarian Rhapsodies

Hungary continues to uphold a centuries-old tradition of turning out many good to fine wines. Many of its grape varieties are indigenous. Others, like the Sylvaner and the Walschriesling, have been successfully adapted to the area. Hungarian wines are quite distinct in style and are geared toward the local populace. But unlike the Greeks, Hungarian taste is a lot more in sync with ours. The result is a wide array of good wines, a lot of them reasonably priced and a good bargain. And they're relatively easy to find.

The most important Hungarian wines are the whites. Some pleasant white wines come from the region of Transdanubia, near Lake Balaton. They're usually labeled *Badacsonyi*, followed by a grape name, such as the widely planted Furmint. The most distinguished wines are made from Botrytis-infected Fermint; these are the legendary whites from Tokay, in the Northern Massif region.

Probably the most well-known of Hungarian wines is the red Egri Bikaver, which literally translates as "Bull's Blood of Eger." The name comes from its deep color, so don't expect it to have some esoteric property. It's a dependable, full-bodied red wine with some potential for aging. Eger also makes a sweet-style Merlot, with the local name Médoc Noir, but it's seldom seen outside of the country.

Important Things to Know

For the wines of Tokay, you'll see the word *aszu* as the descriptor for sweet. Tokay varies from slightly sweet to the richly concentrated celestial wine, Tokay Eszencia, which is made from Botrytis-infected grapes in a manner similar to the German Tröckenbeerenauslese. Rare and always expensive, Eszencia can be close to 50 percent sugar, and often has very low levels of alcohol. Over the centuries, it has been the preferred beverage of the European nobility and was once considered to have curative, therapeutic powers.

On a Tokay Eszencia wine label, you'll see the term *puttonyos*, which refers to the measure of sweetness as determined by the quantity of Botrytis-infected, overripe grapes that were added to the wine. Wines labeled 3 Puttonyos are moderately sweet; those labeled 5 Puttonyos are very sweet and concentrated.

Unsweet versions of Tokay, otherwise known as dry to off-dry wines, are labeled Tokay Szamorodni. They have a slightly nutty, slightly oxidized character.

The Least You Need to Know

➤ German wines range in quality from simple wines to some of the best in the world.

➤ You have to do a lot of memorizing to know German wine.

➤ Good wines are made in Switzerland, but they are expensive.

➤ Good, inexpensive wines come from Austria, Greece, and Hungary.

Chapter 16

The New World

In This Chapter

➤ American wine laws

➤ Wines of California

➤ Oregon wine

➤ Wine from Washington, the state

➤ New York wine

Wine in America is a relatively new industry. Winemaking in Chile, Argentina, and America took off when a wave of immigrants came to their shores in the late 19th century; at this time, there was little quality wine made and little or no regulation. While wine industries thrived elsewhere, wine (and all alcohol) came to an abrupt halt in the U.S. when Congress passed the Volstead Act, otherwise known as Prohibition. Then came the Great Depression, and then World War II, and the '50s was just not an era for major innovation.

It was during the 1970s that winemaking became a full-scale growth industry in California. Before 1970, the state had a handful of operating wineries; today, there are more than 600 wineries—most are small, but they're growing in both quantity and quality. Unlike most wine producing regions, wine growers and wineries in California are often two different animals. Grapes may be grown by ranchers in one area and sent off to a winery in another. Or a winery may grow its own grapes in numerous different regions throughout the state. When it comes to wine in America and in California in particular, reading the wine label is of utmost importance—because of wine regulations without teeth, information on the label is often misleading and may not be an indication of quality. This chapter introduces you to the ins and outs of choosing an American-made wine.

American Wine Laws

Yes, we do have them, although sad to say, U.S. regulations offer consumers the least amount of quality protection of any major wine producing country. American wine laws do not dictate the quality of the wine produced in its appellations like other countries—a region, like Napa, California, may produce some of the finest wine in the country as well as some of the poorest while using the same nomenclature. To buy American wine, you must know your producers.

As for those wine laws, the U.S. does have an appellation system that designates the regions where wine is produced: the American Viticultural Areas (AVAs). Unfortunately, this is about as far as the regulations extend. There are no regulations regarding which grape varieties can be planted where, or the maximum yield of grapes per acre. There's actually very little on an American wine label that's of any help in differentiating a quality wine from an ordinary wine. In addition, there are AVAs within AVAs, adding to the confusion. Many people figure if it has a varietal name, and it doesn't have a screw cap, it must be a quality wine. They're often sadly disappointed.

American wines are only required to state bare essentials on the label. Wines carrying a varietal name have to be made from at least 75 percent of the designated grape, but the grape can come from wines producing in prodigious quantities, thus producing mediocre quality. An AVA indication means at least 85 percent of the grapes must come from the named AVA, but the AVA might include both areas that can produce only mediocre wine as well as areas that produce the finest—Napa Valley in California is an example. When the state designation is California, 100 percent of the grapes used have to be grown within California. Other states require only 75 percent to be grown in-state. "Estate-bottled" or "Grown, produced, and bottled by" means that 100 percent of the grapes were either grown or controlled by the vintner and that he made all the wine. The problem is that the cheapest and most mediocre wine can be "Estate-bottled," so this term is often meaningless. "Produced and bottled by" means the named winery made and bottled at least 75 percent of the wine in the bottle. "Made and bottled by" means the winery made at least 10 percent of the wine. (Pretty big difference, isn't there?) A vintage date means at least 95 percent of the wine was made from grapes grown and fermented during that year. There are no regulations regarding the terms "reserve," "special reserve," or "vintner's reserve," etc.; thus, these terms are often used on a winery's lesser wines to promote the sales of its volume line while its better wines are bottled without any special attributes indicated. Quite a marketing ploy! It's all very confusing, and it's a shame that the U.S. government has not adopted the kind of meaningful regulations found elsewhere in the winemaking community.

Circumventing the California Wine Maze

Unlike France, where each region specializes in a kind of wine or wine made from only one or a few grape varieties, in the United States, you will find that most grape varieties are grown in AVAs. Some grapes excel in certain areas and do poorly in others. In a case where the grape does not create great wine, you are paying for a grape grower's experiment in planting varietal wines. Certain AVAs excel in a particular grape variety or two. I will describe the California AVAs (appellations) next.

The best-known wine regions of California.

Appellation California

This is one of those huge regional categories—it's the broadest tier on the label, and it means the wine comes from anywhere within the Golden State. California alone requires the bottles to contain 100 percent homegrown grapes. Wines from this broad appellation generally range from ordinary everyday to simple-premium quality.

Appellation North Coast

This appellation restricts the growing area to one of the better winegrowing regions within the state. Wines in this category begin in the everyday range and go up to mid-premium quality.

The North Coast AVA contains:

➤ Napa Valley

➤ Sonoma Valley

➤ Mendocino County

➤ Lake County

Central Valley—Home of Inexpensive Wine

This is a hot, sun-drenched region approximately 100 miles long, which produces the majority of bulk wine used in blending, jug, or everyday wine from nondescript high-yielding grape varieties. However some producers, such as Robert Mondavi (known for his high-quality Napa Cabernets), have begun to grow better varietals in the Lodi area that are sold in magnums at a relatively low price and make fine everyday wines.

Top California Wine Regions

California has no less than 13 highly ranked wine-producing regions, some of which have AVAs inside their AVA. Californians do everything in a big way. Each one has its own distinctive style and its preferred grape varieties. The regions range in character from glamorous and palatial Napa Valley to scenic Monterey, the charming village that has become a hub of technology and innovation.

Napa Valley—The Hollywood of Vines

Napa Valley is sort of the Bordeaux region of California, although whether its reputation is warranted or not is up for question as some pretty mediocre wines are produced here along with some of the finest. The region is unquestionably beautiful, lying northeast of

San Francisco. Vineyard land here is at a premium; more than 200 wineries coexist in a relatively small area of growing space, and it is a tourist destination with its own tourist railroad. The most famous of the California growing regions actually produces no more than five percent of its own grapes.

Important Things to Know

Altitude here is an advantage. Wines made from vineyards situated on the slopes of the Mayacamas Mountains in the west and the Howell Mountains in the east are generally better quality than those made from grapes grown on the Valley floor.

Within the broad Napa Valley appellation, there are eight AVAs, plus the Carneros AVA (see below) which is shared by Napa and Sonoma. (There are AVAs within AVAs.) The eight AVAs are

➤ Spring Mountain and Mt. Veeder—in the western mountains.

➤ Howell Mountain, Stags Leap District, Atlas Peak (which are all hilly or mountainous), and Wild Horse Valley—all in the eastern portion of Napa.

➤ Rutherford and Oakville—on the valley floor.

Grape Alert

To many people, an appellation from Napa Valley on a wine label is prestigious, but in reality, the wines range from the ordinary to the sublime. Figuring out which wines fall into the latter category takes some homework. You have to know your wineries and what each produces.

Important Things to Know

The white varietal name most closely associated with Napa is Chardonnay. The finest quality wines have a ripe aroma and flavor that is frequently spicy, with a melange of apricot, pineapple, and citrus flavors. The texture is rich and luscious, and the alcohol levels are high—13 percent or more—giving the wines a headiness when young. Some are fermented in oak barrels in the true Burgundian fashion, or aged in small French oak casks. This regimen endows the Chardonnays with a vanilla character that harmonizes with its varietal personality, as well as a bit of oaky bitterness. Mid-premium Napa Chardonnays are made from less-ripe grapes and/or spend less time aging in those small barrels. They are fruity, appley, and less complex.

Napa's second most celebrated varietal is another white, Sauvignon Blanc (also called Fumé Blanc). The best of these are made in a style resembling their French counterparts. They rarely rival the finest Sauvignon Blanc of the Graves or the Médoc—but then, neither do most of the Sauvignon grown in France.

Napa Valley Sauvignon Blancs range from subtle, light, and moderately oaked to heavy, powerful, warm, and very oaky. It all depends on the winery's style. Most of them fall into the mid-premium category. In general, Napa style leans toward full ripeness in the grapes, producing wines with high alcohol, which are counterbalanced with assertive oak flavors that mingle with the grape's personality. Age is no matter: they're attractive when young and are capable of good bottle aging.

Napa is not too well known for its Rieslings (usually labeled Johannisberg Riesling), but some of its finest Late Harvest wines can stand up to the most noble of Germany's Rieslings. Some vineyards in Napa (along with Sonoma and Monterey counties) will regularly develop Botrytis, which allows for the production of Late Harvest wines in the German tradition. Since there is no U.S. equivalent to the German *prädikat*, you have to look for the term *Late Harvest* on the label. It may also state the percentage of residual sugar. These Late Harvest wines can achieve super-premium or even noble status. They offer the floral Riesling character, along with Botrytis complexity—honeyed aroma, and a hint of almonds with corresponding acid balance to parallel the sweetness. In some instances, it's hard to tell the difference between these wines and their German prototypes.

Few dry or slightly sweet Napa Rieslings can match the unique style and charm of their counterparts from the Rhine and Mosel, but they can equal Rieslings from anywhere else in the world. They tend to be fuller in body, particularly in middle body, and more fruity than the German versions.

Now the reds. Napa Valley Cabernet Sauvignon ranks among California's best when made to be the best. Those made from grapes grown from north of Yountville, a cool area south of St. Helena, generally qualify in the mid- or super-premium range. A select few from sites in Rutherford, Oakville, and the Stags Leap district can achieve noble status. Well-made Napa Cabernets offer a berryish, herbal aroma, fairly full body, ample tannins, and some warmth. The super-premiums have a riper character, reminiscent of cassis, dried sage, and black currants, that often develops a cedary "cigar-box" characteristic with bottle aging. The best of these will benefit from aging for a decade or more.

Merlot is rapidly gaining in stature and popularity. It's easier to enjoy—its tannins are less harsh and less astringent than Cabernet. Napa has the edge on quality Merlots. The best are very ripe and herbaceous in aroma and flavor. They have a round, soft, and voluptuous character, and you'll frequently notice a somewhat sweet finish.

Zinfandel thrives in Napa Valley when grown on hillside sites and allowed to ripen to high sugar levels. It does less well on the valley floor. Super-premium Zinfandels come from hillsides or very old vineyards. Zinfandel reigns in the Calistoga region, the area's warmest sub-region.

Most Napa Valley Zinfandels are berry-like, medium-bodied, with moderate tannins and a tart finish. That's red Zinfandel we're talking about. The blush wine, White Zinfandel, has recently soared to popularity. It's a light, sweet, and fruity wine, good for summer and leisurely drinking.

Important Things to Know

HEY!

Bordeaux-styled blended wines have appeared in greater numbers during the past decade. The reds are usually made from red Bordeaux varieties (Cabernet Sauvignon, Cabernet Franc, Merlot, and sometimes Malbec and Petit Verdot). The whites are usually made from the white Bordeaux grapes (Sauvignon Blanc and Semillon). Some of these blends are known by the name *Meritage* wines, although Meritage rarely appears on the label.

Sonoma—No Glitter, Just Good Wine

The Sonoma winegrowing region lacks the lavish estates that characterize Napa Valley. It may not be prime on the tourist map, but it's certainly on the wine map. Sonoma is home to some of the most successful California wineries.

Sonoma covers a lot more land than Napa. The climate parallels Napa, although some of its coastal areas are noticeably cooler. The grape varieties are largely the same as Napa; the style and character of the wine is often distinctive.

These are the designated AVAs of Sonoma:

➤ Sonoma Valley

➤ Sonoma Mountain

➤ Dry Creek Valley

➤ Alexander Valley

➤ Russian River Valley

➤ Sonoma-Green Valley—contained within Russian River Valley

➤ Chalk Hill—contained within Russian River Valley

➤ Knights Valley

To make things just a bit confusing with the AVA within an AVA business, Sonoma County has two broader AVAs: Northern Sonoma, a somewhat scattered designation encompassing Russian River Valley, Alexander Valley, Dry Creek Valley and Knight's Valley; and Sonoma Coast, which contains a mélange of land situated along the coast in western Sonoma.

Some mid- and super-premium quality Chardonnays come from Sonoma. The Dry Creek and Alexander Valley districts tend to accentuate a very fruity varietal aroma with a lemony flavor; they have a medium-bodied, slightly viscous texture. Sonoma Chardonnays tend to be fruitier and leaner than Napas, and are improved by long bottle aging. Only the Dry Creek district is noted for its Sauvignon Blancs.

Sonoma is the home of many mid-premium Cabernet Sauvignons. Most are vinous and straightforward, medium-bodied, moderately tannic, and early maturing, with a slightly weedy, peppery character. These traits are especially evident in wines from Dry Creek, Alexander Valley, and the Sonoma Valley.

> ## HEY! Important Things to Know
>
> Only a small number of California wineries have managed to handle the finicky Pinot Noir, and some of the best are in Sonoma, particularly Russian River Valley. They offer the characteristic Pinot Noir fruitiness, a slightly cherry, smoky character, medium body, and slight tannins. Making a great Pinot Noir in California has been the result of continuing experimentation.

Super-premium Zinfandels come from a large chunk of hillside vineyards in Dry Creek (see below) and Alexander Valley. Alexander Valley Zinfandels range from super- to mid-premium and offer a distinct, ripe cherry, blackberry character, along with richness and depth.

Dry Creek Valley

This appellation of Sonoma is important enough to deserve its own listing. Dry Creek is celebrated for its Chardonnays, Sauvignon Blancs, Cabernet Sauvignons, and Zinfandels. In fact, it's a Zinfandel haven; its grapes are noted for richness and depth. The best of the Dry Creek red Zinfandels have an earthy, peppery character that distinguishes the region from other regions.

Carneros—Numero Uno

Carneros is the single most important winegrowing district in California. Extending from the southern part of Napa Valley into Sonoma County, it enjoys the cool breezes from the

Pacific and the mists rolling in from San Pablo Bay. Carneros is home to grapes that thrive in a cool climate—Chardonnay, Pinot Noir, and various white varieties—for high-quality sparkling wines.

The winemakers of Carneros have managed to tame the Pinot Noir grape, creating some mid- to super-premium wines. The Pinots are typically deep-colored with herbal, cherryish, and slightly roasted aromas and flavors, a velvety texture, some depth, and a long finish.

Stags Leap—Cabernet Country

Stags Leap in Napa is celebrated for its outstanding Cabernet Sauvignon. (For characteristics, see Napa varietals.)

Monterey—Charm and Ingenuity

Monterey is a scenic area that boasts of the town of Carmel and some excellent vineyard areas and wineries. Monterey has two centers: the Salinas Valley near Soledad, and King City in the south. The northern half is dry, cool, and windy—the kind of climate white grapes favor.

Monterey is a microcosm of California viticulture—a synthesis of experimentation and technology. The growers and winemakers have triumphed over such pitfalls as vegetative Cabernets (in the early 1970s they tasted like uncooked asparagus and smelled like bell peppers), and that nasty little bug, phylloxera. In true California spirit, the winemakers—and the wine—survived and thrived.

HEY!

Important Things to Know

Drawing on the techniques of Burgundy winemaking, Monterey Chardonnay has been coaxed into full potential. Monterey Chardonnays tend to have more varietal character in aroma and flavor than their counterparts produced farther north. They possess depth, texture, and astringency; the accent is on fresh, varietal fruitiness. Many Monterey-grown Chardonnays have a unique green or grassy character, medium body, and a sharp, crisp finish. Small-barrel oak aging is the method of choice to soften the wine's sharp edges.

Monterey is one of the best California regions for Sauvignon Blanc. At mid-premium quality status, these wines yield a characteristic grassy, weedy, or black pepper flavor.

Monterey offers some dry-styled or slightly sweet Rieslings; flowery yet firm, they're similar to the German *kabinett* style. These "Soft Rieslings" can be opulently fruity and flowery; they're low in alcohol and meant for simple sipping.

Gewürztraminer is an important varietal here. Monterey Gewürztraminers can be spicy in fragrance and fruity in flavor. Some retain a slight degree of Muscat character, which adds complexity. The best are well-structured for bottle aging.

Monterey Cabernet Sauvignon has managed to shed its vegetable garden image. Since the late 1970s, innovative winemakers have learned to cope with their unusual regional trait, and even use it to their advantage. The Cabernets have an herbal, spicy flavor; a moderate, peppery overtone; and good varietal character.

Mendocino

The name Mendocino has a lyrical ring, evocative of the quaint, picturesque town itself. Due north of Sonoma, Mendocino County has two main subdivisions. Ukiah is a large area with a prolific growth of vineyards. The smaller Anderson Valley has a cool climate and the highest level of rainfall of all winegrowing regions. A full range of varietals thrive here. Initially best known for Zinfandel and Cabernet Sauvignon, Mendocino now grows Chardonnay, Riesling, Sauvignon Blanc, Gewürztraminer, Pinot Noir, and sparkling wine grapes. Parducci was the first winery to operate in the area; today it shares its renown with Fetzer.

The Anderson Valley has recently made a name for itself in the sparkling wine industry. The sparkling wine operations of Roederer Champagne, Scharffenberger, and Handley are all based in the Anderson Valley.

Mendocino Chardonnays are usually lemony and crisp, and are characterized by a firm, lean style. They don't strive for greatness, but they're enjoyable beverages and the quality is consistent. Mendocino-style Sauvignon Blanc is early-maturing; it's soft and light-bodied, with a somewhat muted grassy, black pepper varietal flavor. The Rieslings are slightly sweet *kabinett* style with low acidity.

There's a lot of Zinfandel grown here, and the range is extensive. They are berrylike, medium-bodied, with moderate tannins and a tart finish. Mendocino-grown Zinfandels vary from simple and berrylike to riper and excessively tannic, depending on climate. Mendocino Cabernet Sauvignons have more tannic astringency and a weightier quality than their counterparts from Sonoma. They often have an appealing ripe fruit aroma, redolent of berries and herbs, but more astringent and tannic. In the mid-premium category and above, they have a fresh violets and plum-like character, and moderate (under 13 percent) alcohol. The regional Pinot Noirs offer varietal fruitiness, a slightly cherry, smoky character, medium body, and slight tannins.

Lake County

To the north of Napa, this area has recently gained in popularity. It's primarily planted in red wine grapes, notably Cabernet Sauvignon and Zinfandel. The regional versions of these varietals tend to be light-bodied, but with straightforward flavor appeal. A few strongly-varietal Sauvignon Blancs are made from Lake County grapes.

San Luis Obispo

San Luis Obispo is another area that's been gaining in importance. Its main subdistricts are the warm and hilly Paso Robles—territory of Zinfandel, Cabernet Sauvignon, and Pinot Noir—and the cool, breezy Edna Valley and Arroyo Grande, planted in Chardonnay and Pinot Noir. Its Cabernets and Chardonnays are similar in style to those from Santa Barbara (see below).

Amador County—Zinfandel Gold

Amador is located in the Sierra foothills where weary but hopeful prospectors once panned for gold. Few of them found it; the winegrowers who discovered the native Zinfandel did a lot better. Zinfandel grapes reach full ripeness in this region. They're generally warm, fruity, and very tannic.

The foothills are located southwest of Sacramento, where Amador shares some of its winemaking fame with El Dorado County. The most prominent grape-growing areas are Shenandoah Valley and Fiddletown in Amador. Vineyards in hot, dry El Dorado are planted at high altitude to counteract the summer heat.

Small amounts of Cabernet Sauvignon, Sauvignon Blanc, and Riesling are also grown and bottled here, but Zinfandel reigns supreme.

Santa Cruz—Rugged and Growing

Santa Cruz is a beautiful, mountainous area that runs from San Francisco south to the town of Santa Cruz. A decade ago, it was home to a dozen small wineries; today, the number is growing, and some of its wineries are the best in California. This is a cool growing region, with sea breezes on both sides. Pinot Noir grows happily on the Pacific side, while Cabernet Sauvignon prefers the San Francisco Bay area. Chardonnay likes them both (so do most tourists).

The appellation Santa Cruz appears on many big-styled, ripe Chardonnays and Pinot Noirs.

Santa Barbara County—A Proud Newcomer

Santa Barbara County is an area of beautiful rolling hills and is a relative newcomer to the wine industry. It's known mostly for wineries using the Santa Ynez appellation. Actually, its first vineyards were planted by Spanish missionaries in the 18th century, but it wasn't until 1975 that the pioneering Firestone Vineyards began producing noteworthy Pinot Noirs, Rieslings, and Chardonnays, paving the way for other modern wineries.

Initially, most of the region's wines used the Santa Ynez Valley appellation, but the Santa Maria and Los Alamos Valleys are also gaining in stature.

Santa Barbara Chardonnays tend to be relatively early maturing; they are often similar in style to their cousins from San Luis Obispo. They have a unique grassiness and, depending on sugar development (which determines the alcoholic content), they range from very firm and hard in style, to rounder and softer (although few have the rich texture that earmarks Napa Chardonnays). They have excellent acidity and a slight silky texture.

Some Sauvignon Blanc is produced in Santa Ynez. It tends to have an aggressive, pronounced aroma of grassiness, black pepper and fruit that needs to be tamed and rounded by cask aging, bottle aging, or blending with a small percentage of Semillon (remember, in California wines are often blended with grapes from other regions).

Santa Barbara Cabernets also share some traits with the San Luis Obispo version. Both have moderate, Bordeaux-like alcohol levels (under 13 percent), and a rich, herbal berry-like aroma and flavor made complex by a weedy overtone, and in some cases, by oakiness from long-aging in small casks. They tend to have a short finish when compared to the regal, lingering aftertaste found in the Cabernets of Napa and the middle Médoc of Bordeaux.

A good portion of Santa Barbara's growing wine reputation is founded on the affinity of the Pinot Noir grape for its soil and ocean air. The Pinots are often deep-colored, with herbal, cherryish, and slightly roasted aroma and flavors, a velvety texture, some depth, and a long finish.

The Golden State's Best Values

California's best values are found in its everyday and simple- to mid-premium wines that are produced in large quantities. California's best wines, the super-premium and noble wines, are produced in small quantities and are sought after by collectors who drive the price up beyond the wine's intrinsic value. At auction, these wines (with a few years behind them) bring astronomical prices. So you should look to California for its lower priced wines and to Bordeaux, Burgundy, Italy and elsewhere for super-premium wines because they will provide comparable wines at lower prices.

HEY!

Important Things to Know

While many California wines are meant to be consumed when bottled, the super-premium and noble quality wines benefit from bottle aging. Chardonnay will benefit from two to four years of aging. Red varieties like Cabernet Sauvignon, Merlot, and the better Zinfandels can benefit from five to ten years of aging or more.

The Pacific Northwest

North of California, there's a thriving wine industry, although wines from Washington and Oregon are not exactly household words. The Cascade Mountains cut through both states, producing distinctive climatic regions. This section covers the winemaking regions in the U.S. Northwest.

Washington—North and Dry

Washington state began growing vinifera varieties in the 1960s, although few wineries existed until two decades later. Most of the vineyards are situated in the east, where rainfall is less prolific and the climate is continental (or even desertlike).

The winegrowing regions of Washington are as follows:

➤ The Yakima Valley in the southeast has cool summer weather and a long growing season; it's not the biggest region in acreage, but it has more wineries (22) than the larger Columbia Valley.

➤ Columbia has the most sizable grape-growing terrain; 11 wineries make their home here. Puget Sound wineries often use grapes from the Columbia region.

➤ The Walla Walla Valley accounts for less than one percent of the state's viticultural output, and only six wineries reside here.

Washington Varietals

Gewürztraminer and Johannisberg Riesling do well here, with excellent varietal character and a less sweet style than their California cousins. Riesling grapes thrive in the few vineyards located west of the Cascades, in the Puget Sound area. Washington state Sauvignon Blancs are noted for their powerful character. The ubiquitous Chardonnay is widely grown, although the quality can be inconsistent. Chenin Blanc, Cabernet Sauvignon, and Merlot round out Washington's most prolific varietals. The Washington-based Columbia Crest Merlot is currently the biggest selling Merlot in the U.S.

Oregon—Taming Pinot Noir

Oregon's main winegrowing region is the Wilamette Valley, followed by the Umqua Valley, and the Rogue River Valley.

Willamette Valley

Willamette encompasses a sizable area south of the city of Portland. It's extremely cool during the summer and often quite rainy during the harvest season. Pinot Noir favors a cool climate, and Oregon winemaking has made its name on this most finicky of grapes.

In Willamette's winery-rich Yamhill County, all of the wineries produce Pinot Noir. Oregon Pinot Noirs first received acclaim in the early 1980s, and their reputation has soared. Recently, Pinot Noir has been joined in Oregon by that other Pinot, Pinot Gris.

Umqua Valley

Warmer than Willamette—although still cool—the Umqua Valley is the home of Oregon's pioneering winery, Hillcrest Vineyards. Pinot Noir also thrives in Umqua, along with Riesling (historically Oregon's second most important varietal), Chardonnay, and Cabernet Sauvignon. Hillcrest, which began Oregon's wine industry in 1962, is noted for its fine Rieslings.

Rogue River Valley

The Roque River Valley is a relative newcomer. It's the warmest of the Oregon growing regions, ideal for Cabernet Sauvignon and Merlot—and of course, Chardonnay, which really took the advice, "Go West!" Pinot Gris is also beginning to make some inroads here.

New York State—Wine from Back East

Remember those "I Love New York" commercials? Do you recall seeing any wineries? They might have included the Brotherhood Winery in the Hudson Valley—founded in 1839; it's the oldest winery in operation anywhere in the U.S. Or they might have shown the Canandaigua Wine Company in the Finger Lakes, the country's second largest winery. But they didn't. To most people, New York State is the home of New York City and Woodstock, and some nifty areas for hiking and climbing. New York is second in wine production to California, but its reputation is vastly eclipsed by the Golden State.

The western states may be relative newcomers to the wine industry, but they dug right in with *Vitus vinifera*, experimenting and cloning, and figuring out how to transcend such regional peculiarities as vegetal Cabernet Sauvignon. By contrast, New York's viticultural staple had always been *Vitus lambrusca*, which is great for jams and jellies and unfermented beverages, but not so great for fine wines. The first vinifera grapes were cultivated in the Finger Lakes in the 1950s, by the Russian Dr. Konstantin Frank. In 1961, the first vinifera wines emerged from his winery, Dr. Frank's Vinifera Wine Cellars (what else would it be called?). Historically, a 1961 vintage might have given New York an edge over its West Coast counterparts, but *terroir*—especially climate—is still a major factor. New York winemakers have had to deal with high production costs and labor-intensive means to protect the vines from the harsh, freezing winter. There's no soothing Pacific here. Hence, except for low-priced champagne, the wines of New York cost more to make than their West Coast counterparts and are more costly in the wine store.

Finger Lakes

The cold climate of the Finger Lakes district in western New York is somewhat tempered by the four large bodies of water. Approximately 85 percent of the state's wines come from this district, although not all are vinifera. Riesling and Chardonnay are the two most successful varietals. During the 1980s, wineries like Glenora and Hermann J. Weimer began paving the way toward high-quality vinifera wines.

Long Island

The Northern Fork AVA, 80 miles from New York City, has shown great promise with several vinifera grapes, notably Riesling, Pinot Noir, and Cabernet Sauvignon. Recently, Merlot and Sauvignon Blanc have been thriving. Long Island's second AVA consists of the Hamptons at the southern fork. It's far more celebrated for its luxurious summer homes than its wine. Wines from these regions tend to be purchased by the trendy, who summer in the Hamptons.

Hudson Valley

The Hudson River Valley, a mere 40 miles from New York City, is home to Benmarl, Clinton, and several other wineries, including the historic Brotherhood, which caters to a tourist crowd. They have shown good progress with better quality French hybrids and occasionally succeed with the vinifera grapes. The region also grows lambrusca varieties, which are often sold to wineries in the Finger Lakes district.

Wines from Other States

Virtually every state within the viticultural temperature zone grows grapes and makes wine from Idaho to Texas, from New Jersey to Virginia. Most of these wines are simple and not much to speak of, but they are interesting to try if you live in the locality where they are made. Besides, you will be providing support to a local winemaker who probably needs it—such local winemaking ventures are rarely very lucrative and the winemaker needs all the sales he can generate. You may find the wines expensive for what is in the bottle, but the pride of serving a locally made wine more than makes up for that when entertaining out-of-towners. Look for wineries in your locality and try their wines—you might be in for a pleasant surprise.

The Least You Need to Know

➤ California produces many varietal wines from many areas. You need to know the producers to know which are good and which are not.

➤ Oregon and Washington produce some very fine wines.

➤ New York produces some very good wines, but they are hard to find outside their locality.

Wines from Down Under

Down Under usually refers to Australia, and it's quickly becoming a key player in the international wine market. It's not the only player, though. The chapter also covers two other up-and-coming viticultural realms in the southern hemisphere: New Zealand and South Africa.

Although Australians may hate to admit it, they have been becoming more refined. Or at least their wines have. Rough-and-tumble wines are being replaced by respectable, good-quality whites and reds that can grace any table. Australian wines offer good value, and an Aussie wine bottle may be a good conversation opener. Australia's neighbor New Zealand has a way to go to catch up, but who knows; in a few years they may be the latest rave and you can claim to have discovered them first. The last stop in this chapter is South Africa. With a new government and a much broader export market, South Africa has the potential to be a key player in the world wine industry. South African wines may not be so easy to find, but they're worth looking for. Your persistance will pay off.

Australia—More Than Kangaroos

Over the past two decades, a wine renaissance has been taking place in Australia. Once reputed only for making cheap, fortified wines, the Australian wine industry has turned around completely, to earn itself a place of high standing in the world wine market. The pattern is not too different from California's. In fact, the main difference is that the screwcap-jug wines that were synonymous with California winemaking for decades were "bag-in-box" wines in Australia. Both areas of the world have a hand in technology and an eye on the future. The macho reds and imbalanced, hot-tasting whites that made up Australia's first varietal efforts have been fine-tuned and styled into wines with style, balance, and charm.

Unlike California, however, which is the first home of Zinfandel, Australia has no unique vines. Vinifera vines first made their appearance in the late 18th and early 19th centuries from Europe and the Cape of Good Hope. Fortified wines are a style common to warm-climate winemaking, especially in the days when spoilage was a serious problem, so it's not surprising that rich, sweet wines dominated production. But that's not to dismiss the native beverage—Australia still makes some of the best Sherry outside of Spain.

> **Wine Words**
> A *bag-in-box* is a wine container that looks like a milk or juice container with a spigot. Inside is a plastic bag that collapses when the wine is poured, keeping air away from the wine. This is a very popular wine container in Australia and is beginning to appear in the United States and elsewhere for simple wines.

Those Aussie Blends

The predominant grape used in Australia for fine wine is Syrah, known here as Shiraz. Shiraz is the name you'll see on the label—which, in California fashion, bears the varietal name. The named grape has to comprise at least 85 percent of the bottle's contents. The Aussies have some unique quirks, though. For example, if you're in the market for Riesling, look for the name "Rhine Riesling." If it just says "Riesling," chances are it's Semillon.

One peculiarly Australian trait is to blend two vinifera and use both varietal names. The dominant grape comes first: Shiraz/Cabernet Sauvignon or Cabernet Sauvignon/Shiraz. Even the blends themselves are unusual. Most winemakers in Australia follow the classic French prototypes: Cabernet Sauvignon with Merlot and Cabernet Franc; or Semillon with Sauvignon Blanc. Having no prior tradition, Australia has created two original styles of wine: Shiraz with Cabernet Sauvignon and Semillon with Chardonnay.

The ever-popular Shirazes are worth exploring because they are made in several styles, from very light, simple-premium quaffable wines to serious, complex wines that require bottle aging. The other mainstay of Australia is Semillon. Some are aged in oak, similar to

Chardonnay, and taste of vanilla and oak with complexity. Others are unoaked, which produces simple white wines when young; yet these same wines become complex and honeyed with bottle age.

For all their idiosyncrasies, Australian wine labels are very consumer-friendly. Most blended wines list their grape varieties on the label, and the percentages of each grape are usually included. There is one catch: There's no restriction on where the grapes used in blended wines are grown, so there are many trans-regional blends. Untamed, sprawling Australia is a long way from historic France in style as well as geography. The great majority of Australian wines carry the appellation *South Eastern Australia*. It means the grapes could have been grown in any one of the three states in this immense territory. You will find others that reveal wines from several appellations, with the percentage of each frequently listed. If you're looking for distinctive, stylistic, regional nuances, you must look for wines from a single appellation.

Viticultural Regions

Australia's main viticultural regions are geographically and climatically similar to Napa and Sonoma Valleys: dry, not very humid, and ranging in temperature from moderate to fairly warm in some parts. The most important wine-producing state is South Australia, which accounts for approximately 60 percent of Australia's wine. It has two distinctively different faces. The Riverlands region produces the inexpensive jug-style wine that is the staple of the bag-in-box industry. Closer to the state capital of Adelaide are the vineyard regions, which are gaining renown for their fine wines. These include the following:

➤ **Barossa Valley.** Located north of Adelaide, this is one of the coolest vineyard regions and one of the first to be associated with fine wines. It's also the largest area, and is highly influenced by Germanic wine styles. Its Rhine Riesling and Riesling are light and delightful. The Shiraz and Cabernet Sauvignon are solid, consistent, and continually improving.

➤ **Coonawarra.** The climate is cool and the region is held in esteem for its classic reds, Cabernet Sauvignon, and Shiraz. There can be wide vintage variations, but in fine years, its Cabernets have been standouts!

➤ **Clare Valley.** The climate here is diverse and the winemaking eclectic, producing a wide variety of wines from crisp Rieslings to full-bodied reds.

➤ **McLaren Vale.** Located south of Adelaide and cooled by the ocean, this is white wine territory. It's known primarily for Chardonnay and Sauvignon Blanc.

➤ **Padthaway.** Another white wine area situated north of Coonawarra.

New South Wales was the first viticultural state; today it accounts for approximately 30 percent of the country's wine. Its main wine region is the Hunter Valley, which is sub-divided into two districts:

➤ **Hunter Valley.** During the 1980s, Hunter Valley began to attract wealthy wineloving investors and lifestyle-seekers, making it sort of a Napa-Down-Under. The Hunter Valley consists of two distinct districts. The Lower Hunter Valley, close to Sydney, is warm and humid with heavy, rich soils. The Upper Hunter Valley is drier and further inland. Shiraz and Semillon are the classic varietals, with Chardonnay recently gaining in stature. Riesling and Pinot Noir have also yielded some impressive efforts.

➤ **Mudgee.** Situated inland near the mountains due west of Hunter Valley is a lesser-known wine region that offers Chardonnay, Merlot, and Cabernet Sauvignon.

Victoria, in eastern Australia, is the site of many small wineries. It offers a quantity of everyday white, red, and sparkling wines, and remains a center for fortified wines. The wines produced here range from stylish Pinot Noirs to rich, fortified dessert wines. Among the key winegrowing regions in the state of Victoria are

➤ **Rutherglen, Glenrowan, and Milawa.** Situated in the northeast, the warm climate lends itself to the making of fortified wines including fortified Muscats and Tokays.

➤ **Goulburn Valley.** This central area is known for its Shiraz and Marsanne.

➤ **Great Western.** This is the mainstay of Australia's sparkling wine industry.

➤ **Yarra Valley.** This cool region located close to Melbourne yields some fine Pinot Noir, Cabernet Sauvignon, and Chardonnay.

What Are Australia's Best Values?

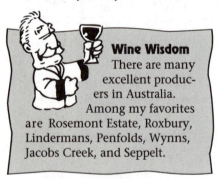

Wine Wisdom
There are many excellent producers in Australia. Among my favorites are Rosemont Estate, Roxbury, Lindermans, Penfolds, Wynns, Jacobs Creek, and Seppelt.

Australian bag-in-box wines are inexpensive and provide good value. They can be found in some markets but are not yet popular in the United States. Australian Chardonnay, Shiraz, and Cabernet Sauvignon, priced around $6 to $8 (U.S.), provide good value and well-made wines. The more expensive Australian wines, $20 or more, compare to their counterparts from other parts of the world but are not bargains like the lower-priced wines.

New Zealand

Think of Australia, and the next name that comes to mind is usually New Zealand. Following Australia, New Zealand is emerging in the world wine market, but it still has a ways to go.

New Zealand is farther south in the Southern Hemisphere than Australia, where's it's cooler. It's actually composed of two large islands, both of which are subject to the effects of the ocean spray. The warmer North Island is known for its red wines, particularly Cabernet Sauvignon, which come from the area around Auckland and Hawkes Bay; along with its less-costly Müller-Thurgau-based wines. The South Island contains Marlborough, New Zealand's largest wine region, which is gaining acclaim for its white wines, notably Sauvignon Blanc and Chardonnay.

New Zealand whites are generally unoaked wines with rich flavors and sharp acidity. Its reds are similar to those of Australia. The wines of New Zealand tend to be priced higher than comparable wines from Australia and elsewhere, but they do provide an interesting wine drinking experience.

South Africa

Since the first Dutch settlers introduced European vines over three centuries ago, South Africa has been producing a variety of wines. The Dutch were shortly joined by French Huguenots who contributed their Gallic winemaking knowledge and techniques. South Africa's rich, dessert-style Muscat wine, Constantia, became legendary during the early history of South Africa, and was considered a delicacy in the royal courts of Europe.

Aside from Constantia, few countries other than Great Britain displayed any interest in South African wines. Up until 1918, quality regulation was poor to non-existent, and overproduction resulted in inferior wines. To combat this effect, the government adopted a regulating body, the KWV (which is not actually a government organization, but a Cooperative Winegrower's Association), to control the over-burgeoning wine industry. The strict quota system of the KWV has come under a lot of criticism, especially in recent years, and in 1992 it finally loosened controls, permitting independent wineries greater production. In 1972, the government implemented a type of appellation system, granting an official "Wine of Origin" seal to certain wines and certain estates to ensure accuracy of label information.

With the death of Apartheid and the election of Nelson Mandela, South Africa has gained new esteem in the world, as well as entry into a commercial market that had been closed to it since the 1970s. One recent trend has been acceleration in the production of table wines. Most of the country's 5,000 grape growers are not wine producers and they take their grapes to one of the 70 cooperatives run by the KWV. Approximately half the crop is turned into distilled alcohol or grape concentrate. Most of the remaining grapes are used mainly for Sherry or Port; however, more and more of this production is being used to make dry, unfortified wines. New independent wineries are cropping up, and South Africa is gaining a reputation for higher-quality, estate-grown wines.

Despite changes in winemaking as well as government policy, the conglomerate still reigns supreme. The growing table wine industry is dominated by the Stellenbosch Farmers' Winery Group (SFW). The Nederburg Estate, regarded as one of South Africa's most esteemed properties, is part of SFW. Another important table wine producer is the Bergkelder Group; 18 wine estates including some of South Africa's best are affiliated with this firm.

Although South Africa ranks eighth in wine production worldwide, only 20 percent is exported. The UK remains its biggest customer.

South Africa's Wine Districts

The implementation of the Wine of Origin (WO) appellation system marked the creation of 10 wine districts (and their subdistricts). The vast body of viticultural land is located in Cape Province near the southeastern coast (in the vicinity of Cape Town) of South Africa. The vineyards are known collectively as the Coastal District vineyards. The two most prominent districts are Paarl and Stellenbosch, but several others are emerging (including one subdistrict). Currently the five key wine districts are

- ➤ **Stellenbosch.** This region is the largest in area and production, and is renowned for its high-quality wines, particularly reds. It's situated east of Cape Town.

- ➤ **Paarl.** Located north of Stellenbosch. It's the site of the KWV and the impressive Nederburg Estate. Paarl is recognized for its high-quality white wines.

- ➤ **Franschloek Valley.** This subdistrict of Paarl is a center for experimentation and innovation in winemaking.

- ➤ **Constantia.** Located south of Cape Town, this historic region created the luscious dessert wine that wowed the nobility of Europe.

- ➤ **Durbanville.** Located north of Cape Town, this region is noted for its rolling hills with well-drained soil.

South Africa's WO legislation is modeled after the French *Appellation Contrôlée* system (that is, it includes strict regulation of vineyard sites, grape varieties, vintage-dating, and so on). By South African law, varietal wines must contain at least 75 percent of the designated grape, although in compliance with EU regulations, those destined for export must have at least 85 percent of the named grape. Roughly 10 percent of South Africa's wines earn the WO seal.

South African Grape Varieties

Chenin Blanc, referred to in South Africa as *Steen*, is the reigning grape variety. And no wonder—it's a versatile vinifera. It is primarily used to make medium-dry to semi-sweet wines, but it also makes dry wines, late-harvest Botrytis wines, rosés, and sparkling wines. Sauvignon Blanc and Chardonnay are also gaining in popularity.

The predominant red grape has traditionally been Cinsault (the same as the Rhône variety), formerly called the Hermitage in South Africa. The Cinsault grape produces an ever-popular wine by the same name. It's been getting a few rivals lately, notably Cabernet and Merlot, and to a lesser degree Pinot Noir and Shiraz.

The table wines of South Africa have always included a few crossbreeds; the best known is the distinctive Pinotage, a hybrid of Cinsault and Pinot Noir. Pinotage combines the berry fruitiness of Pinot Noir with the earthy qualities of a Rhône wine, producing an easy-to-drink, light- to medium-bodied, simple-premium wine.

The Least You Need to Know

➤ Australia produces some interesting white and red varietal wines that provide good value.

➤ The wines from New Zealand tend to provide less value than their counterparts from Australia and elsewhere.

➤ The wines from South Africa are gaining a renewed popularity and are well worth seeking out.

Bubbles and More

Ever since its discovery in 18th-century Champagne by the Benedictine monk and cellarmaster, Dom Perignon, sparkling wine and Champagne have been symbols of elegant lifestyles, celebration, and festivity. From Fred Astaire and Ginger Rogers to James Bond, the movies are replete with sophisticates sipping Champagne; and for most of us ordinary folks, it just wouldn't be New Year's Eve without it. But no one has captured the essence of Champagne more eloquently than Dom Perignon, who looked into the bubbles and exclaimed, "I am drinking stars." This chapter introduces you to the art and science that create those stars.

More than Champagne

If bubbles alone were the key to Champagne's opulent image, we could be celebrating our triumphs and delights with soft drinks. Instead, the exacting standards and costly procedures surrounding the production of Champagne from the French province east of Paris created the aura of the sumptuous beverage best reserved for special occasions. With its precisely delimited growing region, French Champagne is limited in production, and rising prices reinforce its image as a luxury wine. Yet, surrounded by mystique, our associations with Champagne have carried over to encompass just about all sparkling wines, from all regions, over a range of prices. Except in the United States, only wine from the true Champagne region may bear the term "Champagne"; others are called sparkling wine or *vin mousseux*.

Important Things to Know

Under French legislation, Champagne is a sparkling wine produced within the defined geographic boundaries of that district and made under the strict regulations of the Appellation Côntrolée. Only certain grape varieties may be used, and only one technical procedure for creating the Champagne—the *Méthode Champenoise*—is allowed. Sparkling wines from elsewhere in France are called *vin mousseux*, never Champagne, even if the same grapes and same methods are used. Most people use the term champagne to describe any sparkling wine; however, I will be using the term *sparkling wine* throughout this book to describe sparkling wine made outside of the Champagne district of France.

Wine Words

A *cuvée* in Champagne is the name for the first and best juice to flow from the press. It is also used to describe the blend of base wines assembled for second fermentation in bottle. Tête de cuvée means the best of the cuvée.

Good-quality sparkling wines can be purchased today at reasonable prices, comparable to prices for good-quality table wines. You can easily enjoy some effervescence before dinner, with dinner, or to celebrate that special occasion (like finishing that report or giving the dog a bath). Choosing a sparkling wine isn't too different from choosing any other type of wine. It just takes some knowledge, some label-reading, and maybe calling up a wine shop or two. And above all, you have to place your own personal preferences over those of the wine snob who tries to tell you it has to be Dom Perignon or Taittinger.

Styles—From Dry to Sweet

Actually, figuring out champagne labels is the most difficult part of learning about Champagne. Maybe it was meant to enhance the Champagne mystique, but Champagne labels are somewhat enigmatic. Why, you might ask, is *Extra Dry* sweeter than *Brut* (Dry), when in wine, drier means less sweet? Brut itself is no clear indicator; it ranges from zero to 2 percent residual sweetness. Then there's *Demi-Sec*, which suggests half as sweet—only for champagne it means twice as sweet. Before it gets too confusing, these are the label terms from the driest to the sweetest:

➤ Extra Brut, Brut Nature, or Brut Sauvage: Bone dry

➤ Brut: Dry

➤ Extra Dry: Medium dry

➤ Sec: Slightly sweet

➤ Demi-Sec: Fairly sweet

➤ Doux: Very sweet

Grape Alert

You may have heard that Dom Perignon is the best of the best. It is a good *tête de cuvée* Champagne, but it is not the best. It is made in large quantities for a mass market and is somewhat sweeter than what the connoisseur considers appropriate for a *tête de cuvée* bottling. There are better Champagnes for the same or lower price.

Important Things to Know

HEY!

Sweetness in Champagnes can easily mask defects—either a weak *cuvée* (blend) or a winemaking flaw. The drier a Champagne is, the more perfectly it has to be rendered; its flaws and weaknesses can't be concealed. The most delicate Champagnes, particularly those called *Grand Marks* or *Tête de Cuvée* by the producer to signify the best, must be flawless.

Whether it's dry or semi-sweet to you is a matter of personal preference. But there are some things to look for in a quality sparkling wine or Champagne:

➤ First, there are the bubbles (known as the *bead*). They should be tiny and persistent (like those cartoons where the bubbles float skyward from the glass). This should last in the glass for five to ten minutes at a minimum.

➤ Then, there's the mouthfeel. The finer the wine, the tinier the bubbles, which will be less aggressive on your palate.

➤ The balance between sweetness and acidity makes the difference between a good-tasting sparkling wine and one that is unpleasant.

Grape Alert

Sparkling wines produced from areas other than Champagne use the same nomenclature to describe sweetness as Champagne to describe their wines. But while the terms are defined legally in Champagne, they are not necessarily defined elsewhere and their use may be inconsistent.

➤ Sparkling wine made by the *Méthode Champenoise* (described in the following section) will have a slightly creamy mouthfeel as a result of their extended aging on the lees.

➤ Now the finish. It should be crisp, refreshing, and clean. Bitterness on the finish of a sparkling wine is a sign of poorly made wine.

Sparkling the Wine

What Dom Perignon described as stars was actually no more than carbon dioxide retained in the bottle following a refermentation of residual sugar and live yeast cells that had remained after the original fermentation. The same discovery—though a lot less dramatic—is probably made by every home winemaker. Like the resourceful German winemakers who created Eiswein, the early Champagne pioneers essentially parlayed a potential disaster into one of the world's finest beverages. The bubbles added sparkle to wine, but what was needed was a strong closure and special bottle to withstand the pressure. The innovative Madame Cliquot invented the first Champagne cork, and the Champagne industry was born.

For the winemakers in several regions, adding sparkle to wine serves a dual function in turning a liability into an asset. Many sparkling wines come from cool areas where the vines don't ripen well. A still table wine from such a region might be excessively acid, harsh, and thin; in short, it would be an awfully unpalatable beverage. Through an intricate process of refermentation, the potential salad dressing is metamorphosed into a bubbling triumph.

HEY!

Important Things to Know

For wines from the U.S., the term *sparkling wine* on the label is a better indicator of quality than the word *champagne*. Sparkling wine is a perfectly respectable appellation. Beware of cheap imitation champagnes from California and New York State that sell for less than $7 and describe their contents as "champagne."

In the U.S., sparkling wine and champagne (note the lowercase *c*) are made effervescent by undergoing a second fermentation in a closed container. The choice of grape varieties is up to the producer, with no restrictions on growing conditions or bubble-producing technique. The only legal limitation is that the bubbles must be produced naturally and not added by artificial carbonation. The terms *champagne* and *sparkling wine* are often used interchangeably. I prefer to use Champagne the way Madame Cliquot and the Appellation Controlée intended it. All effervescing wines from outside the Champagne district will be referred to as sparkling wine.

French Champagne derives its quality from a series of time-proven, exacting methods. The permissible grape varieties are the noble Chardonnay and Pinot Noir, plus minor blending grapes which, even in Champagne's characteristically cool climate, develop character when picked at low sugar levels ranging from 15 to 19 degrees Brix (normal for table wine is 20 to 23 degrees). The grapes are conventionally fermented into wine, then assembled by the Champagne maker into a base wine or blend known as the *vin de cuvée*. The blend may be entirely from one vintage, but it usually consists of wines from two or more years, acquired to suit different markets. For example, the blend may be drier for export to the U.K., or sweeter for the U.S. palate. Despite the variance, the vin de cuvée is usually made within an established house style.

The *Méthode Champenoise* is the original and the most intricate technique. The sparkles can also be added by the transfer method and the bulk or Charmat process, each of which is described in this section. So we'll divide our hypothetical cuvée into three batches and start with the *Méthode Champenoise*.

Méthode Champenoise

First thing to remember: The winemaker adhering to the *Méthode Champenoise* bottles the wine in the same bottle you'll eventually see in your wine shop. A sugar and yeast solution that will ferment in the bottle is added to the wine. The bottles are sealed, with either a temporary cork or metal crown cap, and then placed on their sides. The second fermentation takes three or four months to complete. That's only the beginning.

By law, the wine must remain in contact with the dead yeast cells for a minimum of one year, though some remain as many as five years. Time "on the yeast" adds flavor complexity through a process of *yeast autolysis*, which contributes richness and a desired yeasty character. Virtually all the top-line French Champagnes spend several years on the yeast.

Once the bubbles are created and the flavors are developed, the problem is to remove the dead yeast cells from each bottle. The technique for doing so, called *degorgement* (disgorgement), distinguishes the *Méthode Champenoise* from a less-costly shortcut method called the transfer process. Prior to *degorgement*, the Champagne undergoes a laborious and time-consuming process called *remuage,* or riddling.

For remuage, the bottles are placed neck-down in special A-frame racks. Each day, cellar workers riddle (slightly shake and rotate) each bottle, causing the sediment to creep gradually from the side of the bottle to the neck area. After about six weeks, the sediment is lodged in the neck, up against the closure. At this stage, the bottles are carefully removed—neck down—and taken to the *degorgement* room.

HEY!

Important Things to Know

French Champagne is ready to drink when you buy it. It changes a little in bottle, but it does not improve much with cellaring. (Besides, unless you're a collector, why wait?)

Degorgement can either be done by hand or machine; the principle remains the same. The neck of the bottle is immersed in a freezing brine solution, trapping the sediment in a plug of ice. The bottle is opened, the plug expelled by the pressure, and *voilà!*—no more sediment.

Some liquid is always lost by the process, and it's replaced according to house style—either with Champagne or a solution of Cognac and a sugar syrup. This tiny squirt plays a role in determining the sweetness of the finished Champagne. Known as the *dosage*, it contains some degree of added sugar.

Following *degorgement*, a special multi-layered cork is inserted, the protective wire hood attached, and the Champagne set aside for further bottle aging to allow *dosage* and wine to *marry*.

Transfer Method

If you follow the steps of the *Méthode Champenoise*, it's not difficult to see why fine French Champagne is *très cher* (expensive). The second method for making sparkling wine (note the distinction) is the transfer method, a time- and labor-saving shortcut to bottle-fermented wine. It differs from the *Méthode Champenoise* in two ways. First, though the wine undergoes its second fermentation in a bottle, it's not the bottle you'll see on the shelf. Second, there's no riddling or disgorging; both steps are replaced by filtration.

During the transfer process, the wine is transferred into a large, pressurized tank via a special machine designed to prevent loss of pressure. Once in the tank, it's filtered to remove the yeast cells and all other sediment, and finally bottled. The process ensures that the sparkling product is free from sediment, and it's far less costly than the *Méthode Champenoise*. The catch is that some of the character developed during fermentation may be filtered out along with the yeast.

Actually, the distinction can be quite subtle. If the *cuvées* are similar, the distinguishing factors are the length of time the wine spends on the yeast and the degree of filtration used. Both influence flavor. But unless you've got the bottle in front of you, it can be difficult to distinguish between a quality sparkling wine made by the transfer method and one made by the *Méthode Champenoise*—even for a wine expert, regardless of what they may have you believe. The transfer method can still give us sparkling beverages with the sought-after tiny beads and persistent effervescence that are the hallmarks of fine sparkling wine.

Charmat Process

With our third batch of *cuvée*, we come to the Charmat, or bulk process (named for Eugene Charmat, the Frenchman who invented it). After its initial fermentation, the *cuvée* is poured directly into a closed tank, with an added solution of yeast and sugar. The size of the tank varies, but it's usually several thousand gallons (or immense). The second fermentation takes three to four weeks, at which point the wine is filtered and bottled.

The bulk process makes sparkling wine, but it's unlikely Madame Cliquot would have approved. Bulk process sparkling wines generally have large bubbles that dissipate quickly. They also lack the traditional yeasty character since they spend little time, if any, in contact with the yeast. It's basically wine made bubbly—and not always pleasantly so. Charmat lends itself to large volume and an efficient use of time, labor, and equipment. It's used to make inexpensive sparkling wine, often from neutral or even poor-quality grapes.

> **Grape Alert**
> All U.S. sparkling wine labels are required to indicate which technique was followed. The French Champagne method will be designated by one of two phrases: *Méthode Champenoise* or *Fermented in this Bottle*. The transfer process is usually identified by the phrase *Fermented in the Bottle*. Note the subtle difference in wording. For domestic sparkling wines, either *Charmat* or *bulk* must be declared if this process is used.

Champagne—The True Champagne

Champagne's opulent aura may be a bit overdone, but just like in Hollywood, there is such a thing as star quality. And just like a great director brings out the best in a star, a great Champagne maker is truly a great artist!

What Makes Champagne So Good?

Making Champagne really is more of an art than a science. The *cuvée* is carefully selected by tasting and retasting potential components (which may be up to 200 different wines!). Monitoring the time on the yeast, carefully riddling the bottles, and finally disgorging the sediment are all acts that require more than simple manual labor. But the final product, with its small, delicate bead, persistent effervescence, subtle yeastiness, and intricate balance justifies the extraordinary time and labor involved in the *Méthode Champenoise*.

Geographically, Champagne is the northernmost wine growing region in France. Its cool climate makes grape-growing (especially red grapes) for table wines a gamble, but it's ideal for adding those sparkles. And its chalky limestone soil is perfect for the Pinot Noir that adds fullness and body to the *cuvée*.

Most of the major Champagne houses reside in two cities within the district. The first is historic Rheims, where Joan of Arc led the Dauphin Charles to be crowned King of France. The second is the smaller Epernay, located south of Rheims. Surrounding them are the vineyard sites where the three Champagne grape varieties—Pinot Noir, Chardonnay, and Pinot Meunier—are lovingly cultivated.

➤ The Montagne de Reims (south of Rheims), where the best Pinot Noir grapes grow.

➤ The Côte des Blancs (south of Epernay), the area for the best Chardonnay.

➤ The Vallée de la Marne (west of Epernay), most favorable to Pinot Meunier (a black grape); however, all three varieties are grown here.

French Champagne makers are perfectionists (and under French law they have to be). Both the grape varieties and their yields are closely regulated with quality uppermost in mind. Pinot Noir contributes fullness, body, structure, and longevity; Chardonnay offers finesse, backbone, delicacy, freshness, and elegance; and Pinot Meunier provides floral scents and fruitiness. But ultimately, the combination depends on the Champagne maker's preferred style.

Important Things to Know

HEY! The highest quality comes from the free-run juice, the juice that runs off the grapes from their own weight before pressing. Pressing is an art in Champagne because it is essential to avoid tainting the juice of the dark-skinned grapes with anything more than the slightest hint of color or bitterness of flavor (if any). Champagne has about 300 *crus*, and the vineyards are graded on a quality basis. The highest ranked vineyards are sought after by the prestigious houses especially for their top-of-the-line Grand Mark. Certain vineyards are es-teemed for Pinot Noir, while others are cherished for Chardonnay. Except for the Blancs de Blancs, which are made entirely from white grapes, the usual ratio is two-thirds black grapes to one-third Chardonnay. Of the two black grapes, it's Pinot Noir that dominates; only a small amount of Pinot Meunier is used. There's also a Blanc de Noir, made entirely from black grapes.

Non-Vintage Champagnes

Contrary to legend, most Champagne (85 percent of all produced) is non-vintage (NV); that is, there's no vintage year on the label. It's all in the blending. In addition to the myriad of wines in the *cuvée*, NV Champagnes are allowed to contain wine from three or more harvests.

Non-vintage Champagnes are created according to the favored house style. One house may seek elegance and finesse, another will strive for fruitiness, and a third might consider body and full flavor as paramount. Every Champagne house has its own style, and it's rarely tampered with. After all, Champagne drinkers are no different from most consumers. Most people remain loyal to their preferred style of Champagne.

As noted in the earlier discussion about the *Méthode Champenoise,* most Champagne producers age their product long after the one-year minimum. The usual time for NV Champagne is two and one-half to three years. This additional aging provides greater marrying time for the blend and enhances the wine's flavor and complexity as it absorbs the lees in the bottle.

Vintage Champagne

It occurs roughly four or five times a decade: a year when the weather in Champagne is so grower-friendly that a good *cuvée* can be made exclusively from the vines of that year without blending with reserve wines from previous harvests to create Champagne.

There are two categories of vintage Champagnes:

> **Regular vintage:** within the $25 to $50 a bottle price range. The label carries the name of the house plus the vintage date.

> **Premium vintage (*tête de cuvée* or *prestige cuvée*):** examples are Taittinger's Comtes de Champagne, Roederer's Cristal, Veuve Clicquot's La Grande Dame; these range from $50 to $200 per bottle.

No doubt you'd like some reasons for spending a substantial sum for a vintage year on the label. Here's why vintage Champagne is unquestionably superior:

> ➤ The cuvée is made from the finest grapes from the finest vineyards (without exception for *tête de cuvée*).

Grape Alert
Prolonged refrigeration may be great for your carbonated soft drinks, but it's lethal for sparkling wine. The prolonged exposure to extreme cold temperature will flatten the bubbles and dull the flavor of any Champagne or good sparkling wine. You should chill your sparklers just before serving.

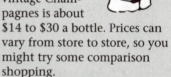

Wine Wisdom
The going price for most non-vintage Champagnes is about $14 to $30 a bottle. Prices can vary from store to store, so you might try some comparison shopping.

➤ Vintage Champagne is usually made from the two noble varieties only, Pinot Noir and Chardonnay.

➤ Vintage Champagnes are usually aged for two or more years longer than non-vintage Champagne, giving them greater complexity and finesse.

➤ The grapes all come from a superior, if not superlative, vintage.

Vintage Champagne is richer in flavor than non-vintage Champagne. It may also be more full-bodied and more complex, with a longer finish. Whether a vintage Champagne is worth its extra cost is a question you have to decide for yourself after trying one.

Blanc de Noirs

This rare and exotic Champagne specimen is made exclusively from black grapes—sometimes 100 percent Pinot Noir. It's at the upper end of the *tête de cuvée* price range. Bollinger's Blanc de Noirs *Vielles Vignes* (old vines) is the crème de la crème of the Blanc de Noirs.

Blanc de Blancs

Blanc de Blancs literally translates as white from white (if you're feeling artistic, think of it as white on white). Blanc de blancs is made from 100 percent noble Chardonnay grapes. It can be either vintage or non-vintage, and is usually priced a bit higher than other Champagnes in the same class. Blanc de blancs are lighter and more delicate than other Champagnes.

Rosé Champagne

Commonly (maybe too commonly) known as pink Champagne, rosé Champagnes are actually a cut above average. Unfortunately, being pink and sparkling makes people take them less seriously. They're usually made from Pinot Noir and Chardonnay only. Like blanc de blancs, they can be either vintage or non-vintage, and they cost a bit more than regular Champagnes in the same category.

Top Champagne Producers

As explained earlier in this section, all of the best Champagne houses develop their own signature style. Here's a list of premier producers categorized according to style:

Light and elegant style

➤ Billecart-Salmon

➤ Charles de Cazanove

➤ de Castellane

➤ Jacquesson

➤ Laurent-Perrier

➤ Perrier-Jouet

➤ Philipponnat

➤ Ruinart

➤ Taittinger

Medium-bodied style

➤ Charles Heidsieck

➤ Deutz

➤ Hiedsieck Monopole

➤ Möet & Chandon

➤ Mumm

➤ Pol Roger

➤ Pommery

Full-bodied Style

➤ Bollinger

➤ Gosset

➤ Henriot

➤ Krug

➤ Louis Roederer

➤ Salon

➤ Veuve Clicquot

If you're in the market for *tête de cuvée*, here's a guide to some of the best, so you'll know you're getting superior quality for your investment:

➤ Billecart-Salmon: Blanc de Blancs (1986, 1985)

➤ Bollinger: Blancs de Noirs Vielles Vignes (1985)

➤ Cattier: Clos du Moulin (the only non-vintage on the list)

➤ Charbaut: Certificate Blanc de Blancs (1985)

➤ Charles de Cazanove: Stradivarius (1989)

➤ Charles Heidsieck: Blanc des Millenaires (1983)

➤ Gosset: Grand Millesime and Rosé (1985)

➤ Hiedsieck Monopole: Diamant Bleu and Rosé (1985, 1982)

➤ Jacquesson: Signature (1985)

➤ Laurent-Perrier: Grand Siecle (1988, 1985)

➤ Louis Roederer: Cristal (1988, 1986, 1985)

➤ Möet & Chandon: Dom Perignon (1988, 1985, 1982)

➤ Mumm: Rene Lalou (1985, 1982)

➤ Philipponnat: Clos de Goisses (1986, 1985, 1982)

➤ Pol Roger: cuvée Sir Winston Churchill (1986, 1985)

➤ Pommery: cuvée Louise Pommery (1988, 1987, 1985)

➤ Ruinart: Dom Ruinart Blanc de Blancs (1988, 1985)

➤ Salon: Le Mesnil (1983, 1982, 1979)

➤ Taittinger: Compte de Champagne (1988, 1985)

➤ Veuve Clicquot: La Grande Dame (1988, 1985, 1983)

The Great Pretender: Vin Mousseux

As noted earlier, most sparkling wines made in France outside of the Champagne region are called *vin mousseux*. The most popular wines come from the Loire Valley, with a few appearing from the Rhône and Midi regions. The Loire sparklers can be quite good and relatively inexpensive. The difference is they are made from different grape varieties than Champagne, and spend less time on the yeast. Saumur is the Loire Valley's biggest appellation for *vin mousseux*, which may or may not be made by the *Méthode Champenoise*. A word of caution: It tends toward over-sweet and quality varies.

When made by the *Méthode Champenoise*, the wine is often labeled *Crémant*. Grape varieties do not have to be the ones used for true Champagne and usually are those typical of the region. Most sell in the $8 to $15 price range.

Other Sparkling Wines

You've probably imbibed California sparkling wine, and chances are you've had some Italian sparkles from the famous Asti wine zone. And maybe you've tried some of the Spanish sparkling wine that's become increasingly popular in recent years. They may not be Champagne, but they're good-quality beverages in their own right.

The Cavas of Spain

Spain is the up-and-comer in the sparkling wine market, and most of its wine is available for under $8. Sparkling wine is called *Cava* in Spain, and the best of it comes from the Penedes region near Barcelona.

> ### Important Things to Know
>
> Cava made by the *Méthode Champenoise* can be well-balanced with a fine, steady bead. The distinction is in the grapes. Most Cavas use local Spanish varieties, although the finer *cuvées* contain Chardonnay. Cava production is dominated by two huge wineries, both of whose catchy commercials have made them well-known to U.S. consumers: Freixenet and Codorniu.

German Sekt

Theoretically, the cool German climate should make it a perfect place for sparkling wines. Unfortunately, theory does not necessarily translate into practice. Germany produces some of the finest white wines in the entire wine world, but Sekt just isn't one of them. It's produced by the Charmat method, which can make it coarsely bubbly. The better brands can be fruity and fresh, but only a handful of brands make quality Sekt. The best are made from Riesling grapes, which can provide an interesting taste experience.

Italian Spumante

Italy is one of the leading volume producers of sparkling wines, formerly known as *spumante* (literally, sparkling). The term *spumante* came to be associated with a fruity, oversweet beverage resembling a soft drink, so sparkling wines now bear the regional name without the spumante stigma. The Italians do prefer their sparkling wines sweet, so even those labeled Brut tend to be on the sweet side; but it's not impossible to find good Italian sparkling wines that are bone-dry.

The major production center is the Piedmont, which gives the world Asti. This well-known Italian sparkler is made from the Muscat grape, which has a musklike or pinelike aroma that's attractive but not overpowering in a well-balanced wine. A good Asti is delicious and fruity, with flavors reminiscent of pine. Made by the Charmat method, Asti is non-vintage and is meant to be consumed when purchased.

Some very good-quality sparkling wine is produced by the *Méthode Champenoise* in the Oltrepo-Pavese and Franciacorta wine zones of Lombardy. Until recently, only small quantities were exported, but they should not be too difficult to find. This is where you'll find the bone-dry bubbly; the dry sparkling wines are made with little to no *dosage*.

Domestic Bubbles

Most of the domestic sparklers you'll find in your wine shop come from California and New York State. Happily, both producers have outlived a reputation for making inferior, mass-produced, grapey imitations of the real thing. Made by the *Méthode Champenoise*, the bubbles have gotten smaller and more persistent, and the quality has vastly improved.

Some of the best California sparkling wines come from Champagne houses that have set up shop on the West Coast. Led by Möet & Chandon, which began California production in 1973, Roederer, Taittinger, and others have all heard the siren song of the Golden State.

HEY!

Important Things to Know

The California bubbly made by the French Champagne houses is definitely a different wine than the Champagne they make in Champagne—the California versions are fruitier and more direct.

Remember, for the best quality, look for the words *sparkling wine* on the label, not champagne. The only bottle-fermented bubbly that uses the name champagne is Korbel, which sells for about $9. Two quality sparkling wine producers in New York State are Château Frank and Glenora. Their wines retail in the $12 to $14 price range, and both are made by the *Méthode Champenoise*.

The Least You Need to Know

➤ All sparkling wine is not Champagne.

➤ True Champagne can come from only the Champagne district of France.

➤ Sparkling wines from regions other than Champagne can be quite good.

➤ American wines labeled as champagne (with a lowercase *c*) are usually inferior and go flat quickly.

OOOH...

Chapter 19

Fortified Wines

In This Chapter

➤ Porto wines from Portugal

➤ Ports of the world

➤ Sherry—sunshine from Spain

➤ Madeira—from the island of Madeira

In this chapter you will learn all about fortified wines from Portugal, Spain, and Madeira. The chief distinctions between table and fortified wines are the style and alcohol content. By definition, a fortified wine is a wine whose alcohol content is increased by the addition of brandy or neutral spirits. Fortified wines usually range from 17–21 percent alcohol by volume—a few points over the 14 percent limit for table wine.

Historically, wines were fortified for stability. No bubbles wanted here; the added alcohol killed off the yeast population and prevented refermentation. It also ensured the survival of wines that were transported over long distances.

Certain countries like Portugal and Spain insist that the fortifying agent must come from within their borders, often within a delineated region, and be made from specified grape varieties. This is not a strict form of quality control—it's a way of keeping business at home. It's not a quality indicator like a *cru*.

Fortifying the Wine: Giving it Muscle

Fortified wines can be made in two ways. In the first, the grapes are chosen carefully for their ability to develop high sugar content and potential to ferment to high alcohol levels. The must from the select grapes is inoculated with special, powerful yeasts, capable of thriving in high alcohol ranges. The alcohol level will naturally reach 17 or 18 percent, which automatically inhibits fermentation. Sweetness can be adjusted later.

In the second and much more common traditional method, a fortifying agent is used to raise the level of alcohol and, where necessary, halt fermentation. Most Ports, Sherries, Marsalas, and Madeiras start with grapes high in natural sugars. They may be fermented dry, or, when sweetness is desired, be fortified to stop fermentation at a particular point and still retain some sweetness. The selection of the brandy or neutral spirits used as the fortifying agent is a crucial quality factor. Some fortified wines are aged in wood for smoothness, while others are raw and rough.

Porto—Port from Portugal

A decade or two ago, the Portugese changed the name of *their* Port to Porto to avoid confusion in a marketplace filled with Ports from many other countries. Only Port from Portugal can be called Porto. For the purposes of this chapter, I will refer to Porto as Port, but remember that we are speaking of authentic Port from Portugal.

The foremost authority on Port is H. Warner Allen, a noted wine writer during the early part of the century. He wrote: "Vintage Port…has a lushness, unctuousness, delicacy, and refinement that make Port unparalleled by any wine of its type in the world."

Wine Wisdom
For a list of recommended Port producers, see Appendix A.

Port has long been the favorite of fine English gentlemen, and some swear it's a British invention. When faced with a shortage of French wine in the late 17th century, the resourceful (and thirsty) British imported wine from Portugal. To ensure its stability on the journey to England, they added a touch of brandy to the finished wine. In 1670, the first English Port house, Warre, opened its doors in the seaport city of Oporto, Portugal. Oporto is still the home of true Port. As Port became an important commodity, the process for making it became more refined. Instead of adding the brandy as an afterthought the (mainly British) producers began fortifying the wine with brandy during the fermentation process. A Port producer today can make as many as five or six different styles of Port depending on the taste preferences of the intended market. True Port has gotten sweeter by design to meet market demands, but the process remains the same.

Port is made from a blend of grapes grown on the steep slopes of Portugal's Douro region, where the soils are gravelly schist in composition and the climate is warm to hot. Anywhere from 12 to 15 different grape varieties go into the making of Port; they're local varieties and something of unsung heroes. Even the most important are relative unknowns: Touriga, Sousão, Bastardo, and the Tinta versions—Tinta Cão, Tinta Madeira, and Tinta Francisca. They're chosen for their ability to develop high sugars, good color, and, when used in concert, character and finesse. After being gathered from the terraced hillsides, the grapes are fermented and brought to Oporto for prolonged aging, blending, and bottling. The quality of Port is derived from the vintage, the aging, and the blending; variations in these elements account for nuances in style.

Vintage Port

Vintage Port is the *crème de la crème* and is produced only in exceptional vintages; that is, vintages capable of producing wines of great depth and complexity. The standards are set by individual producers, but a vintage year is generally declared by consensus. It's unusual to find a lone producer declaring a vintage year (although it's not impossible).

Usually made from selected lots, Vintage Port is capable of aging and developing complexity for many, many years. Once it's been fermented, fortified, and adjusted for sweetness, Vintage Port must be aged for two years in wood before bottling. At that time, it's concentrated and rich, to the point of being undrinkable. In bottle aging, the spirits and flavors marry, and the wine throws a heavy deposit or sediment. Ten years in bottle usually yields a mere infant at most. It takes 20 or 30 years before Vintage Port earns its name. Some of the best Vintage Ports are 70 years old or older.

> **Grape Alert**
> As the normal deposit from bottle-aging forms a crust on the bottom and along the sides of the bottle, Vintage Port really has to be opened carefully and decanted (or you'll be sipping sediment). Another type of Port that develops a crust is called Crusted Port, usually made from a blend of vintages that the producer chooses to approximate the richness of Vintage Port. Crusted Port will develop in bottle for six to eight years, but rarely achieves the heights of a fine Vintage Port.

Most good Vintage Ports sell in the $30 to $50 range when they are young (and years away from being ready to drink). You can expect to pay $50 or more for a Port with a decade or more age. A fully mature port can cost from $80 to $200 a bottle in a great vintage.

Late-Bottled Vintage

Late-Bottled Vintage Port comes from one vintage that is cask-aged for at least four or often five years before being bottled. Most of the sediment falls during cask-aging, making Late-Bottled Vintage Port a compromise between Vintage and non-Vintage varieties. It is less expensive, less complex, and sometimes made from young vines or less traditional grape varieties and sells for about $15 to $20.

Ruby Port

Ruby Port is a blend of vintages, usually lacking the intense purple colors and flavors of a better-quality Port to begin with. It's cask-aged for roughly three years. Ruby Ports are blended for consistent color and style, and are usually the least expensive Ports (around $8 or $10). They're the youngest of the Port family, and are rougher and less harmonious than their Tawny cousins, described next.

Tawny Port

Some Tawny Ports are deep garnet or brownish in color and need spend no more time aging than a Ruby. But the best lie in cask for many years, until the color becomes light or tawny through oxidation. Some well-aged Tawny Ports can be marvelous and subtle. Expect to pay about $15 for a longer-aged Tawny; the lesser-quality Tawnies can be found for as low as $6 or $8.

The very best Tawnies state their average age (the average of the ages of wines from which they were blended) on the label—10, 20, 30, or 40 years. Ten-year-old Tawnies cost about $15 to $25, and 20-year-olds sell for $35.

Important Things to Know

HEY!

Occasionally, a Tawny Port will be so outstanding that it is not blended with Ports of other vintages but aged individually. This single-vintage Tawny will be labeled either *Port of the Vintage* (as opposed to Vintage Port) or *Colheita Port*. An exceptional Colheita can be a fine example of an aged Port, but it is distinctively different from Vintage Port.

White Port

White Port is rarely seen outside of Portugal and France. Made from white grape varieties, it has a golden color and is usually finished dry, bottled young, and drunk as an apèritif. The sweet-finished version is usually inferior in quality; there are much better apèritifs.

Vintage Character Port

Vintage Character Port is a blend of premium Ruby ports from several vintages, cask-aged for about five years. They are full-bodied, rich, ready to drink when bottled, and sell for about $12 to $15. Vintage Character Ports are sold under a proprietary name like Board-room (made by Dow).

Port at Home

Like other fine red wines, Vintage Ports should be stored on their sides in a cool environment. Other Ports may be stored upright like liquor; they're already fully developed. With the exception of Ruby and White, all Ports will keep for several weeks after opening.

Port should be served at cool room temperature, 66 to 68 degrees F. Ports go well with nuts, such as walnuts, and strong cheeses, such as Stilton or Roquefort.

Ports of the World

The name "Port" is supposed to refer to the pride of the city of Oporto, only it's one of those terms that's been borrowed incessantly, like "Kleenex" or "Coke." Non-Oporto Ports are generic dessert wines that are made in many countries; some are good, some are adequate, and some are cheap, baked-tasting sweet wines bearing little resemblance to the real thing.

Perhaps the best ports to be seen outside of Portugal come from Australia. Look for Yalumba, Chateau Reynella, and Lindemans.

After an unfortunate history of producing dull and ordinary Ports, tainted by baked qualities that come from inappropriate grapes grown in a hot climate, California and South Africa have both set their sights on producing high-quality Port. Both regions have planted the traditional grape varieties and searched for finer fortifying spirits.

In California, several very interesting Ports have been made either from blended grapes or from blends in which Zinfandel predominates. Among the Port revivalists, Amador County and parts of Sonoma County have gained attention as respected Port wine regions. South Africa, a country traditionally noted for making fortified wines, has been coming alive with finer Port wines. Some South African versions have been virtually indistinguishable from the Oporto models.

Sherry, Baby

Originating in the Jerez (Andalucia) region of southern Spain, Sherry is said to be an Anglicized pronunciation of Jerez. The ancient Moorish town of Jerez is the site of many Sherry *bodegas* (wineries), but it is just one part of the Sherry-producing region. The coastal village of Puerto de Santa Maria, located southwest of Jerez, also boasts several bodegas. The sea air is believed to be an important element in the making of dry *fino* (a type of Sherry). Ten miles northwest of Jerez, another coastal village, Sanlucar de

Barrameda, is so renowned for its sea breezes that the lightest and driest of Sherries, *Manzanilla*, can legally be made only there. It does not appear possible to make wine of this quality elsewhere.

The most prized soil in the region is *albariza*, a soil that is predominately chalk, with limestone and magnesium. Easily recognizable by its white topsoil layer, *albariza* sections bear the best Sherry grapes, and by law at least 40 percent of the grapes used in Sherry must come from *albariza* soil. (See Chapter 14, "Olé!—Wines in the Spanish Style," for more).

The predominant grape variety used in Sherry is the Palomino, a prolific vine whose fruit is delicious to eat, but which normally yields thin, neutral, and sometimes harsh table wines. Once again, inventive winemakers have turned a liability into a plus. The wine oxidizes easily during aging, yielding the characteristic and desirable nutty aroma and flavor that are the hallmarks of a fine Sherry. Pedro Ximenez is a secondary grape for Sherry, yielding a very sweet wine that is often used as a blending or sweetening agent. Moscatel (Muscat) is sometimes used for dessert Sherries.

Dona Flor and Her Two Sherries

Sherry is a fortified wine made in large volume and most producers use modern, efficient methods of crushing and vinification. The Sherry-to-be begins as a wine that is fermented in stainless-steel tanks. The first-year wine is then aged in the *bodega* in butts (U.S.-made oak barrels with a capacity of 158 gallons), filled to about one-third capacity. What evolves over the next year or two is a drama of self-fulfillment. Some butts will reveal a propensity toward developing the unique, thick, white film yeast called *flor* in Jerez. Others won't. The appearance of the flor yeast (technically known as *Saccharomyces fermenti*) is unpredictable, discerned only by frequent tastings, and found nowhere else in the world. Call it kismet. During the aging process, the *bodega* master (vintner) tastes the contents of each butt and rates it on the basis of its propensity to develop flor on the wine's surface. Essentially, the developing wine is telling the experienced vintner where it wants to go.

The wine's progress in each butt is chronicled, and based on the intrinsic character and development of the *flor*, the wine is channeled into one of three directions:

➤ Wines without any *flor* character and with weak flavors will either be distilled into spirits or made into vinegar.

➤ Wines that develop only a small degree of *flor*, but have good body and flavors are marked as Olorosos and introduced into a *solera*. (You'll learn shortly what a "solera" is.)

➤ Wines that are light in color with a thick layer of *flor* are marked as Finos and sent to another *solera*.

Within the *bodegas*, butts marked Fino will be made into three different styles of Sherry: Fino, Manzanilla, and Amontillado. The Olorosos will be made into Oloroso, Cream Sherry, or Brown Sherry.

The crucial factor in achieving quality in a Sherry lies in the aging process. Most Sherries are non-vintage wines, and almost all are the product of the *solera* system of blending and aging in butts. The *solera* itself is a configuration (usually triangular in shape) of barrels containing Sherry of various ages. It's usually composed of three tiers or rows, with each successive tier representing a younger wine. There is a method behind this. The system is based on the premise that newer wines "refresh" the older ones, and the union releases a host of flavors. This procedure, called *fractional blending*, marries old wine with newer wine from different tiers of the *solera* (incidentally, *solera* is derived from *suelo*, the word for bottom or ground, referring to the bottom tier of the *solera*).

The oldest Sherry resides on the bottom tier. Above it are the *criada*, sort of a nursery in which the Sherry matures. In an established *solera*, the butts remain; the wine moves first diagonally, and then down from one tier to the next (think of it as a liquid chess game). When the wine is bottled, the *bodega* master drains off part (no more than one-third from each butt) from the bottom tier and replaces it with wine from the tier above. As Sherry moves throughout the *solera*, it's continually in the process of fractional blending.

Fino

Fino, the finest Sherry, is always produced and aged within Jerez or in Puerto de Santa Maria. It has a pale color, a yeasty, slightly nutty aroma, delicate flavors, and is usually dry, sometimes slightly bitter. Its scent is often reminiscent of almonds. The alcohol content ranges from 15.5 to 17 percent alcohol. Finos average about three to five years in *solera* before bottling. They do not develop in the bottle and once opened, lose freshness within a week or so. If you're going to keep them at all, refrigerate after opening. They should be served chilled, and it is best to finish the bottle within a day or two to enjoy the best attributes of the wine.

Manzanilla

Manzanilla is best described as Fino produced in Sanlucar de Barrameda. It is pale, straw-colored, delicate, and light-bodied. Some say the wine's slightly bitter, tangy, and pungent character is due to the salty flavors picked up from the sea air. Wines made in Sanlucar but sent to Jerez for aging in *solera* do not develop the typical character of Manzanilla, so there may be something to it. One explanation is that the temperate sea climate causes the flor to grow more thickly in this area. Manzanilla is the driest and most intense of all the Sherries. It should be served chilled.

Amontillado

Amontillado is an amber-colored, aged Fino that's spent a longer time in the *solera*. It's medium-bodied with a more pronounced, nutty flavor. Amontillado is dry and pungent. True amontillado is not often seen and is expensive, while cheaper Sherries labeled amontillado are commonplace. If you find an amontillado selling for $6 or less, it is not worth buying. Serve amontillado slightly chilled.

Oloroso

Oloroso is deep in color and boasts a rich, full-bodied style with a scent of walnuts. Because of its prolonged aging, it lacks the yeasty flor pungency. Olorosos are customarily dry wines, but are sometimes sweetened to suit market demands. They usually contain between 18 and 20 percent alcohol. Serve at room temperature or very slightly chilled.

Palo Cortado

This rare breed of Sherry is the best of the non-flor Sherries. It begins life as a fino with a flor and develops as an amontillado after having lost its flor. Then it begins to resemble the richer, more fragrant oloroso style, while retaining the elegance of an amontillado. Palo Cortado is similar to an oloroso in color, but its aroma is like amontillado. Serve at room temperature or slightly chilled.

Medium Sherry

Medium Sherry is an amontillado or light oloroso that has been slightly sweetened.

Pale Cream

Pale Cream Sherry is a slightly sweetened blend of fino and light amontillado Sherries.

Cream Sherry

Cream Sherry is made from oloroso wine, often of poor quality; once sweetened, the sweetness will mask the defects. The wine is sweetened and the color darkened by the addition of wines from Pedro Ximenez grapes, which are left to sun-dry for seven to ten days for extra sugar development. Pedro Ximenez is a thick, concentrated, very sweet wine, and not much is required to make a Cream Sherry. However, its character is a key factor in the quality of the finished product. Cream Sherries are very popular.

Brown Sherry

This is a blend of oloroso, Pedro Ximenez, and an added sweetening agent. It's very dark, very syrupy, and very, very sweet. The style is far more common in the U.K. than the U.S. East India is a type of Brown Sherry that is even sweeter and darker in color.

Pedro Ximenez and Moscatel

This is an extremely sweet, dark brown, syrupy dessert wine that can be used as a sauce on desserts. It is made from raisined grapes of these two varieties and is low in alcohol.

Montilla

Located northeast of the Jerez region, the wines made here are similar to the *fino*, *amontillado*, and *oloroso* styles of Sherry. Unlike Sherry, they are not fortified to higher alcohol levels, but derive their strength naturally during fermentation. The main grape variety is the Pedro Ximenez. The leading brand for Montilla is Alvear, usually priced at $8 to $9. Once seldom seen in the U.S., it's now widely distributed.

Grape Alert

There are quite a few impostors labeled "Sherry" that come from countries other than Spain. Few are made by the *solera* system of aging and blending. A few decent Sherries have come out of California, but they are still ordinary, lacking the flavor complexities and textures of the real thing. If you're looking for real Sherry, stick with Spain.

Enjoying Sherry at Home

Always buy Fino and Manzanilla when you're ready to serve them. They're at peak flavor and complexity when first opened, but an open bottle can keep in the refrigerator for up to a month. It won't taste quite like the intricate blend the *bodega* master intended, but it can still be a drinkable and delightful beverage. Appendix A lists recommended Sherry producers.

Madeira—The Making of a Legend

Once famous as the beverage of choice in colonial America, Madeira is named for its island home off the coast of North Africa. The grapes for this legendary fortified wine are grown on very steep hillsides that ring the perimeter of the island. The wines of Madeira are often identified by their predominant grape variety. These include, principally: Verdelho, Sercial, Bual (or Boal), and Malvasia.

To say that Madeira is hardy is an understatement. It's not just its robust character, but also its ability to age. If a wine can be called a survivor, Madeira is it. The prime Madeiras are vintage-dated from 1920 all the way back to 1795 when the colonists were still around to enjoy their favorite drink. Even the rarest, most noble Château Lafite is a mere infant by comparison.

The styles of Madeira range from sweet to moderately dry. As the juice of the grapes, or *mosto*, is fermented in large vats, the wines destined for a dry style will complete fermentation, while the sweeter versions will have fermentation arrested through the addition of

223

brandy. Madeira follows one unusual production technique that accounts for its unique character: a system of baking or heating the wine known as *estufagem* (from *estufas*, or ovens). The technique was originally discovered accidentally back in the days when the wine was stored in the hold of a sailing vessel. En route to the East Indies, the ship passed through the tropical heat and in the overheated hold, lo and behold!—the wine changed character. The resulting heady flavor was such a hit that the winemakers began to duplicate these conditions by aging the wine in large casks in the sun for gentle baking.

Today, the slightly roasted or smoky tang is achieved by aging in heat-controlled vats. In the *estufas*, the temperature increases gradually until it reaches about 110 degrees F, where it remains for several months. The sugars in the wine become carmelized, resulting in a completely *maderized* (oxidized) wine that has not developed any unpleasant aroma or taste. *Post-estufagem*, the Madeira is allowed to cool and recover for the same period of time. Finally, it is fortified and aged in wood casks before being bottled.

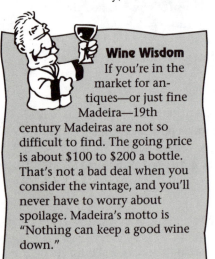

Wine Wisdom

If you're in the market for antiques—or just fine Madeira—19th century Madeiras are not so difficult to find. The going price is about $100 to $200 a bottle. That's not a bad deal when you consider the vintage, and you'll never have to worry about spoilage. Madeira's motto is "Nothing can keep a good wine down."

I admit it: Appreciating high-quality Madeira is an acquired taste. Technically, it's a white wine, although the most robust Chardonnay literally pales before it. Its characteristic color is a dark, rich amber. Madeira has a rich, nutty aroma, a sharp tang to its flavors, and a finish as long as its age. Most Madeira is sold under proprietary names. Authentic vintage Madeira (the kind described earlier) usually comes from a single cask. Many Madeiras are aged in *solera,* and those labeled as *solera* with dates refer to when the *solera* was established, not the entire contents of the bottle.

Twenty years is the designated cask-aging time for a vintage Madeira, although the old wines were aged even longer. *Special Reserve* Maderias are a blend of wines about 10 years old and are less expensive. *Reserve* Madeira is about five years old.

The styles of Madeira are differentiated by both the grape and the level of sweetness. These names reflect either the grape variety or style:

➤ Sercial, the finest dry Madeira, has a lightness and delicacy that lends itself well to enjoyment as an apèritif. The grape is grown at the highest altitude, and is thus one of the latest to ripen. It offers the most distinctive aroma and dry, tangy taste on the palate.

➤ Verdelho is slightly sweeter and rounder on the palate than Sercial. It has a more typical Madeira aroma that can be best described as a toasted, nutty character.

➤ Bual (Boal) is sweeter than Sercial or Verdelho, much fuller in body, and darker in color with flavors of raisins and almonds. It makes for a nice wine to serve with dessert.

➤ Malmsey, made from the Malvasia grape, is the sweetest of all, dark amber in color, and with a smooth, luxurious texture and a very long finish.

➤ Rainwater is well-known in the U.S. (not surprising, from its name, which was coined by a renowned Madeira collector in Savannah, Georgia). It can be variable in sweetness, but as its name implies, should be rather pale in color.

➤ Terrantez is between Verdelho and Bual in style. It is a powerful, medium-sweet, fragrant Madeira with a lot of acidity. It is rarely seen these days.

Setúbal

This is a Portuguese dessert wine from the town of Azeitao, south of Lisbon. Made from the Muscat grape, it is somewhat similar to Port, with grape spirit added to halt fermentation. It is a rich wine with longevity.

Marsala

Italy's most famous fortified wine takes its name from its prime production center, the town of Marsala in western Sicily. In vogue as a chic beverage in the late 18th century, it has since been reduced to the status of a cooking ingredient—a common dessert wine at best.

Despite its tarnished reputation, Marsala does bear some resemblance to Madeira, and devotees (and producers) are bent on a Marsala revival. It is dark in color with amber, red, or gold versions. It has a caramel aroma; it tends to be very sweet, although there are dry and semi-dry versions. The sugar comes from allowing the grapes to dry in the sun prior to fermentation or, more commonly, from the addition of grape concentrate after fermentation. Dry Marsala is often blended in a *solera* system. Dates on Marsala bottles refer to the founding of the *solera*, not a particular vintage.

The best Marsalas are labeled *Superiore* or *Vergine*. Marsala Vergine is unsweetened and uncolored and is aged longer than other styles.

Vin Santo

From Tuscany comes Vin Santo, which is rich golden amber in color and also made from dried grapes, then barrel-aged several years. Vin Santo comes in dry, medium-dry, and sweet versions.

Vermouth

This flavored, fortified wine derives its name from the German word *wermut* (worms-wood). It is made in many wine regions throughout the world. It boasts an intriguing list of flavoring agents: herbs, juniper, coriander and of course, wormwood, to name but a few.

Vermouth normally begins as inexpensive, bland white wine. The herb infusion, which has been steeped in alcohol, is then added, and the whole is quickly blended together to marry. The herb formula varies from brand to brand, and Vermouths vary from fairly dry to quite sweet. It is inexpensive, ubiquitous, and used as an apèritif or mixer. After all, without Vermouth, a martini would be nothing but gin and an olive.

The Least You Need to Know

➤ Fortified wine is made by adding alcohol to wine to raise its alcoholic content.

➤ Port is produced throughout the world, but authentic Port is produced only in Portugal and is officially called Porto.

➤ Sherry is also produced throughout the world, but authentic Sherry is made in the Jerez region of Spain.

➤ Madeira is produced only on the island of Madeira off the coast of North Africa.

Part 4
Wine and You

You may have heard of surfing the Internet. Similarly, you can surf the wine market, looking for new wines to try and good values to stock up on. This part will explain how to pick a knowledgeable wine merchant. It will tell you all about wine ratings and why you should treat those rated on a 100-point scale (like high school) with a grain of salt. You'll learn about private labels and direct imports that are sold at a discount over similar wines with brand names. You'll also learn how to evaluate a restaurant wine list, how to recognize price gouging, and what to do about it. You will gain the confidence necessary to reject a bad bottle and stand your ground in the presence of an inflexible sommelier.

This part tells you which wine magazines and newsletters are worthwhile. It also provides you with a list of wine books for further reading on topics that are beyond the scope of this book.

In short, after reading this part, you will be a knowledgeable wine purchaser armed with the inside information to find the best values at the best prices, both in wine shops and in restaurants.

Chapter 20

Wine Bottle Secrets

> **In This Chapter**
>
> ➤ Basic wine bottle shapes
>
> ➤ How to read a label
>
> ➤ Bottling terms that describe origin, style, and quality of wine

At one time, the shape of a wine bottle provided a good indication of what the bottle contained. As bottles become more and more standardized, this indication has become less and less apparent. Interestingly, the most unusual bottle types tend to fall at opposite ends of the quality spectrum. The most expensive Champagnes are typically bottled in special shapes that are unique to the brand. At the other end of the scale, some cheaply made wines attempt to disguise their lack of character with an attention-getting container.

This chapter introduces you to the key things you need to know about wine bottles. You learn how to decipher what the shape of the bottle means and also what to look for on the label.

The Basic Shapes

Wine bottles come in several predominant shapes, each with its own variations. You find these shapes most often:

➤ **Claret.** The Claret bottle, also called Red Bordeaux, has straight sides and sharp shoulders. This shape is used for wines made in the Bordeaux style, as well as wines grown and bottled on Bordeaux soil. Red Bordeaux, Sauternes, and Graves wines are all packaged in this angular bottle. So are California varietals such as Cabernet Sauvignon, Merlot, Sauvignon Blanc, Semillon (all Bordeaux vinifera), and Zinfandel, considered a Bordeaux style.

➤ **Burgundy.** Wines fuller in body or richer in perfume than Claret-styled wines are generally bottled in the narrow-shoulder, rounder Burgundy bottle. California Chardonnay and Pinot Noir—Burgundy varietals—are sold in the Burgundy bottle. Fuller-bodied Spanish wines and the sturdier Italian wines (such as Barolo and Barbaresco) find their way into variants of this shape.

➤ **Hock.** The German Hock bottle is tall, slender, and brown in color. Its variant is the green Mosel. The traditional rule in Germany is Rhine wine in brown bottles, Mosel in green. This rule is no longer 100 percent true, but it still serves as a good guide. Most wines from Alsace are bottled in a shape similar to the Hock. So are many California Rieslings, Gewürztraminers, and Sylvaner varietals. The Hock shape is used throughout the world, but be warned: It is not always an indicator of the kind or quality of wine within.

➤ **Bubbly bottles.** The Champagne bottle is a variant of the Burgundy bottle—sort of a bigger and sturdier cousin. It usually has an indentation or *punt* at the bottom, and thick walls to withstand the pressure of the carbonation. If you're the proud owner of a brand-new pleasure vessel or vehicle you'd like to christen with a magnum of bubbly, champagne companies make special christening bottles for the purpose. You would need an awful lot of muscle to smash the solid, reinforced glass of a real Champagne bottle. As mentioned at the beginning of the chapter, the most expensive Champagnes are usually bottled in signature shapes. The flaring Champagne cork—the legacy of Madame Cliquot, along with the sparkling wine bearing her name—is a laminated seven-piece closure constructed to guarantee a tight seal with plenty of strength once it is in the bottle neck.

The reason for the deep green or brown color of most wine bottles is more than aesthetic: The color protects the wine from sunlight. (You wear sunglasses—why shouldn't your wine?) Brown glass is believed to offer even more protection than green, and it is often used for low-alcohol, sweet-finished white wines. All in all, though, technology is supplanting tradition. With advances in winemaking and better methods of stabilizing wines for bottle aging, clear glass is becoming more popular. Even traditional winemakers are giving in to the adage, "What you see is what you get."

The varied shapes of wine bottles.

Claret or Red Bordeaux   Burgundy   Magnum   Hock   Champagne

Magnums and More

In addition to different shapes, wine bottles come in varying sizes. The standard size is 750 ml, which is approximately four-fifths of a quart. The most common other sizes are 375 ml, which is called a half-bottle, and a magnum (1.50 liters), which contains two standard bottles. A double magnum (3 liters) contains four standard bottles. A wine bottle containing six standard bottles is called a Jeroboam, and a bottle containing eight standard bottles is called an Impériale.

In Champagne, bottle usage is somewhat different. A magnum is still a magnum, but a bottle containing four standard bottles is called a Jeroboam. A Rehoboam contains six standard bottles; a Methuselah contains eight standard bottles; a Salmanazar contains 12 standard bottles; a Balthazar contains 16 standard bottles; and a Nebuchadnezzar contains 20 standard bottles, perfect for large weddings or other momentous occasions.

The Vintage Makes It Right

The date on the bottle is the wine's vintage. It tells you the year the grapes were harvested and nothing more. The fact that there is a date on a bottle is not an indication of quality by itself; however, most wines with a vintage are quality wines. Some everyday wines for which the vintage is of no importance will carry a vintage date to make them appear better than they are. To determine whether the vintage is a good, great, or poor one for the region in question, you need to consult a vintage chart such as the one on the tearout card in the front of this book or wine magazines or newsletters, which provide the scoop on the latest vintages.

Earlier chapters already discussed the requisite for a great vintage: Certain weather conditions were met the entire year. Mother Nature smiled on the tender succulents, allowing them to bathe, nap, and gradually reawaken refreshed and energetic, with just the right balance of acid, sugar, and flavors.

Important Things to Know

HEY!

Avoid poor vintages; the wines will be feeble, insipid, and vapid—not exactly what you want to start your wine collection. However, some exceptions exist. Every poor vintage has some properties that still manage to make a good wine. You can find out which wines are good by reading reviews in wine magazines, newsletters, or surfing the online services or the Net. Wine drinkers tend to malign average vintages, but doing so is really unfair. True, average vintages lack the complexity and finesse of a great vintage, but they're quite capable of providing a savvy consumer with some perfectly delightful wine-drinking, and usually at reasonable prices.

Then there are the great vintages. Every flavor nuance is ready and waiting to incite your nose and taste buds into a peak sensory mode. The balance is perfect, the breed has been bred, and the wine has a body and concentration that other wines only dream of. The catch: How do you know what vintages have been so favored? As I said earlier, simply consult a vintage chart like the one on the tearout card at the front of this book. Investing in a fine wine should not be a matter of trial and error. Sometimes it's just a good idea to let someone else do the work.

Back Label Secrets

The back label is the one that *doesn't* have the picturesque scene of the vineyard or the name like *Château d'Yquem* with its royal crown that immediately stands out. The back label frequently contains information that is useful or at least interesting. If one exists, the back label is where bottlers who are so inclined tell you things like what foods are a good match for the wine or what temperature brings out its peak flavor. The label may offer an engaging story about the wine or the winery. Or it may tell you nothing more than the pH balance, if that. Front labels are regulated; back labels are a little more whimsical.

Bottling Terms

You've been studying up on your A.O.C., QmP, D.O.C.G., and V.D.Q.S., and starting to think that a wine label resembles a legal document or a Web site. Terms like these appear on the label, most by legal designation, to let you know what is in the bottle you're contemplating taking home with you.

All labels on wines sold in the U.S. must be approved by the Bureau of Alcohol, Tobacco, and Firearms (BATF), a division of the Treasury Department. In addition to collecting alcohol taxes, BATF is charged with ensuring that the information on a wine bottle is truthful, accurate, and not misleading. All wines must conform both to the mandatory label requirement of the U.S. and to the regulations of the country of origin. Each state may impose its own individual regulations, but these must also conform to federal standards.

The philosophy in our country seems to be *keep it simple*. This practice has its good and bad points. On the negative side is the fact that the domestic wine label is by far the least useful guide for determining the contents of the bottle (although many producers choose to provide precise technical information). On the plus side is the fact that the more concise the terms on the label, the less likely they are to be misleading. All of the EU (European Union) countries have strict standards for labeling, which make labels relatively easy to decipher. You just need to know what to look for.

Origin Descriptors

An origin descriptor refers to the words on the label that indicate where the wine comes from. The descriptor starts with the designation *Product of France* or *Product of Spain*, and so on, which is legally required of all imported wines. Then the descriptor goes on down through region, state, vineyard, château—whatever level of description is required for the particular type or quality of the wine. Some renowned French wines, such as Château d'Yquem, list only the vineyard and the name of its producer. After all, the winemakers contend, what more than the name and a vintage date is needed? On the other hand, reading the origin descriptors on a superior German wine can be like singing *The Twelve Days of Christmas*—it goes on and on.

Quality Descriptors

By EU regulations, the wine with the vineyard name on the label is inherently a better quality than the wine that lists only a vast region. A.O.C, D.O.C., D.O.C.G., and QmP are all quality indicators at the most basic (you learn about these terms later in this chapter). Then in France, there are the *crus*: *Cru Classé* (classified growth), *Premier Cru*, *Grand Cru*. This descriptor is an indicator of both origin and quality. In Italy there is *Classico*, referring to a special inner wine zone, and *Riserva*, which indicates extra aging. Spain has *Reserva* and *Gran Reserva*; in Portugal these words translate to *Reserva* and *Garrafeira* (although requirements differ). In Germany there is *prädikat*, which means the wine has something special (sweetness) and signifies quality and style. Domestic wines carry quality descriptors like *Late Harvest* or *Botrytis*, and sparkling wines are required to state whether they are produced by the *Méthode Champenoise* (*fermented in this bottle*) or the *transfer method* (*fermented in the bottle*). (Only true Champagne is permitted to use the french term *Méthode Champenoise* on the label.) Other than these quality descriptors, you're on your own. Some domestic wines carry the label *Classic*, but it's virtually meaningless—they rarely *are* classic.

Style Descriptors

Style descriptors legally are required only on German wines and Champagne. These descriptors indicate the wine's sweetness or dryness (percentage of residual sugar). Some non-German wine labels do include style descriptors, but it is up to the individual producer. The absence of a style descriptor is just one more reason to know your wines.

General Terms

The most basic general terms are white, red, and rosé in the language of the wine's native land. A few variations exist; for example, Italian wines may be labeled *Nero*, which means very dark red. But usually, you need to judge color gradations for yourself. General terms include virtually anything that does not fall into the other categories, from *Table Wine* (required on imports; optional on domestic wines) to *Serve at room temperature* or *Serve chilled* (entirely optional). The vintage also can fall into the category of general information, although if you know your vintages, it is a quality descriptor as well.

Mandatory Information

Along with the country of origin, the alcoholic content and content by volume are absolutely imperative on all labels. Volume of imported wines is listed in standard metric measure and conforms to approved size. The name and address of the importer, producer, and/or *négociant* (described in a later section) are required on all labels. For California wines, the name and address of the bottler and the Bonded Winery (BW) license number are required. Only on American wines are varietal names mandatory.

Important Things to Know

HEY!

Classification on EU wines according to EU, national, and local regulations is always designated. This is the quality indicator domestic wines do not have. American labels provide the consumer with a lot of data concerning who the grapes belonged to and who selected, bottled, produced, and cellared the contents, but if you're looking for information to help you choose the right wine, you may feel like you're reading a weather report for every city but your own.

The French Wine Label

The French wine label provides a lot of information that gives you clues as to the ultimate quality of the wine. The label provides exacting information as to certain minimum quality standards through its system of Appellation Controlée regulations, which are linked to carefully defined geography. By law, the smaller the piece of property named, the more stringent the regulations are for methods of cultivation and production. Other than names of properties and estates, the names of the négociant (if any) and importer must appear on the label, so knowing the reputations of these companies is useful. Frequently, the name of the négociant or shipper is a clue to the quality of a wine from an unknown property.

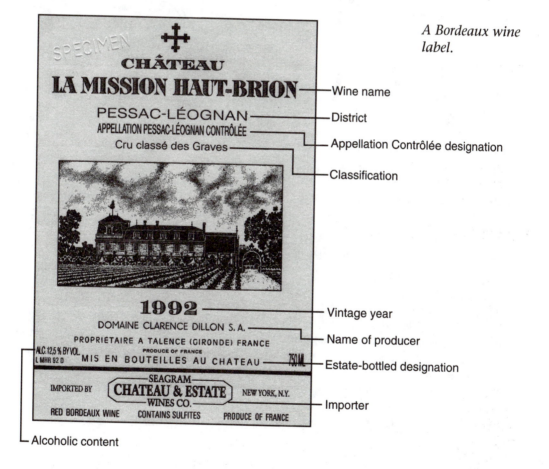

A Bordeaux wine label.

A Burgundy wine label.

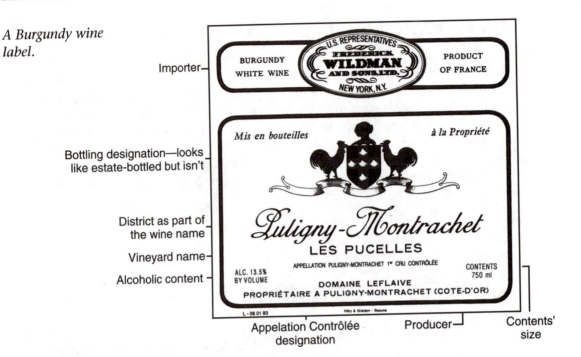

Importer—

BURGUNDY
WHITE WINE

U.S. REPRESENTATIVES
FREDERICK
WILDMAN
AND SONS, LTD.
NEW YORK, N.Y.

PRODUCT
OF FRANCE

Bottling designation—looks like estate-bottled but isn't

Mis en bouteilles   *à la Propriété*

District as part of the wine name—

Vineyard name—

Alcoholic content—

Puligny-Montrachet
LES PUCELLES
APPELLATION PULIGNY-MONTRACHET 1er CRU CONTRÔLÉE

ALC. 13.5%
BY VOLUME

CONTENTS
750 ml

DOMAINE LEFLAIVE
PROPRIÉTAIRE A PULIGNY-MONTRACHET (COTE-D'OR)

L - 06 01 93   Héry & Granjon · Beaune

Appelation Contrôlée designation   Producer—   Contents' size

French Origin Descriptors

The term *A.O.C.* or *A.C.* on a label is an abbreviation of *Appellation d'Origin Controlée.* *V.D.Q.S.* stands for *Vins Délimités de qualite Supérieure*, the second rank below A.C. of delimited wine areas. *Vin de pays* is the third rank below A.C. *Cave* is the French word for cellar. *Château-bottled, Mis au Château, Mis en bouteilles au Château, Mis au (or du) Domaine,* and *Mis en bouteilles au (or du) Domaine* all mean estate-bottled and have legal significance. *Mis dans nos caves, Mis par le propriétaire,* and *Mis en bouteille a la propriete* sound like estate-bottled wine but are not and are usually put on a label to deceive the consumer into believing that the wine is estate-bottled when it is not. These terms are not legally regulated. *Négociant* is a businessperson who purchases wine from growers and bottles it under their own brand or for resale under the individual Château name. *Eleveur* is a négociant who buys young wine from the grower and matures it in his own cellars. *Propriétaire-Récolant* means owner and manager of a property.

French Quality Descriptors

Appellation Controlée is both an origin descriptor and a quality descriptor, as French geographical designations are linked to quality regulations. *Cru Bourgeois* in Bordeaux refers to the many good vineyards just below the classified growths in quality. *Cru Classé* is a classified growth of Bordeaux, the most famous of which is the 1855 classification of the wines of the Médoc. It is preceeded by the level of the cru such as Premier Cru Classé.

Cru Exceptionnel is a Bordeaux classification between cru Bourgeois and Cru Classé. *Grand Cru* means great growth—in Burgundy the highest level of classified vineyards, in Bordeaux the highest of the five levels of classified growths.

Grand Vin means great wine. As it has no legal definition, this term is used with impunity for any wine, good or otherwise. *Premier Cru* means first growth—in Burgundy the second level of classified growth, in Bordeaux any of the five levels of classified growths. *Méthode Champenoise (fermented in this bottle)* is the legally defined term for the champagne method of sparkling wine production. *Supérieure* indicates that the wine is at least one degree of alcohol above the minimum allowed for a particular A.C. The term does not mean that the wine is *better* or *superior*. *V.D.Q.S.* and *Vin de pays* relate to the quality of a non A.C. wine.

French Style Descriptors

Vin Blanc means white wine, *Vin Rouge* means red wine, and *Vin Rosé* means rosé wine. *Sur lie* refers to wines bottled off the lees without racking or filtering. *Pétillant* means slightly sparkling or crackling. *Mousseux* refers to sparkling wine other than Champagne. *Blanc de Blancs* refers to a white wine made entirely from white grapes; you usually see the term on Champagne bottles. With Champagne and Mousseux, *Brut* means almost dry; *Extra* Dry means slightly sweeter than Brut; Brut *Sauvage* or *Sauvage* means completely dry; *Demi Sec* means semi-sweet; and *Doux* means quite sweet.

French General Terms

Année means year. *Recolte* means crop or harvest, and *Vendange* means grape harvest, used synonymously with année. *Chai* is an above-ground building where wine is stored in cask. *Chambré* is the French word for bringing a red wine from cellar temperature to room temperature (as in *Servir Chambre*). *Servir Frais* means to serve chilled. *Château* in Bordeaux refers to a single estate—elsewhere it may be part of a brand name. *Domaine* means wine estate. *Clos* means walled vineyard. *Côte* refers to a slope with vineyards as opposed to graves or flatter land. *Cru* means growth and refers to a legally defined vineyard. *Cuvée* is a vat or batch of wine.

The German Wine Label

The German wine label is exceedingly precise as to quality specifications; the descriptions are linked closely to growing regions, large and tiny; to a designation of quality; and also to the degree of ripeness achieved by the grapes that went into the wine. The labels often appear more complicated than they are, but they are less intimidating once you learn the system. The region in which the wine is produced and the ripeness of the grapes are the two main concerns, and both items play important roles on the label.

*The German
Grosslage wine label.*

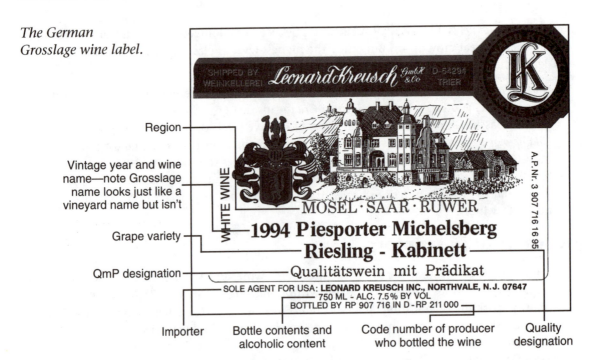

Region

Vintage year and wine
name—note Grosslage
name looks just like a
vineyard name but isn't

Grape variety

QmP designation

Importer

Bottle contents and
alcoholic content

Code number of producer
who bottled the wine

Quality
designation

*The German
Einzellage wine label.*

Vintage year and
wine name—this is
an authentic
vineyard name

German Origin Descriptors

Gebiet is a term indicating one of the 13 major German wine regions. A *Bereich* is a large subregion of a Gebiet. A *Grosslage* is a subdivision of a Bereich consisting of numerous adjoining vineyards that may span the boundaries of many villages. Grosslage wines are designated with a name that sounds like an individual vineyard wine; therefore, you need to memorize Grosslage names to avoid buying a village wine when you want higher-quality wine (see Appendix A). An *Einzellage* is an individual vineyard site of a minimum size of approximately 12 acres. Vineyards smaller than 12 acres are given the name of a nearby Einzellage and are of similar quality and style.

Abfüller means bottler, and *Abfüllung* means from the producer's own estate. *Aus Eigenem Lesegut* and *Erzeuger Abfüllung* mean estate-bottled. *Eigene Abfüllung* means bottled by the producer. *Keller* is a cellar and *Weinkellerei* is a wine cellar. *Weingut* means wine estate. *Weinhandler* refers to a wine shipper or merchant. *Winzergenossenschaft* and *Winzerverein* mean winegrower's cooperative. A.P. (*Amtliche Prufungsunummer*) is the official testing number found on all better German wines; it indicates the place of origin, the producer's individual number, the individual lot number, and the year (not necessarily the vintage) that the lot was submitted for testing.

German Quality Descriptors

Tafelwein is table wine, the lowest level of quality. Tafelwein may not bear a vineyard site name. *QbA* (*Qualitätswein bestimmter Anbaugebiete*) refers to a wine from a specific origin and is the middle level of German wine quality. *QmP* (*Qualitätswein mit Prädikat*) refers to wine with special attributes, the top level of wine quality consisting of six degrees of ripeness. No chaptalization is permitted for these wines.

German Style Descriptors

Kabinet is the basic grade for QmP wine that must be made from grapes with sufficient natural sugar to produce a wine with a minimum of 9 ½ percent alcohol. *Spätlese* means late picked and refers to a wine made from fully ripened grapes. *Auslese* is a term describing very ripe late-picked grapes that render a fairly sweet and luscious dessert wine. *Beerenauslese* is a very sweet wine made from even later-picked, overripe grapes, some of which have been shriveled by Botrytis (noble rot). *Tröckenbeerenauslese* is wine made entirely from grapes shriveled by Botrytis. During the harvest, the pickers keep these grapes separate from the others. *Eiswein* is a sweet, concentrated wine made from frozen grapes that may not be affected with Botrytis. *Tröcken* refers to a complete dry wine. *Halbtröcken* is a half-dry or off-dry wine. *Perlwein* is a slightly sparkling wine, and *seck* means sparkling wine.

German General Terms

Moselblumchen is the generic wine from the Mosel that is in the Tafelwein class. *Liebfraumilch* is the generic wine from the Rhein region that is in the QbA class. *Fass* and *fuder* mean cask. *Rotwein* means red wine, and *weisswein* means white wine. *Schloss* means castle. *Staatswein* refers to wine from government-owned vineyards.

The Italian Wine Label

Italian wine labels provide a fair amount of meaningful information regarding what is in the bottle. Nomenclature for certain wines is regulated under laws enacted in 1967, modeled after the French concept but without the refinement of official classifications. The Italian wine-regulating system, the *Denominazione di Origine Controllata (D.O.C.)* is government approved and defines growing regions. For several types of wine, the D.O.C. guarantees certain minimum standards of production. Good-quality Italian wines indicate the place, either as the name of the wine itself (Chianti, for example) or linked to a grape variety, such as Barbera D'Asti or through a D.O.C. designation. Not all places have earned D.O.C. status, but most better Italian wines sold within the United States are D.O.C. wines. If a grape name is not referenced by a place, (such as Nebbiolo d'Alba), chances are that the wine lacks distinction. *Denominazione di Origine Controllata e Garantita (D.O.C.G.)* is the highest grade of Italian wine and is granted only to regions making the highest quality wine.

The Italian wine label.

Wine name

Wine district

D.O.C.G. quality designation

Riserva Quality designation with vintage date

Estate-bottled designation

Producer

NOZZOLE

CHIANTI CLASSICO

DENOMINAZIONE DI ORIGINE CONTROLLATA E GARANTITA

RISERVA 1993

ESTATE BOTTLED BY
TENIMENTI AGRICOLI VALDIGREVE S.A.S.
GREVE - ITALIA

RED WINE
PRODUCT OF ITALY

750 ML
13% ALC. BY VOL.

Alcoholic content   Bottle contents

Italian Origin Descriptors

Classico refers to a wine made in a legally defined inner section of a wine district and ostensibly denotes a higher quality. *D.O.C.* refers to a wine from a delimited wine district and produced in accordance with D.O.C. wine laws. *D.O.C.G.* is wine made from a delimited district that has earned this higher-quality designation. *Cantina* means winery or cellars. *Cantina Sociale* is a winegrowers cooperative. *Casa Vinicola* means wine company. *Consorzio* is a local winegrowers association with legal recognition. *Infiascato alla fattoria, Imbottigliato nel'origine, Imbottigliato del produttore,* and *Messo in bottiglia nel'origine* mean estate-bottled. *Imbottigliato nello stabilimento della ditta* means bottled on the premises of the company and is not estate-bottled. *Tenuta* refers to a farm or agricultural holding.

Italian Quality Descriptors

D.O.C. and *D.O.C.G,* explained earlier, are quality descriptors. *Riserva* means aged in wood for a time specified by law. *Riserva Speciale* means aged one year longer than Riserva. *Stravecchio* means very old and is rarely seen.

Italian Style Descriptors

Secco means dry. *Amaro* means very dry (bitter). *Abboccato* and *amabile* mean off-dry or semi-sweet with *amabile* being sweeter than *abboccato*. *Dolce* means sweet. *Cotto* refers to a concentrated wine. *Passito* refers to wine made from semi-dried grapes. *Spumante* is sparkling wine and *Frizzante* is semi-sparkling wine. *Vin santo* is wine made from grapes dried indoors.

Italian General Terms

Vino da Tavola means table wine. *Bianco* means white wine; *rosso* means red wine; and *rosato* means rosé wine. *Nero* is very dark red. *Fiasco* is a flask.

The United States Wine Label

In terms of legally defined nomenclature, very little on an American wine label is useful in differentiating a high-quality wine from an ordinary wine. Terms such as Reserve, Special Reserve, Vintner's Reserve, and so on, have no legal regulation and may be used with impunity on mediocre or low-quality wines. American wine districts are limited solely to defining geography and do not have any concomitant regulations as to grape variety that may be grown, yield, or production methods as do the French, Italian, and German counterparts. Thus the American label has very little information to guide you to a high-quality wine. To tell the difference between two wines from a particular wine district (Napa Valley, for example), you must have an intimate knowledge of the individual producers. Although some districts are reputed to be better than others, a well-made wine from a lesser district can be far superior to a wine made from large yields in a more respected district. With American wine, *caveat emptor* is the rule, and our government has no interest in establishing regulations that can give you clues as to which wine is better than another.

The American wine label.

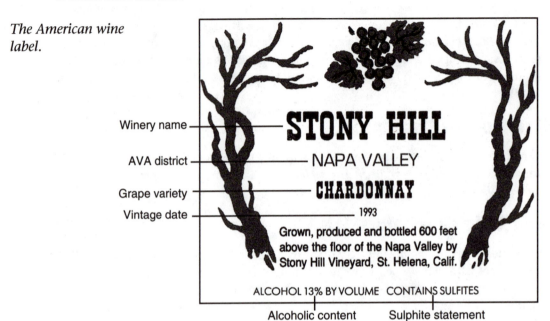

Winery name — STONY HILL
AVA district — NAPA VALLEY
Grape variety — CHARDONNAY
Vintage date — 1993
Grown, produced and bottled 600 feet above the floor of the Napa Valley by Stony Hill Vineyard, St. Helena, Calif.
ALCOHOL 13% BY VOLUME   CONTAINS SULFITES
Alcoholic content   Sulphite statement

American Origin Descriptors

American means that the wine can be a blend of wines from different states. *State* means that 75 percent of the wine must be from the named state; however, California regulations require that California wine be 100 percent Californian. *County* means that 75 percent of the wine must be from the named county. *Valley, District,* and *Region* must be a BATF-approved viticultural area (*AVA*) to be used on the label, and at least 75 percent of the wine must come from the named area. The general rule of thumb is that the smaller the geographical area specified, the better the reputed quality; however, as stated earlier, this descriptor provides no guarantee of quality. *B.W. No. 0000* is the bonded winery's license number. *Grown by* means that the grapes were grown by the named winery. *Selected by* means that the wine was purchased by the named winery. *Made and Bottled by* means that the named winery fermented at least 10 percent of the wine and bottled all the wine. *Cellared and Bottled by* means that the named party blended and/or aged or otherwise treated and bottled all the wine. *Produced and Bottled by, Proprietor or Vintner*

Grown, and *Bottled by* mean that the named party fermented at least 75 percent of the wine and bottled all the wine. *Estate Bottled* means that the named party fermented all the wine from grapes 100 percent from the named AVA; that the grapes came entirely from the party's own vineyards or vineyards in which the party controls the viticultural practices; and that the wine was bottled on the same premises where it was made.

American Quality Descriptors

Reserve, Vintner's Reserve, and *Special Reserve* are label puffery that have no legal definition. In some cases, this term designates the best of the producer's wine, and in other cases, the wine is no different or is actually lesser in quality than the producer's regular line of wine. *Rare* and *Classic,* usually seen on the most inexpensive wine, has no legal definition—the wine so labeled is rarely "rare" or "classic." *Nouveau* refers to wines that are quickly fermented by carbonic maceration and bottled immediately after fermentation. *Late Harvest* refers to wine made from overripe grapes that may or may not be affected with Botrytis. *Brix* is a measure of potential alcohol based on the sugar content of the grape when it was harvested. *Residual sugar* refers to the amount of remaining natural sugar in the wine after fermentation is completed—more than one percent tastes sweet. *Off-dry* refers to wine that has a little residual sugar but not enough to be sweet. *Botrytis* means the grapes were affected with Botrytis. *Fermented in the bottle* refers to sparkling wine made by the transfer method. *Fermented in this bottle* refers to sparkling wine made by Méthode Champenoise.

American General Terms

Table wine refers to wine that is less than 14.5 percent alcohol and made without additional alcohol. *Dessert wine* is above 14.5 percent alcohol and is usually sweet wine fortified with additional alcohol. *White* is white wine; *red* is red wine; and *rosé* or *blush* wine is rosé wine.

The Least You Need to Know

➤ Wine bottle shapes are a clue as to what is in the bottle.

➤ A magnum contains two standard wine bottles. Standard bottles hold 750 ml.

➤ Wine labels must contain certain information as a matter of law such as the country of origin and the alcoholic content.

➤ Back labels frequently provide some very useful and interesting information such as the history of the winery or wine region or a description of the taste of the wine.

Chapter 21

Surfing the Wine Market

> **In This Chapter**
>
> ➤ The value of a good wine merchant
>
> ➤ Money-saving techniques for buying wine
>
> ➤ Wine auctions
>
> ➤ Secrets of the wine trade

Finding a Good Wine Merchant

A good wine merchant is one who really understands wines and can advise you on wine selections that meet your budget and complement your palate. Be careful when selecting a merchant, however. Unlike stockbrokers, who know their business depends on matching the right customer with the right commodity, some wine merchants are more concerned with eye-catching window displays and ringing up quick sales at the cash register. A merchant may be quick to provide advice and sound authoritative on the surface, but in reality, the merchant may know little or nothing about the wines he or she stocks. More than 30,000 different wines are sold in the United States—even the pros can't be familiar with all of them. Visiting a wine store can be like visiting a foreign country. I had that experience more than once in wine stores that feature private brands and obscure producers. Just think of wine-buying as a challenge. If you're buying software or athletic shoes or audio components, what do you do to make sure the salespeople know their stuff? You ask questions. Most of us shop around for car dealers, lawyers, and hairstylists. Don't feel intimidated about shopping around for a wine merchant. You don't need to set your sights on the ideal, but a few strategic questions should guarantee that you find a merchant who is knowledgeable, reputable, and user-friendly.

Consider asking these few sample test questions:

➤ What is the difference between a Bordeaux and a Burgundy?

➤ Why is a bottle of French Burgundy more expensive than a comparable bottle of French Bordeaux?

➤ Ask about a few wine and food combinations.

➤ Specify your wine needs (such as a bottle of dry white wine for under $10, or a domestic sparkling wine for under $16 to go with roast chicken) and see what the merchant suggests.

By using this tactic, you are not only testing the merchant but testing your wings as a savvy wine consumer. And if all goes well, this could be the start of a beautiful friendship.

If the Price Is Right

Price is another reason for shopping around—and for knowing your wines. Prices are set by the retailer, not the producer or importer. Generally, you won't see a massive difference from one shop to another except in some shops that are known for rock-bottom prices. But a couple dollars here and there can add up—especially if you're just beginning to build a wine cellar.

Important Things to Know

HEY!

If you know in advance what you want, check out one of the large "supermarket" wine and liquor emporiums. The owners or sales help in these giants are not always knowledgeable about their wares, but the prices can be the best around. With a bit of homework, you can find substantial rewards.

On the other hand, if you do need advice to help with your selection, it is worth paying slightly more for the right bottle of wine than paying less for the wrong one. In choosing wines, as in most other items, a fine balance exists between consumer loyalty and shopping around. It's virtually impossible for one retailer to satisfy all of your wine needs.

Service, Service, Service

When you shop for wines, you don't want to feel like you're in a twilight zone of wine bottles, wondering if you're invisible to all but yourself. You want somebody to make you feel like you've come to the right place. Willingness to assist is important. A cordial attitude from the wine shop's personnel is any consumer's right.

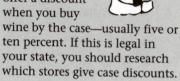

Wine Widsom
It is customary for wine shops to offer a discount when you buy wine by the case—usually five or ten percent. If this is legal in your state, you should research which stores give case discounts.

Beware of the helpful merchant who goes too far, however. You don't want to feel pressured. And you need to know that the person who is helping you choose the right Bordeaux for the boss's party or the California white for the barbecue is someone you can *trust*. Never mind a willingness to give advice; can you rely on it? Do the suggestions parallel your desires and requirements? Are you hearing about new arrivals and good bargains?

Some of your decision should be savvy, and some of it pure gut instinct. You may feel an immediate rapport with a merchant who seems informed, friendly, and willing to show you around. Just be sure you're sold on more than charm. Never be afraid to apply your own knowledge. Building your confidence is as important as building your wine cellar, and it keeps you from depleting your bank book as well.

Naming Your Price

I strongly recommend framing your questions within a particular price range to indicate you are a value hunter, not a candidate for a quick, high-profit sale. If the merchant meets you with a haughty look or an immediate attempt to steer you to a higher price range, you'll know this merchant's attitude toward building a clientele.

Explaining What You Need

Asking the right questions is not only the way to test the merchant's expertise and customer-friendly attitude, it's the only way to get what you need. Some people who have no problem asking for help to find the perfect wardrobe for a certain occasion wilt at the thought of having to explain their wine preferences. It's all part of the wine mystique. You may think, "What if they think my taste is gauche? Or worse yet, cheap? What if I use the wrong language? Or what if they think I'm just plain ignorant?" Forget that voice. Listen to the voice that says, "I know what I want and I'm going to find it."

You are relying on the expertise of someone who is there to help you—and to gain a good customer. One way to assure yourself that you'll be explaining your needs correctly—and directly—is to make a checklist of all the points you need to cover to get the right wine:

➤ Is the occasion informal, formal, or momentous?

➤ What foods are being served?

➤ What are my personal preferences and my guests' preferences?

➤ Will more than one wine be served?

➤ Do I expect to have leftover bottles?

➤ What is my budget for the occasion?

Don't be afraid to use words like fruity, oaky, truffles, vanilla, or any of the things you've learned. A knowledgeable merchant won't be judging your taste. And if the merchant does not understand these terms, you are definitely not in the right place.

Always keep an open mind. If the merchant suggests something different than the type of wine you were thinking of, don't dismiss the suggestion as poor listening. That wine may work. On the other hand, if the advice seems to be way off-track, you may need to be more specific. If the suggested wine seems a bit pricey, the merchant's intent may not be to make more money, but to tactfully imply that a better wine may be more appropriate for your occasion. Buying wine should be an interactive experience. Establish a dialogue with the retailer. Explain your needs, listen to answers, and don't be afraid to question advice. A good wine merchant will be as happy as you are to see you go home with the right wine.

The Importance of Selection

The type, range, and assortment of wines is a key consideration in choosing your retailer. Some people stay away from the big emporiums when they're in the market for something special. If you're after a vintage Madeira or the right Tröckenbeerenauslese to complement your Bavarian pastries, you may not find it in some establishments. But a good wine store should have a selection of wines to meet the needs of discerning customers. Most large wine stores stock an array of fine wines—at lower prices than you may find in a smaller shop. Many stores stock expensive and rare wines that are not on display, so make sure to inquire. Recently, I found an $85 Château Haut-Brion Blanc for $25 less at a discounter who kept the wine in his basement and did not bother to display it.

Shops with a limited selection often neglect many important wines. These shops may have a large selection of several popular wines such as Chardonnay, Beaujolais, and Pouilly-Fuissé, along with quick-selling California jug wines. You also may find a few expensive Champagnes and big names (usually off-vintages) from Bordeaux; but beware. This merchant probably hasn't taken the time or effort to learn much about wine. Another example is the merchant who stocks mainly well-advertised brands. Then there are the stores that feature unknown brands from producers or importers who specialize in bargain versions of well-known wine types. These wines may offer good drinking and value, but they are typically not up to snuff.

Important Things to Know

HEY!

A good selection of wines is one that encompasses a variety of tastes, styles, occasions, and budgets. The shop should be not only be well-stocked but well-organized. This is an excellent guideline to use when choosing your wine shop. A well-run shop groups wines by country and wine type, and frequently by price. Rack or aisle markers or signs enable you to easily locate the section you want.

A useful innovation favored by some shops is to arrange wines by similar characteristics: Red Bordeaux with California Cabernet Sauvignon; German Rieslings with California Johannisberg Rieslings; Chardonnays and White Burgundies, and so on. This method makes comparison-shopping easier. It also encourages comparative tastings by type, nationality, and by smaller regions and sub-regions.

Wine Storage at the Store

Wine bottles may look good shelved upright in rows like liquor bottles, but stocking better wine this way is deplorable if the inventory doesn't turn over rapidly. Shops should store wines just as you store them at home. The bottles should be protected from direct sunlight, and bottles with corks (anything over jug quality) should be lying on their sides.

Window dressing is a key part of selling, but no wines belong in sun-drenched windows. The better shops display empty or sample bottles. No good merchant ever sells a bottle from a window display. A store should display wines inside, however. Most of us like to touch and handle bottles while shopping—how else do you read the back label? The better shops keep a bottle of each available wine in a large rack or stacked in such a way that you can reach for it without risking an avalanche. The rest of the stock should be kept in perfect, temperature-controlled storage space.

Temperature control for wine is always important. In the main area, you usually find the temperature is constant and cool. If the entire stock is not within

Grape Alert
Wine shops, like supermarkets and bookstores, try to appeal to the impulse buyer. Shops typically display wine near the checkout or cash register area, frequently in a large basket or halved wine barrel. These wines may be bargains or may not, even when reduced in price. Outdated inventory or close-outs from wholesalers that have little merit frequently inhabit this section.

sight, I often check to see where the cases are stored. Sometimes, the back rooms of a shop or central warehouse area are far from ideal in climate and general storage conditions. In short, you want to know where the wine has been. Storage is especially important if you are buying wines by the case or purchasing old and rare wines.

Important Things to Know

Most wine shops offer a chilled wine section featuring whites, rosés, and Champagnes. This section is offered as a convenience to customers buying wines for immediate drinking. On the surface, these wines look tempting, but you don't know how long the wines have been chilled. If they have been in a chiller for weeks, chances are the wines have lost some of their freshness or liveliness. (At worst, the wines may be undrinkable, although this situation is rare.) Some shops have a chilling machine that can chill your wine in three or four minutes without harming it. If they do, great. If not, buying a bottle and chilling it yourself for about half an hour is far better than taking a chance with pre-chilled wine.

Considering Wine Ratings

Have you ever gone to a movie that received unanimous raves, four stars proudly preceding its title, only to be disappointed, dismayed, or just plain disgusted? Fortunately, rating wines is not as subjective as rating movies. Critics evaluate wines using standard criteria that was developed to assess acidity, tannins, sweetness, and so on. In recent times, a 100-point system has been adopted by most wine publications and wine critics. Beware—no one can accurately evaluate wine on such a system with any degree of accuracy (more on this subject in Chapter 22). When reading wine reviews, look for complete and comprehensive tasting notes to guide you to the wines you like. Trouble is that many wine critics do not fully describe a wine in their published tasting notes; however, their critique is better than nothing.

Because magazines survive on advertising, they may not be the best source for wine ratings. Newsletters and updated consumer guides are more impartial and generally more thorough. The important thing is to look beyond the numbers. A wine may have a superlative rating, but when you go through the adjectives you may realize the wine is not going to titillate your tannic taste buds or awaken your oaky aesthetic. A judicial assessment of words and numbers can help you combine your own knowledge and preferences with the critic's. Studying critiques also helps you to become a better rater yourself. For a list of wine publications, see Chapter 22.

Saving Money

Nowadays, very few wine shops sell wine at a full markup. Some sell at better prices than others. Here are some ways to save money when you buy wine.

Discount Stores

Wine Wisdom
Some supermarkets are stocking better wines, even classified growths of Bordeaux and Burgundy and expensive California wines, sometimes at bargain prices, sometimes not. Don't think that just because the wine is sold in a supermarket without a sales staff it will be cheaper than your favorite wine merchant. Comparison-shop before you make your supermarket your regular stop for wine.

A discount or mass merchandiser is a good source for bargains. If you're in the market for an everyday wine, don't be afraid to try unknown or private-label brands. And if you decide you like them, don't be afraid to say so! Never be intimidated by wine snobs. You may live in a locality where wines are sold in supermarkets, convenience stores, and in some places, drug stores; these places are usually good sources for everyday wines. The prices are reasonable, and you can match the wine with the food right at the source.

Private Labels

Some popular wine shops or those that are part of a chain or franchise often carry *private-label* wines that carry either the name of the establishment selling them or some registered trademark the retailer owns. Some private labels can represent good value. The merchant buys a certain percentage of wines in bulk and has them bottled under the store label. Without the prestigious name of the winery, the wines can be sold for much less. This concept is the vinous equivalent of designer fashions without the designer prices. Quality can vary from batch to batch, but chances are that the merchant who seeks to build a reputation on the store name or exclusive trademark will choose wisely. You may come home with a great bargain.

Second Labels

When a winery selects its wines to make its brand name wine, it frequently has lesser-quality but good wine left over. These wines may be from younger vines or vineyard sites that did not ripen to optimum maturity. Often these products are sold under another name, such as Les Forts de Latour (Château Latour's second label), or an unrelated name. These wines can provide excellent drinking. Some wineries also want to increase the amount of wine they sell, making optimum use of their marketing personnel, but they lack sufficient wine to meet the standards for their primary label. The winery may create a second label to market wines of a lesser quality. Because the winemaking expertise from

251

the making of the prime label goes into the making of second-label wines, they are frequently quite good at bargain prices.

Returning a Bottle of Wine

Returning a purchase in any retail field falls under the heading of customer service. You've paid for your wine, lovingly taken it home, cooked the perfect meal, used your best corkscrew technique, and voilà! The odor of rancid corn chips hits you. The smell usually is not that drastic, but you are entitled to a product without flaws. You would return a defective CD or a spoiled container of milk. You also should return wine that is not up to snuff.

A reputable wine merchant is in business to please consumers, not alienate them. If the wine seems flawed or the bottle damaged, you will generally have no problem returning it. If you are returning an unopened bottle (you've changed the menu or found out your guest hates Cabernet Sauvignon), use the same principle that guides the return of most retail items: Return it within a few days of purchase. After a week or two, the merchant is justified in not accepting the bottle. Aside from consumer ethics, how does the retailer know how *you* stored the bottle?

Buying Old Wines

Many wine enthusiasts feel the lure sooner or later. It's like the people who start with a few nostalgic knickknacks and suddenly find themselves drawn to the finest antique shops. If you are a fan of vintage Ports or Madeiras, you may one day survey your collection and think you should have a few. You may be looking to old and rare wines with the sole purpose of financial investment. Or you may be having a dinner that calls for a mature bottle from a great vintage. Those *Grand Crus* Bordeaux from an excellent vintage can provide for some very exciting wine experiences.

These wines are frequently quite expensive, but when you factor in the value of long-term storage, you may consider the price for some of these wines quite reasonable. When buying older wines, the storage and handling is of utmost importance. Inquire how the wine was stored and where it came from. Inquire about getting a refund if the bottle is not what it should be, because older bottles can have considerable bottle variation. Some wines from a case can be superb, and other bottles in the same case can be as dead as a doornail. Just remember that when you buy, buy with caution.

Can I Make Money Investing in Wine?

Only a miniscule percentage of wines are great investment wines. The wines that are really sure investments have certain qualities you should heed:

➤ They have excellent potential for longevity.

➤ The wine press and the wine industry have given these wines unanimous commendations.

➤ They are from good to superlative vintages.

➤ They have a track record for becoming more valuable with time.

➤ They have such a rarity factor that the demand escalates the price in greater proportion than other wines. Romanée Conti and Château Pétrus are prime examples of wines that command astronomical prices after a decade or so.

Important Things to Know

HEY!

Even careful attention to the guidelines in this section does not ensure that you are making a good investment. No matter how careful your selections, you always face a major risk. More potential investment wines depreciate than appreciate in value when you factor in the cost of storage. If you are seriously thinking of becoming an investor, do the same thing you would if you were investing in stocks or commodities: Seek the help of a qualified expert. Some large retail firms can offer advice on investment wines.

An Insider's View of Buying and Selling Wine at Auctions

The conditions for buying or selling wine at auction are determined individually by each state. Auctioning wine is totally legal in Illinois and California (of course) and has recently been permitted in New York. The lifting of restrictions in New York has made it a haven for wine-lovers, eager to bid on those beckoning bottles or to sell from their own collections. Many other states permit charity wine auctions, but some states prohibit wine auctions altogether. Check with your local wine merchant to find out the story in your locality.

Regardless of how modest or expansive your desires, you want assurance that you are dealing with a reputable auction house. In New York, call these places:

➤ Morrell & Company (212) 688-9370

➤ Sherry-Lehmann/Sotheby's Auction House (212) 606-7207

➤ Zachy's/Christie's Auction House (914) 723-0241

➤ Acker, Merrall & Condit (212) 787-1700

In the Midwest:

➤ Chicago Wine Company (847) 647-8789

➤ Davis & Company Wine Auctioneers (312) 587-9500

In California:

➤ Butterfield & Butterfield Auction House (415) 861-7500

If you want to sell your wine, bear in mind a few factors about most auction houses and retail stores:

➤ They are mainly concerned with valuable, prestigious, or rare wine.

➤ They want to know where the wine comes from. Be able to prove that the wine has had optimum storage.

➤ They charge a commission for their services, ranging from 10 percent to 25 percent of the sale price depending on the deal you make; 25 percent is customary. Some auction houses charge a buyer's premium of 10 percent or 15 percent.

➤ Some retailers pay you only after they sell your wine; others pay you when they receive the wine. Look for the best deal.

Buying wines at auction has one great advantage: You can find wines you won't find in most wine shops. In most instances, you can purchase old and rare wines only at auction or from a wine company specializing in buying wine collections for resale.

The main disadvantage of buying wine at auction is that you frequently don't know the provenance (storage history and ownership) of the wine. If the wine comes from a well-known collector or an establishment known for impeccable storage and care, the auction catalog says so, and such wines usually command a premium price.

Important Things to Know

HEY! An auction is *not* the place to buy younger wines or mature wines that are in the pipeline. With few exceptions, you can find these wines at better prices elsewhere, as auction fever frequently results in paying higher than market price. In addition to the bidding price itself—which is frequently more than reasonable—you need to pay a buyer's premium, a charge of 10 percent to 15 percent in excess of your bid.

Mail-Order Wine

Many large wine shops can sell wine by mail or telephone order. They ship to any state that subscribes to a reciprocity agreement with their state; some may ship the wine even if your state doesn't permit it, so check out your local regulations. The following list of wine shops are worth exploring:

➤ Ambrosia, Napa, CA (800) 435-2225

➤ Bel-Air Wine Merchant, West Los Angeles, CA (310) 474-9518

➤ Big Y Liquor Super Market, Northampton, MA (413) 584-7775

➤ Brookline Liquor Mart, Allston, MA (617) 734-7700

➤ Calvert Woodley, Washington, D.C. (202) 966-4400

➤ Central Liquors, Washington, D.C. (800) 835-7928

➤ Chicago Wine Co., Niles, IL (847) 647-8789

➤ Crossroads, New York, NY (212) 633-2863

➤ Duke Of Bourbon, Canoga Park, CA (800) 434-6394

➤ Garnet Wines & Liquors, New York, NY (800) 872-8466

➤ Geerlings and Wade, Sommers, CT (800) 782-9463

➤ Golden West International, San Francisco, CA (800) 722-7020

➤ Horseneck Wines and Liquors, Greenwich, CT (800) 667-6529

➤ John Hart Fine Wine, Chicago, IL (312) 944-5385

➤ Kermit Lynch Wine Merchant, Berkeley, CA (510) 524-1524

➤ MacArthur Liquors, Washington, D.C. (202) 388-1433

➤ Marin Wine Cellar, San Rafael, CA (415) 459-3823

➤ Morell & Company, New York, NY (212) 688-9370

➤ New York Wine Warehouse, New York, NY (212) 956-2250

➤ North Berkeley Wine, Berkeley, CA (800) 266-6585

➤ Northridge Hills Liquor & Wine, Northridge, CA (800) 678-9463

➤ Pop's Wines & Spirits, Island Park, NY (516) 431-0025

➤ Red Carpet Wine & Spirits, Glendale, CA (800) 339-0609

➤ Rosenthal Wine Merchant, New York, NY (212) 249-6650

➤ Royal Wine Merchants, New York, NY (212) 689-4855

➤ Sam's Wine Warehouse, Chicago, IL (800) 777-9137

➤ Schneider's of Capitol Hill, Washington, D.C. (800) 377-1461

➤ Sherry-Lehmann, New York, NY (212) 838-7500

➤ Silver Spirits, Saint James, NY (800) 998-4411

➤ Stafford's Wine Warehouse, Irvine, CA (800) 723-9463

➤ The Wine Connection, Westchester, NY (914) 764-9463

➤ The Wine Stop, Burlingame, CA (800) 283-9463

➤ Tinamou Wine Company, Sonoma, CA (800) 388-6390

➤ Wine Cask, Santa Barbara, CA (800) 436-9463

➤ William Sokolin & Co., Southampton, NY (800) 946-3947

➤ Wine Country, Signal Hill, CA (800) 505-5564

➤ Wine Exchange, Orange, CA (800) 769-4639

➤ Wine Spectrum, Santa Rosa, CA (800) 933-8466

Another recent innovation is the wine-of-the-month club, which ships a selection of two to six different wines each month. If you like the wine, you can usually buy more. These clubs are worth exploring:

➤ Ahlgren Vineyard Wine Club (408) 338-6071

➤ Ambrosia Wine Club (800) 435-2225

➤ California Wine Club (800) 777-4443

➤ California Winemaker's Guild (800) 858-9463

➤ Gold Medal Wine Club (800) 266-8888

➤ Oregon Pinot Noir Club (800) 847-4474

➤ Passport Wine Club (800) 867-9463

One operation that calls itself a "club" but is merely a mail-order operation is the Wine Enthusiast Wine Club. I do not recommend this organization because in my opinion, it offers lackluster wines from obscure or unknown producers at higher-than-market prices for well-known brands.

Wine Trade Secrets

A knowledge of the inner workings of the wine trade is not only useful in understanding how wines get to your store and how they are priced, but is in and of itself fascinating.

Importers

Although each state has its own regulations, the imported wine trade in the U.S. is basically a three-tier system. Wine importers and producers sell to a distributor/whole-saler, who sells it to a retail merchant or restaurant, who sells it to you. Of course the price of wine increases with each middleman.

Needless to say, the wine industry loves this type of system. It provides the industry players with limited competition and guaranteed profits and debt collection that are legally legislated. This system especially benefits retailers in states where minimum profits are maintained. Can you blame a merchant who is protected from supermarket competition for fighting to keep the status quo? Unfortunately, consumers pay millions of dollars a year for this legally sanctioned abuse of our rights.

There was a time following the repeal of Prohibition that liquor companies concentrated on high-profit liquor and left imported wines to smaller specialists (remember, there was no domestic wine industry as we know it today). During this period, names such as Frank Schoonmaker and Alexis Lichine became famous for their high-quality imported French or German wines. The renowned Lichine literally barnstormed the country, going from city to city persuading restaurants to serve French wines. He also convinced the French to package their wines to appeal to American consumers. Other wine promoters soon joined in courting American buyers.

During the mid-1960s and early 1970s, giant conglomerates began taking a serious interest in the wine business and bought several of the fabled wine companies renowned for excellent wines. The result was that liquor executives, unknowledgeable about wine or the wine trade, were unable to exercise control over their suppliers or choose new ones with any expertise. With several exceptions, the fabled wine importers became bastard-ized trade names submerged in an industry devoid of any wine savvy. Today, many wine importers offer a mixed bag of goods—some bad, some good, and some superb. Ironically, the names of some of the most prestigious importers of years gone by have become symbols of what to avoid rather than what to buy.

If you're starting to get a bit cynical about the wine trade, be assured that you still can count on a few importing firms to maintain the tradition of quality by selling only dependable merchandise. These firms are few in number, but they specialize in selecting fine wines and particular vintages on a personal level. Using these importers, you can buy any wine with the confidence that you are buying a superb bottle (some importers distribute domestic wines as well):

- ➤ Admiral Wines
- ➤ Banfi Vintners
- ➤ Dreyfus, Ashby & Co.
- ➤ Frederick Wildman & Co.
- ➤ Jorge Ordonez/Fine Estates from Spain
- ➤ Kobrand Corp.
- ➤ Louis/Dresner Selections
- ➤ Neil Empson Selections
- ➤ Peter Vezan Selections
- ➤ Robert Kacher Selections
- ➤ Select Vineyards
- ➤ Terry Theise Selections
- ➤ W. J. Deutsch & Sons
- ➤ William Grant & Sons
- ➤ Wines of France/Alain Junguenet Selections

- ➤ Austin Nichols
- ➤ Clicquot, Inc.
- ➤ European Cellars (Eric Solomon)
- ➤ Jeffrey Davies/Signature Selections
- ➤ Kermit Lynch Selections
- ➤ Kysela, Père et Fils
- ➤ Marc de Grazia
- ➤ Parliament Imports
- ➤ Robert Chadderdon Selections
- ➤ Seagrams Château & Estate Wine Co.
- ➤ Steve Metzler/Classical Wines from Spain
- ➤ Vineyard Brands
- ➤ Weygandt-Metzler Importing
- ➤ Winebow

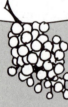

Grape Alert

Although Paterno Imports offers superb wines frequently at resonable prices, it sells its Santa Marguerita Pinot Grigio at outrageous prices—double what it's worth. You can buy a comparable wine from other importers at a much lower price.

Distributors

The distributor is the wholesaler who sells the wine to the retailers and restaurants. Sometimes distributors import wine for distribution limited to their market area.

Direct Import

Some wine merchants have discovered clever loopholes in the regulations that give them an edge over their competition, provide better value for customers, and still earn them generous profits. The most significant example of this tactic is *direct import*, which works this way: The merchant buys wines abroad (these wines are unavailable in the U.S.) and arranges for an importer/wholesaler to bring them into the country. Although many states rule that the wines must be "posted" at a legal resale price to everyone, these wines belong to the merchant, who is free to set the price. For doing the paperwork, the importer receives a stipend per case, sometimes as low as a dollar or two and sometimes as much as $20 depending on importing and warehousing costs.

The importer tells other retailers that these wines are out of stock—which they are, because the entire shipment went to only one merchant. The merchant can sell these wines for roughly 30 percent below the price of comparable wines from a national importer. Frequently these wines are even better—a merchant who goes to so much trouble generally has a good palate and an eye for a good deal.

Similar arrangements exist for domestic wines. This situation can complicate your comparison shopping, because a higher-priced wine can be notably lower in quality than a little-known bargain brand. If you play your cards right, however, you can emerge the winner. The two keys to bargain-finding success are an experienced palate and good book knowledge. If you have a novice palate, don't despair. Just do a little more homework.

Master of Wine

Master of Wine (MW) is a title bestowed by the Institute of Masters of Wine in London. To qualify, candidates must have considerable knowledge of wine and the wine trade. They need to be well-versed in the wines of the world and in each country's wine regulations and requirements. The MW is awarded only after passing a rigorous written and tasting examination. The title is prestigious and demands a certain level of competence; however, not all MWs are created equal.

Once the sole province of the United Kingdom, preparatory programs for the MW are currently offered in the U.S., Australia, and continental Europe. Only a small number of Americans have so far qualified for the title. Most of the 195 Masters of Wine are in the U.K.

For information on how to study for and take the test, write to Institute of Masters of Wine, Five Kings House, 1 Queen Street Place, London EC4R 1QS, England.

Boutique Wineries

California and other states have many small wineries, called *boutique wineries*, that specialize in finer quality wines. Many of these wineries were established in the late 1970s and 1980s. For years, many of California's finest wines rarely left the state. There was no conspiracy by Californians to keep the good stuff from going east. Instead, the lack of national attention reflected a prejudice against domestic wines by the rest of the country, coupled with a weak or nonexistent chain of distribution. But as the number of California wineries grew, the local market could not absorb all the wine produced, and the wineries were not equipped to market their wines nationally.

Marketing organizations quickly cropped up to fill the void. Today, many boutique wineries are promoted by these marketing firms or by national wine importers who have shrewdly recognized these small wineries as a good source of profit. Spotty distribution still remains a problem with many small California, Washington, Oregon, and New York state producers. Some wineries just do not produce enough wine to spread around. Others don't care to be involved with the regulations—which vary from state to state—imposed on the sale and movement of wine. Still others simply can't afford to pay the prohibitive fees imposed by states for registering a brand for sale within its borders. American wines remain one of the few domestically produced products to face severe restraints in interstate trade. A number of these wineries sell direct to the consumer in their tasting room or by mail or telephone order. Some producers offer their wines through mail-order organizations that feature wines in attractive and informative catalogs.

The Giants

In terms of winemaking itself, domestic production is dominated by a handful of large and powerful producers in California and New York state. Some of these vast producers are owned by importing firms or have their own national distribution network, usually through wholesalers.

You can find wines from these producers in virtually every wine store throughout the United States. (How's that for marketing strategy?) Gallo, which has recently successfully achieved a more upscale image than its jug wine reputation with its wines from Sonoma County, commands the largest share of the market. Next in size is Almaden and Paul Masson. Along with a few other biggies, this group occupies the lion's share of space in American wine stores. Most of these wines are ordinary jug or simple-premium quality; however, Gallo has produced some superb mid- and super-premium wines in its Sonoma County line.

The Least You Need to Know

> ➤ Shopping around for a good wine merchant is an important step in your involvement with wine.

> ➤ You can return a bad bottle if you don't wait too long.

> ➤ Private labels and direct imports can provide some bargains.

> ➤ You can buy wine by mail or telephone if permitted in your state.

HMMMN...

Chapter 22

The Best Sources of Information

In This Chapter

➤ Scoring systems

➤ Wine magazines and newsletters

➤ Wine online

➤ Books for advanced reading

The selection of sources for information about buying wine is almost as big as the selection of wines available. With the explosive growth of online information services, certainly one of the best places to get current information is on the Internet. The number of forums for wine enthusiasts keeps growing. But going online is only one way to get up-to-date information. Old-fashioned hard copy information sources are proliferating as well. The biggest problem for today's wine consumer is finding the time to choose and go through all the resources. This chapter gives you some ideas about how to find and weigh the relative importance of information from various sources.

A Word on Scoring Systems

When you pick up computer magazines to see computers rated on a 100-point scale, you know the computers were subject to extensive and exhaustive performance tests in specifically designed laboratories. Wine magazines and newsletters act as if their 100-point rating systems were similarly statistically accurate. However, wine publishers are not rating Champagne bottles for their ability to withstand pressure. The laboratory in wine evaluation is the human palate, and thus, scientific accuracy is virtually impossible.

The 100-point wine rating system was conceived by Robert Parker, a government lawyer who decided to publish a newsletter titled *The Wine Advocate*. Parker must have been aware that such a system cannot be statistically accurate; however, he bet that the system's appeal would sell newsletters. He was right—Parker's newsletter is one of the foremost in the field. Today, however, the newsletter's numerical ratings are considered unreliable and controversial by many experts. (Based on Parker's success, virtually all the wine magazines adopted the system despite the impossibility of reliable ratings.)

The problem with wine rating stems from the fact that human beings are the laboratory testing instruments. As wine critics taste wines, they become fatigued from the stress and effort of concentration. And, spitting aside, alcohol is still absorbed into the bloodstream through the membranes in the mouth. Wines sampled later in the tasting are at a serious disadvantage, as the palate can no longer fully perceive their attributes; rarely will these wines appear as good to the taster as the wines tasted earlier. Thus an extraordinary wine tasted late in a tasting of a large number of wines may be considered mediocre. As publisher of *Vintage Magazine*, I had the opportunity to test the palates of some of the A-list tasters who write for magazines and newsletters. Unknown to the participants, I put the same wine in the tasting several times. The expert critics scored the same wine vastly differently each time—in a 100-point system, some scores varied as much as 30 points!

The bottom line is that you should take rating systems with a grain of salt. Rely on the wine descriptions in the publications and see if your tastes coincide with those of the writers—use your taste buds to judge which wines appeal to you and which offer good value for the price you paid.

Important Things to Know

HEY!

For the most part, the scores you see in wine magazines like *Wine Spectator*, Robert Parker's *The Wine Advocate* and *Wine Enthusiast* are guesstimates. None of these tasters have a system to calibrate their palate or their evaluations to a set standard. Some experiments have demonstrated that tasters cannot match their tasting notes or numerical ratings with the wine when it is presented a second time. Thus the tasters' scores are all over the place. You don't need to discard the scoring system entirely; just take it with a grain of salt. One helpful clue is to give each score an accuracy rating of plus or minus 5 points (or more). For example, a wine rated 87 may range from 82 to 92. Add in your own knowledge and taste preferences for best results.

I advocate a letter system: A, B, C, D, F, just like high school. This system is a concise way for getting the point across. A five-point or five-star system also works well. The *Connoisseur's Guide to California Wine* newsletter uses this type of system. The wines are evaluated in a manner similar to movie or restaurant ratings. You're given a point rating with enough information to assist you in making a decision. No pretensions, no fuss, just clear and concise information. You probably would consider rating movies or restaurants on a 100-point scale as ridiculous—consider such a system for wine in similar terms.

Wine Magazines

Wine magazines are a good source for information about wines that have just arrived on the market, plus you get articles and commentary on topics of interest to wine enthusiasts. Some magazines specialize in providing up-to-the-minute information, and others offer a more leisurely read. You also can find ads about wine tours, wine education programs, and related equipment and products. These magazines are among the most popular:

➤ *Decanter.* Published in London, *Decanter* is of primary interest to the British market. The magazine audaciously proclaims on its stationery that it is the "best" wine magazine. *Decanter* does succeed in being the most authoritative magazine, as many writers are professionals in the trade or full-time wine writers. Monthly, $80 a year. Telephone (USA): (800) 875-2997.

➤ *Wine Spectator.* This publication is arguably the best wine magazine in terms of production values and graphics with more pages, features, and wine recommendations than any other, however it publishes incorrect information, inaccurate vintage assessments and bizarre and laughable wine reviews and has an underlying tone of arrogance and self-congratulation. The *Wine Spectator* employs a staff of full-time writers both in America and Europe to provide on-the-scene coverage. However, the writers do not have professional training in wine or the wine trade. No one on the staff is a Master of Wine. The *Wine Spectator* rarely uses freelance writers for its most important coverage. The magazine rates its wines on an untenable 100-point system that is rarely accurate, and its tasting notes are frequently incomplete but nevertheless useful. It does cover the insider's view of the wine world, and for this reason everyone in the wine trade reads it, as do I. *Decanter* is more authoritative, but the slick, full-color design of the *Wine Spectator* has no equal. Large format, 18 issues, $40 a year. Telephone: (800) 752-7799.

➤ *Wine Enthusiast.* This publication is a *Wine Spectator* wannabe published by a rival of the *Wine Spectator*'s publisher who was denied access to advertising in that publication and decided to publish a wine magazine himself. The main business of the publisher is wine accessories, and it shows. The features are frequently written by freelancers who have wine as an avocation and are employed full-time in other professions. The *Wine Enthusiast*'s poor paper quality, quality of what's on the paper, and ratings on an untenable 100-point system do not hold a candle to the *Wine Spectator*. I do not recommend this publication. Large format, 14 issues, $16.95 a year. Telephone: (914) 345-8463.

➤ *The Wine News.* This attractive magazine covers the world's major wine regions and includes tasting notes. *The Wine News* is not up to par with the *Wine Spectator,* but it's worth reading and I recommend it. Large format, bimonthly, $24 a year. Telephone: (305) 444-7250.

➤ *Wine & Spirits.* This publication covers spirits as well as wine. Its writers are mainly freelancers who are employed full-time in other professions. Wine reviews use the untenable 100-point system. Not much is of interest here. 8 issues a year, $22 a year.

Newsletters

Newsletters are precise, up-to-date, and informative. Many newsletters reflect the opinion of one expert (whom you may or may not agree with), and others present the views of several writers. You won't find picturesque accounts of a holiday in Bordeaux or a weekend in sunny Sonoma, but you will find extensive tasting notes and buying guides. You might consider these newsletters:

➤ *The Wine Advocate.* This newsletter is probably the most influential publication in the wine world. *The Wine Advocate* achieved this status by instituting an untenable 100-point system to score the wines. Retailers quickly jumped on the bandwagon, quoting Parker's rating in their advertisement, and his name became prominently known. Despite Parker's use of the 100-point system, he does provide solid, useful information and tasting notes that are usually on the mark. Bimonthly, $40 a year. Telephone: (410) 329-6477.

➤ *Stephen Tanzer's International Wine Cellar.* This is the most influential newsletter after Parker's and in my opinion a better read. In addition to wine reviews, Tanzer publishes interviews with important members of the winemaking community, more background information on the vintages, and he has guest experts writing on various subjects. This publication is a must-have if you are serious about wine. Bimonthly, $48 a year. Telephone: (800) 946-3123.

➤ *Connoisseur's Guide to California Wine.* As its name implies, this publication specializes in California wine. Its writers tend to have a California palate (they prefer big chewy wines). Wines are evaluated by a panel and are rated on a five-point scoring system. Monthly, $42 a year. Telephone: (510) 865-3150.

➤ *The Vine.* England's Clive Cotes, MW is a Master of Wine and his expertise is apparent in this excellent publication. Cotes is an authority on Bordeaux and Burgundy and one of the world's best wine tasters and wine writers. I highly recommend this newsletter for the avid wine enthusiast. Monthly, $120 per year. Telephone (USA): (801) 995-8962.

Free Winery Newsletters

A number of small and large wineries publish their own newsletters. These handy sheets contain announcements of new releases, news of happenings at the winery, and opportunities to buy wine direct from the winery. These newsletters are too numerous to list here, but if you want, you may send me your name and address, and I will forward it to the wineries on your behalf. Send your name and address on a postcard to Winery Newsletters, 217 E. 86th Street, Suite 103, New York, NY 10028.

Wine Online

All the major online services (Prodigy, America Online, CompuServe) have wine forums where wine hobbyists meet to post their tasting notes, read news of the wine world, chat, and exchange ideas. All forums are similar with minor variations. My favorite is CompuServe because its forum leader is the most knowledgeable and adept.

More and more wineries, wine shops, and wine entrepreneurs are creating pages on the Internet or joining a larger Web site with a wine focus. At latest count more than 500 sites were devoted to wine. Several of these pages have links to hundreds of other sites. The Smart Wine site (http://smartwine.com) is one of the most comprehensive with hundreds of links including a large number of California wineries, wine stores, newspaper wine columns from major cities, and its own wine magazine. These other sites are worth visiting:

Fujiwine (http://www.netins.net/showcase/fujiwine)

Pascal's Wine Page (http://www.speakeasy.org/~winepage)

Burgundy Cellar (http://www.burgcellar.com)

Mark Squires' E-Zine (http://pages.prodigy.com/squires/marksq.htm)

Wine Bargain Page (http://www.iglou.com/why/wine.html)

Virtual Vineyards (http://www.virtualvin.com)

Wine Accessory Catalogs

The *Wine Enthusiast* (800-356-8466) and *International Wine Accessories* (800-527-4072) mail order companies both produce slick full-color catalogs with a wide variety of cork-screws, wine racks, wine storage units, glassware, and other accessories. Both sell the same merchandise and are pricey with high markups, but the *International Wine Accessories* tends to be less expensive than the *Wine Enthusiast*, and it provides better service. Both catalogs highly promote the Vacu-Vin wine-keeping device, which scientific studies have demonstrated to be completely ineffective. The *Culinary Arts Society* (217 E. 86th Street, New York, NY 10028) is a no-frills wholesale warehouse operation that sells similar merchandise at deep discounts from a bare-bones price list. The *Culinary Arts Society* does not sell the Vacu-Vin device or any other item it considers to be useless. This wholesaler also sells a large variety of hard-to-find wine books.

Wine Courses

Wine courses can range from informal tastings, which are conducted by a wine expert, to professional-level courses. The latter are not restricted to members of the wine trade, but some level of proficiency is a requisite. Wine courses of various lengths and levels are conducted at numerous locations throughout the country. For information on the courses offered in your area, write to the Society of Wine Educators, 132 Shaker Road, East Longmeadow, MA (413) 567-8272.

Wine Clubs

A wine club is an organization where wine lovers get together at wine tastings and gourmet dinners to enjoy the fruit of the vine. A large national wine club by the name of Les Amis du Vin used to exist. The club had more than 30,000 members, but it went bankrupt and the individual chapters across the nation either disbanded or went their own way. A wine club may exist in your locality; the best way to find out is to contact the wine and food editor of your local newspaper or your local wine retailer. If no wine club is in your area and you want to start one, your local newspaper may publish information regarding your plans so that others in your area may contact you. After you get started, use your local newspaper to publish notices of your meetings so your organization can grow. You may find a local wine retailer who wants to get involved providing wine for free or at a discount. Wine clubs provide an excellent way to exchange information about wine, make new friends, and pursue your interest in wine as a hobby.

Books for Advanced Reading

In addition to encyclopedias, pocket guides, and general reading, you can find a wealth of books offering in-depth information on specific topics related to wine. Books are available on Burgundy, Bordeaux, Cabernet Sauvignon, and Chardonnay. You can find books on old wines like Port and Madeira, and books hailing the pleasures of wine from obscure wine regions. Here is a listing of some books that can enhance your enjoyment and appreciation of wine:

➤ *Bordeaux* (second edition), by Robert M. Parker, Jr. This book reviews thousands of wines and vintages and provides comprehensive information about the region. Unfortunately, this book uses an untenable 100-point system to rate the wines.

➤ *Bordeaux* (second edition), by David Peppercorn, 1991. This book offers sketches of whatever the author deems important—good vintages, history, general characteristics of the wine, and information on several hundred wineries of the region.

➤ *Burgundy* (second edition), by Anthony Hanson, 1995. Mr. Hanson is deeply immersed in the Burgundy wine trade and shares his immense knowledge of the subject in this book. It includes considerable detail on the practices and growers of the region.

➤ *Burgundy* (second edition), by Robert M. Parker, Jr., 1996. Parker rates the growers and reviews their wines. He provides an in-depth evaluation as well as comprehensive details on the region.

➤ *Hugh Johnson's Modern Encyclopedia of Wine*, by Hugh Johnson, 1991. A complete explanation of wines, including grape growing and winemaking, of all wine-producing areas of the world.

➤ *Hugh Johnson's Pocket Encyclopedia of Wine*, by Hugh Johnson, 1996. This annually updated book provides country-by-country ratings of many vintages of over 5,000 wines. The book has maps, label guides, vintage charts, and more.

➤ *Parker's Wine Buyer's Guide* (fourth edition), by Robert M. Parker, Jr., 1995. This comprehensive guide rates more than 7,500 wines. Parker rates the producers of every wine-growing region on a five-star system, then reviews specific wines on his untenable 100-point system. Read the reviews but take the accuracy of the ratings with a grain of salt.

➤ *Pick the Right Wine*, by Daniel McCarthy, 1991. Wine merchant McCarthy makes specific recommendations of wine to serve with over 150 dishes. The book is well thought out with viable recommendations.

➤ *Port* (fourth edition), by George Robertson, 1992. A very readable account of the whole winemaking and maturing process by the chairman of Croft & Co.

➤ *Sherry* (fourth edition), by Julian Jeffs, 1992. Includes the history of Sherry from Chaucer's time to present and the entire grape growing and winemaking process.

➤ *The New Connoisseur's Handbook of California Wines* (third edition), by Norman S. Roby and Charles E. Olken. Comprehensive and authoritative coverage of more than 800 wineries with critical ratings of thousands of individual wines and vintages. The book uses a viable three-star system to rate wines.

➤ *The Oxford Companion to Wine*, edited by Jancis Robinson, 1994. This 1,086-page tome includes just about every detail you want to know about wine. The book is written by experts in each field.

➤ *The Wine Atlas of California*, by James Halliday, 1993. An excellent book on California wine as well as a comprehensive and detailed compendium of maps of the region.

➤ *The Wines of Italy*, by David Gleave, 1989. An in-depth coverage of the wines of Italy providing details of all the important regions.

➤ *Vintage Talk: Conversations with California's New Winemakers*, by Dennis Schaefer, 1994. Conversations with winemakers from 20 wineries such as Simi, Sterling, Acacia, and Au Bon Climat. Excellent insight into the role of the winemaker.

➤ *Wine Price File*, by William Edgerton, 1995. This is a data book of wine auction and retail store prices with 70,000 listings of over 15,000 fine and rare wines.

➤ *World Atlas of Wine* (fourth edition), by Hugh Johnson, 1994. This book provides detailed maps of the major wine regions of the world, along with informative commentary.

The Least You Need to Know

➤ You can further your wine education by reading wine magazines, newsletters, and books and participating in online forums.

➤ The 100-point system used by most wine publications can't be reliable or statistically accurate, primarily because it's based on the organileptic evaluation of human tasters.

➤ Look for a wine course or wine club in your locality. These are an enjoyable, social way to increase your wine knowledge.

Chapter 23

Wine in Restaurants

In This Chapter

➤ Wine by the glass

➤ Evaluating the wine list

➤ Bringing your own bottle

➤ Assessing the sommelier (wine steward)

There is truly no finer experience in life than a superb meal with a great noble wine in the ambiance of a three-star restaurant such as Montrachet in New York City with good dining companions who share your love for good wine and cuisine.

Sadly, unless you are independently wealthy with money to throw away, your visions of the nectar of the wine will quickly dissapate when you discover that a $400 bottle of Le Montrachet is $1,200, a $30 bottle of Volnay is $95, a $26 bottle of Champagne is $65, and a mere $8 Beaujolais Village is $20. A three- to five-time retail markup is not unusual at a great restaurant. I will not pay such prices and I recommend that you do not either. I have discovered that the full body, silky mouthfeel, and complex aromas of the expensive coffee blends these restaurants serve are an acceptable substitute for a wine experience. You may want to do what I do—order a cup of coffee during the meal and enjoy two or three refills for a dollar or two.

Nevertheless, most wine lovers agree that no fine dining experience is truly complete without wine. But trying to complement a restaurant menu can be a frustrating and sometimes futile experience. Three notorious occurrences work toward rousing dining displeasure: 1) Exorbitant prices resulting from unjustified markups; 2) A small wine list that is limited to a choice of run-of-the-mill wines varied only in their degrees of mediocrity; and 3) The appearance of a key-jangling *sommelier* (wine steward) who is overtly condescending and, pretensions to the contrary, not necessarily familiar with the wines, their vintages, and availability. When all three factors coincide—or collide—they make a great case for ordering a cold beer or a cup of coffee as I said above.

To be fair, some restaurants do offer a wide variety of carefully selected wines, meticulously matched to the cuisine. A few even afford an opportunity to try wines unobtainable elsewhere. When the wines are fairly priced (some restaurants have realized that well-priced wines often encourage people to enjoy more than one bottle), dining with wine, as you learn in this chapter, can live up to your greatest expectations—or even surpass them.

Wine by the Glass

Ordering wine by the glass *seems* like a good idea. For one thing, it's easy. Your choices are red or white (sometimes rosé). Ordering wine is as trouble-free as choosing between tea or coffee, cola or 7-Up. The problem is, after you taste the house wine, you may wish you had chosen the cola. And depending on the restaurant, your single glass of mediocre wine can cost anywhere from $3 to $7.50.

But what if you are the only person at your table who wants wine? Or the red wine chosen by your meat-eating companions would easily overpower your delicate filet of fish? As the next section explains, you *can* order wine by the glass without being disappointed (or ripped off).

House Wine

House wines are sold by the glass or carafe. Rarely do you find a house wine that is a superb choice. You may, possibly, if you are dining in wine country (that is, Napa or Sonoma), but for most of us, that's a long way off, and you still need to be very sure of your restaurant. House wines are generally your ordinary California or Italian generic wines, purchased in large containers and then marked up—frequently to *10 times* over cost. Think of it: You're paying for your nondescript wine more money per glass than the restaurateur pays for the whole bottle! The word for most house wines is *avoid*.

Better Pours

Some restaurants include a selection of *premium wines by the glass*. Yes, it does mean a higher price but it also means better quality. Premium wines by the glass usually range from $5 to $10 or more per glass for wines that retail for $5 or $6 a bottle.

The wine-by-the-glass menu may list only one premium white and one premium red, or it may include several of each. Other restaurants have no such listing at all, but that does not mean premium wines are not available. The trick is to be enterprising. If you see no premium listing—or if only one or two wines are listed and they are not to your taste—don't be afraid to ask about other selections. Specify what type of wine you want. The worst your server can say is that something is not available, and a helpful and knowledge-able server may suggest something comparable.

Pricing Bottles of Wine

Determining a "fair" restaurant price for a bottle of wine is difficult. Here's one guideline I offer: For wines that require neither aging nor special handling, twice the retail price is probably more than fair—for the more expensive wines full retail price plus $5. Generally, most restaurants mark up wine to three times the retail, which is four to five times their cost. In other words, you can expect to pay $20 for a bottle of wine retailing for about $7 at your local wine shop. When they think they can get away with it, some restaurateurs go six or seven times above cost. For prestigious and often scarce bottles, the markup can be even higher—an expensive wine may have a markup of several hundred dollars or more. All this for no greater effort than buying the wine by phone and pulling the cork at the table.

In my opinion, no wine, no matter how rare or expensive, should be marked up more than $50 over retail. After all, the restaurant only needs to store the wine, but the retailer must store the wine and provide costly display space. If the retailer can make a profit selling the wine at retail, the restaurant can do so, too. For a restaurant, wine sales are profit that go directly to the bottom line; overhead, advertising, and staff expenses are calculated in setting the food prices. When a restaurant charges from $12 to $20 for $2 worth of chicken, it should not gouge the customer who wants to enjoy a bottle of fine wine with his dinner. I refuse to pay these prices and instead seek out restaurants that permit you to bring your own wines, either for free or for a modest corkage charge ranging from $5 to $10 a bottle.

Wine Wisdom
As a rule, most mid-priced wines listed for $1 or $2 above the lowest group on the list present the best value.

Important Things to Know

To the unwary consumer, older wines can present a potentially nasty pitfall. Cashing in on the vintage mystique, many restaurants insist that their old wine is better, and therefore worthy of exorbitant prices. *Old is not necessarily better, nor is it always good.* Poor or "past their prime" vintages of prestigious labels like Château Lafite-Rothschild or La Romanée-Conti can be offered at astronomical prices. Several years ago, I found a 1965 Lafite-Rothschild—one of the worst vintages in many years and sold retail for $4 a bottle when released—listed at $70 a bottle. At this particular resort hotel, the wine was selling quite briskly, although it was nothing short of dead!

Rating the Wine List

There is an old joke among wine lovers about the restaurant that has a wine list reading this way:

1. Chablis

2. Burgundy

3. Rosé

Please Order Wine by Number

The list is not all that funny when you're trying to select a wine that will complement your meal and enhance your dining experience. Variations on this theme are all too common. My motto for ordering wine in a restaurant is "Be prepared!"

Being treated fairly pricewise over a bottle of wine contributes to positive ambiance, and a well-matched wine enhances the total dining experience. The first step of course is the wine selection. The verb *select* means to choose, pick, or prefer. To make a good selection, you need to an agreeable list of wines from which to select.

Important Things to Know

Whenever I decide not to order wine in a restaurant, I make my objections clear to the owner, manager, or maitre d'. I feel they ought to know my reasons. Then again, many restaurants with a poor wine policy attract me frequently, anyway. The ambiance is excellent, the cuisine superior, or both.

When pricing is outrageous, I try to strike a bargain by ordering two bottles at a price somewhere between the retail and the wine price list. Sometimes this strategy works but usually it doesn't. I feel a small profit on each of two bottles is better than none at all, and the savvy restaurateur is liable to get a loyal customer out of the deal. As they say in the lotto game, you never know! It's worth a try. But call in advance to negotiate a deal to avoid an embarrassing confrontation in front of your guests.

The Short List

The list of one white, one red, and one rosé may be a joke, but in all humor there is truth. Abbreviated wine lists with maybe two wines per color, one or two wines from an "exotic" location (anything more exotic than France, Italy, or California), and perhaps some sparkling variety are still too common. A restaurant with this type of list is one that goes through the motions of serving wine without any sensitivity to its customers or desire to attract wine lovers.

The Familiar List

Do you experience a strong sense of *déjà vu* as you stare at the wine list? The red leatherette cover is strikingly familiar. You know what the wines are before you even get to the first page. You don't even check for the vintages next to the wine names because you already know they won't be there. In this situation, the list usually was developed, printed, and supplied by a wholesaler or distributor whose primary motive is self-interest. Why not throw in the binder and typesetting when the list is stocked with the distributor's most profitable wines? You may see such a list in an Italian restaurant one weekend, in a small French restaurant the next. The restaurateur employing this list opts for economy, convenience, and minimal personal effort. Don't just ignore the wine—watch out for the food!

The Brand List

This is a variation on the familiar list. Suspect any wine list with a preponderance of major, nationally distributed brands—B&G, Mouton Cadet, Bolla, Paul Masson, for example. The wines are not necessarily bad, but a list dominated by one or two popular brands is much too restrictive. Offering wines that are commonly available and all too familiar suggests the restaurateur prefers to allow a sales representative to prepare the wine list and makes no effort to match the wine with the cuisine. The wine cellar has neither imagination nor creativity, and chances are both features are missing from the kitchen as well. Check to see if most California wines come from one producer or if most imported wines are from one shipper/importer. If so, you have a brand-dictated list.

The Fat Wine List

Although an extensive wine list is always nice, one that reads like a doctoral thesis or a Henry James novel can bog you down when you're trying to make a simple selection to go with dinner. The well-run restaurants provide the extended list for patrons willing to lose themselves in wineland, and the abridged version for those who are simply trying to match their meal.

The Good Wine List

I love wine lists that offer variety and global appeal—that is, a wide selection of wines from the major wine regions of the world. Of course, I also like an indication that the owner exercised a modicum of caution in the wine selection. Here's an example:

> **Wine Wisdom**
> A well-assembled wine list and informed staff usually go hand-in-hand with a properly run kitchen and fine cuisine.

➤ Bordeaux from different châteaux

➤ Different vintages of the same wine

➤ Wines in a wide price range

➤ Wines from a local producer

➤ Wines chosen to complement the restaurant's menu

These wines are the beginning of a good wine list. This type of list shows that the owner or beverage manager is quite knowledgeable about wines. Generally, he or she is enthusiastic in suggesting wines within your price range.

The Reserve Wine List

No, a reserve wine list does not mean that all the wines on the list are reserve wines. A few upscale restaurants offer a special list of rare wines in addition to the regular wine list. If the occasion is really special and cost is no object, well, why not? On the other hand, if you have any doubts, stick with the regular list. Should you choose the reserve list, ask for assistance from the sommelier. You do not want to be stuck with a very expensive mistake.

Bringing Your Own Bottle

We all know about BYOB (bringing your own bottle) when the restaurant has no liquor license. Small ethnic restaurants often fall into this category, along with restaurants that have just opened and whose license is still pending. What most people don't realize is that BYOB is also a time-honored tradition at a restaurant with a weak wine list, or even a restaurant with an adequate list, when you want to enjoy a special wine of your own. First check your local regulations to be sure it is permissible to bring a bottle of wine to a licensed restaurant. Some districts say no, others say yes. Second, be sure you follow a sensible protocol and are prepared to pay a corkage fee. You are not out to alienate the proprietor. I suggest BYOB is appropriate under the following conditions:

> ➤ The wine you are bringing is something special and *not* on the list.

> ➤ You consider ordering another bottle from the list to maintain goodwill.

> ➤ You call ahead to ask for approval and find out the corkage fee.

> ➤ You are a fairly regular client.

> ➤ You include a reasonable value for the wine when you are calculating your tip.

Wine Wisdom

The key to obtaining the best value from a restaurant wine list is a familiarity with the prices, vintages, châteaux, and producers, as well as the importers and shippers. If the wine list omits specific information about vintages, importers, and so on, the wines may not be worth ordering. It never hurts to ask questions of your server or wine steward.

Important Things to Know

HEY!

A reasonable corkage fee is anywhere from $5 to $10. Some restaurants try to discourage the practice by charging an exorbitant fee. If this is the case, visit a different restaurant that knows a reasonable fee makes for a loyal customer.

Have No Fear—Send Your Wine Back

This situation is the biggest concern for many restaurant goers: Under what conditions can you refuse and return a bottle of wine? This option is exercised too often by an elite few and not at all by the vast majority of diners. Don't break out in hives. The decision simply comes down to this: Do not accept defective or flawed wines. The confusion for some people lies in deciding whether a wine's taste and smell are defective or just unfamiliar and unusual. But isn't this one supposed to smell like skunk?

Important Things to Know

HEY! You definitely should refuse a wine past its peak. If a white wine is dark yellow or brown in color and smells like Sherry, it is not some rare treasure. It is over-the-hill and likely maderized. Red wines past their prime are somewhat brown in color, often orange around the rim. A dull flavor, like the smell of dead leaves, and a sharp, short finish are sure indicators to send the wine back. If you see, smell, or taste any of the defects mentioned in this book (Chapter 7), do not hesitate. Send the bottle back by all means.

Experience is the best teacher for helping you detect the most common off-aromas. When in doubt, ask the server to sample the wine. If she or he is confused about its merits and acceptability, then you are off the hook and another bottle should be forthcoming. Remember to never return a wine you ordered out of curiosity but then did not like.

In my experience, a well-run restaurant will not quibble or get into a battle of wills with its customers. Customer service is the hallmark of the hospitality trade. "The customer is always right," has always been the policy with food and is used more often these days with wine. Just remember: Do not abuse the policy.

Evaluating Your Sommelier

In many higher-priced restaurants, the wine list and your order are handled by a sommelier. By definition, a *sommelier*, or wine steward, is knowledgeable and familiar with the wines listed. Better yet, the sommelier may have bought, stored, and cared for the beloved wines and even trained the rest of the staff in wine protocol. France, Italy, and a few other countries have professional schools to train sommeliers. A few comparable programs exist in the U.S., but it has yet to catch up with the Old World.

Therefore, you must learn to distinguish between the well-informed, full-fledged sommeliers and the impostors who strut around with pomp, ceremony, and haughtiness (and whose sole purpose is to intimidate and ultimately coerce people into buying wines with high markups and/or wines purchased in great quantities). (Try out a few of the questions you used to evaluate your wine shop.) Worst of all, these characters survive because customers, unsure in their own knowledge, are afraid to speak up.

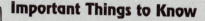

Important Things to Know

A good sommelier is supposed to taste the wine to determine its quality *before* serving it to you. When a sommelier is present, the practice of tasting wine at your table is an acceptable ritual and not a charade.

Taking Home the Rest of the Bottle

You have half a bottle of wine left and you're sure that one more glass will cause you to stumble out the door. Wine is an awfully expensive investment to leave sitting on the table. How do you ask for a doggie bag for your wine? Wine etiquette has no protocol that forbids requesting to take your unfinished bottle home with you. In some states, however, the practice is restricted by law, so your request for the bottle may be turned down. Don't blame the owner or manager for being difficult or haughty. You might ask the restaurateur to keep the corked bottle in his refrigerator for your next visit.

Ensuring Good Service

As a paying customer—and especially at the price restaurateurs charge for wine—you are entitled to fair service. These few suggestions can help you get a fair deal:

➤ Make sure you see the bottle you order. Check producer, type, vintage, etc.

➤ See that the wine arrives with cork and foil capsule intact. The possibility exists that a bottle may have been refilled with inferior wine or returned by another diner.

➤ Take the time away from your friends and guests to study the bottle. Slow the sommelier or server down to your pace—it is your money.

➤ Hold the bottle and check its temperature. A red wine, unless it is Beaujolais Nouveau, should be at room temperature. A bottle that's too warm can indicate poor storage. White wines should be chilled, not frigid. If it's iced like a beer bottle, beware. Wines kept too cold for too long lose their verve; you don't want an over-priced flat wine. You are better off to have white wine delivered to your table at room temperature, then placed in an ice bucket—*for 15 minutes*.

➤ Do not let the sommelier open the wine bottle until you have given your official approval. Do not let the sommelier pour the wine into other glasses until you have tasted and accepted it. My advice: Don't rush.

➤ Check the wine glasses for size and type. If you are not satisfied, ask for others. Champagnes and sparkling wines are best served in glasses without hollow stems. Flutes are preferred, but an all-purpose wine glass may be your only alternative.

Important Things to Know

HEY!

Smell the empty glass. This may sound silly, but the slightest smell of soap or detergent ruins Champagne and impairs most table wine. If you detect a detergent smell, ask the waiter to scrub the glasses carefully. When he returns, don't be afraid to recheck—a once-over light rinse won't always do the trick.

➤ Make certain the capsule is cut neatly and the cork is removed cleanly. The cork should be offered to you, and you should smell and feel it. The cork should not smell of vinegar or feel dried out, and it certainly should not crumble under your touch. Incidentally, Champagnes should be uncorked with a minimal pop, if any. That movieland pop will land half your expensive bubbles on the ceiling.

The wine should not just smell clean and free of defects; it should be consistent with its type. These characteristics assume some knowledge on your part (which you have if you've read this far).

If you randomly select a wine unfamiliar to you and discover it's not to your taste, that's your problem. Live and learn.

If you followed the sommelier or server's recommendation and description, but the wine does not resemble what was described, the problem is the restaurant's. You can refuse the wine. Be persistent.

Important Things to Know

HEY!

A word about timing. Far too often, about the time your food arrives, you are informed that the wine you ordered is not available. Because some of us plan the meal around the wine selected, this news is not good. You can avoid this dilemma by requesting that the wine or wines be presented and brought to the table well ahead of the food.

Vintage wines deserve special mention. If you intend to bring an old vintage with you or are contemplating ordering a really old wine from the list, check ahead for several reasons. Old wines mean old bottles, and they are subject to enormous variations in storage.

Find out if the management stands by the quality of the vintage bottles in its cellar. If you're bringing your own dowager wine, inquire if the restaurant has the necessary decanter, glasses, and a person experienced in decanting old wines.

An old wine is like a special entrée: it should be ordered ahead of time, allowing the staff to make proper preparations that include standing the bottle upright for several hours or more, preferably the day before. The wines should be ready to decant when you arrive.

The Least You Need to Know

➤ You can get better wines by the glass in restaurants if you ask for premium pours.

➤ Most restaurants gouge the consumer on wine prices. A fair price for a $6 retail bottle of wine is $12 in a restaurant. A fair price for a wine selling for $25 or more in a wine store is full retail price plus $5.

➤ The wine list gives you an immediate indication of the competence of the restaurateur. A mediocre wine list or one prepared by the wholesaler is an indication of a restuarateur who is not fully conversant with his craft.

➤ You may be able to bring your own bottle into a restaurant by paying a corkage charge of about $10 or so.

➤ In many states, you can take home a partially filled bottle if you have not finished it during your meal.

Part 5
Wine at Home

You may have heard that you must store your wine at a constant 55 degrees F. This is malarkey. This part delves into the details about storing your wine safely so that it can mature in perfect condition as it ages. It will tell you what temperatures to avoid so that your wine won't become "roasted." You will also learn how to collect wine and maintain your own wine cellar, either for daily drinking or for the future. You will learn how to insure your valuable wine so that you are fully covered in case of fire, flood, theft, or an air conditioning failure.

Because wine tastings are fun and provide an excellent opportunity to entertain in a unique style while learning what different wines taste like, this part shows how to conduct a wine tasting like a pro, as well as how to match the right food with the right meals when dining or entertaining.

Finally, a glass or two of wine a day may indeed keep the doctor away. This part concludes by giving you the latest information on how wine can reduce the incidence of heart attack and cancer, and possibly add extra years to your life.

SCOO-
DOOP

ICE
CREAM

Chapter 24

Wine à la Mode

> **In This Chapter**
>
> ➤ Storing your wine
>
> ➤ Stocking your own wine cellar
>
> ➤ Entertaining with wine
>
> ➤ Conducting a wine tasting

You started with one innocent-looking bottle. Then you had two, then five, and suddenly—the Sorcerer's Apprentice. You're not about to forsake your newfound avocation. The question is, how do you keep all those bottles? This chapter provides some guidance about creating your at-home wine cellar and caring for your wine supply.

How Should I Store My Wine?

For information on choosing the perfect wine rack or climate-controlled home storage unit, see Chapter 4. Numerous models are available, and they seem to just keep proliferating. Whether your taste is conservative, antique, or futuristic, and whether your budget is modest or limitless, you're sure to find a storage unit to suit your needs and taste.

You won't find too many ads in the classified sections advertising castles for sale or rent: *Great hillside location; spacious, airy with deep, dark cellar for storing wine.* Lacking a natural storage cellar, most of us need to be resourceful. The rest of this section recaps some of the information in Chapter 4.

Keep It Dark

Wines are maturing in the bottle, not hibernating. They don't need total darkness, but they do need a place away from direct sunlight.

Keep It Cool

Prolonged storage in very warm or hot conditions will seriously damage your wine. Extreme heat causes wine to mature precociously; it goes from adolescence to senility without ever reaching a golden age. The ideal temperature is 55 degrees Fahrenheit; a range of 50 degrees to 60 degrees is fine.

Keep It Humid

Wines like humidity even if you don't. Your cellar should have a minimum of 75 percent humidity and a maximum of 90 percent (give or take a percentage point). Humidity above 95 percent encourages mold.

> **Important Things to Know**
>
> If the air is dry, the wine can evaporate or leech out through the cork. The resulting condition is called *ullage*, space between the wine and the cork. Ullage can allow the wine to oxidize—the last thing you want for your collection.

You can buy a hygrometer, the instrument used to measure atmospheric humidity, specially designed for wine storage areas. Some hygrometers are single units; others are coupled with a thermometer (required equipment). You can find hygrometers in wine accessories catalogs and some sophisticated retailers.

Is Perfect Temperature a Must?

The ideal of a constant 55-degree temperature is good to shoot for when you are selecting your storage space, but remember—we live in a less than ideal world. Uniformity of temperature is the key point. Avoid any area with dramatic temperature fluctuations over a short period of time. Slow, incremental changes, free of extremes, offer no threat. If your storage conditions vary from about 50 degrees in winter to a high of about 70 degrees in summer, you don't need to worry too much. If your high is less than 70 degrees, don't worry at all.

> **Wine Wisdom**
> Vibration is an enemy of wine, causing it to age poorly and prematurely. Remember, keep the storage area free of vibrations.

Your Own Wine Cellar

Does the idea make you feel like the renowned Dom Perignon, lovingly tending his cellar, or do you feel overwhelmed at the thought of those bottles maturing under your care? Your perspective on wine collecting is a big consideration when you are choosing how, where, or how many.

How Much Wine Do I Want to Keep?

If all you really want is a ready bottle for casual drinking or an emergency stash for unexpected visitors, chances are you'll be happier with a small rack (many hold 10 to 15 bottles) or the case in which your wine arrived (see Chapter 4). If you're starting to feel the collector's urge, especially if you're thinking of buying long-aging wines as an investment, just remember you do need to put some effort into the upkeep. A bit of honest introspection should give you the answer to how much wine you need.

Basic Cellar for Everyday Drinking

A basic cellar should include a diverse collection for everyday drinking as well as for special events. For your everyday collection, select the styles you prefer in your usual price range for everyday wines. Supplement this group with a few bottles of better-quality wines for when the occasion demands something extra. Non-vintage Champagnes and good-quality sparkling wines also fall into this category. Then for those momentous occasions, keep a bottle or two of tête de cuvée Champagne on hand. For occasions when the bubbly may not be appropriate, the perfect choice is a Premier or Grand Cru Burgundy, or Cru Classé Bordeaux from vintages that are ready to drink.

The $1,000 Cellar

This cellar includes the selections mentioned in the preceding section, with a few additions. In this collection, the ready-to-drink Premier and Grand Crus Burgundies and Cru Classés Bordeaux are joined by their less mature cousins, who will be ready for drinking in a few years. Include some white Bordeaux, a selection of German wines, red and white Burgundy, and from the U.S.: California Cabernet, Chardonnay, and Zinfandel.

The $2,500 Cellar

Now we're building on the $1,000 cellar. A case of Cru Classé Bordeaux, red and white Burgundies, and California reds that need 5 to 10 years of aging are the mark of this cellar. Include several bottles of mature, ready-to-drink vintage Port; mature, ready-to-drink Sauternes; and a few bottles of German Late-Harvest wines. This collection comprises the first stage in the Connoisseur's Cellar.

The Connoisseur's Cellar

The Connoisseur's Cellar is what you wish every restaurant or hotel maintained (in fact, many establishments probably wish they could maintain such a cellar). The collection includes an array of wines for everyday drinking and encompasses noble and rare wines of the utmost breed and finesse. Lay down your Bordeaux, Burgundies, California agers, and vintage Ports for future consumption, along with the sweet Sauternes, Beerenauslese, and Tröckenbeerenauslese. (This last category is optional. Your taste may not go to sweet wines. Remember, it's your cellar.)

The Connoisseur's Cellar also can include some esoteric wines like vintage Madeiras, high-quality Sherries, and perhaps a curiosity or two. Try Hungarian Tokay, 5 Puttonos.

How Can I Insure My Wine?

Insurers generally expect you to own a television or two, audio equipment, and these days, a personal computer. They do not expect you to stock an extensive wine cellar. Very few regular homeowners' policies cover wine in case of fire, theft, breakage, or other damage. Some policies may cover up to a few thousand dollars. To ensure coverage on your collection, you can purchase a rider on your home-insurance policy. For optimum coverage, it pays to get an all-risk rider. Then you're covered if your home air-conditioning or your wine refrigeration unit fails and your wine cooks—or you have another dreaded disaster. Figure the cost of wine insurance to be about 40 to 50 cents per $100 of wine insured per year. For instance, if your wine inventory is worth $75,000, your annual premium might be about $315.

HEY!

Important Things to Know

You can appraise your collection yourself by checking out catalog prices for younger wines, and auction house prices for the older ones. However, I strongly advise you to seek professional appraisal. That way you avoid contention with the insurer should a loss occur. I recommend Roger Livdahl

(213-460-6999), a well-respected certified appraiser, or William Edgerton (203-655-0566), publisher of the *Wine Price File*, a book listing 70,000 recent sale prices of thousands of fine and rare wines.

Two major insurers that are experienced in wine coverage are the Chubb Group of Insurance Companies and Sedgewick James.

Entertaining with Wine

This is the moment every wine enthusiast looks forward to. The following few guidelines can help ensure that you plan your event with confidence and verve, not apprehension.

Which Wines Should I Serve?

The kinds of wines depend on the nature of the gathering, the type of guests, the number of guests, and the atmosphere you want to create. Don't get too carried away with the last category. You will not create an upscale impression by serving vintage Bordeaux or Burgundy to a disco crowd. Instead of being impressed by your taste in wine, your guests will be begging for water to fill out their puckered cheeks. And despite its association with gaiety and festivity, Champagne is not always the right choice. At an informal party, understatement should be the rule.

For a party where the food is incidental (traditional snack foods, a plate of crudités here, a Chinese entrée there), it's best to stick with wines that are easily consumed without culinary accompaniment. An inexpensive California Chardonnay is an excellent bet. This wine is fruity, refreshing, and very popular. For a red wine, choose a Beaujolais. If it's holiday season, Beaujolais Nouveau is perfect.

At a formal dinner party, it is traditional to serve one wine with each course. Some more elegant dinners serve two wines with each course. If you own different glasses for different wines, make sure to wash them carefully (no trace of detergent!) and bring them out. If not, you don't need to go buy them; the basic styles recommended in Chapter 2 are fine.

Wine Wisdom
Some invitations specify BYOB, but even those that don't will never turn down a gift wine. If you're the guest at a party and not sure of your host's taste in wine, feel free to bring your own choice. Just be sure you're the one to open the bottle, or it may disappear before you get to enjoy it.

Popping the Cork

Serving Champagne has been surrounded for too long by silly rituals and unnecessary pomp. The occasion may be special, but opening the bottle should be no more ceremonious than opening any other type of wine. Be cautious, however. The contents are under tremendous pressure. Forget the rituals and misconceptions and keep the uncorking safe.

Treat an unopened Champagne bottle with the same respect as a loaded gun. Never point the bottle in anyone's direction, including your own. Hold the bottle at a 45-degree angle away from everyone. Because temperature can possibly cause a bottle to fracture, take special care when handling iced or over-chilled Champagne (some people like it that way). Use these simple guidelines:

➤ Always inspect a Champagne bottle for deep scratches or nicks. A badly scratched bottle has the potential to explode.

➤ Never chill Champagne lower than 45 degrees. A colder temperature increases the risk of a bursting bottle if it has deep scratches.

➤ When removing the wire cage around the cork, always place your palm over the cork to prevent its shooting out of the bottle.

➤ Always point the neck of the bottle away from yourself and others. A flying Champagne cork works only in the movies. In real life you run the risk of seriously injuring someone.

➤ Remove the cork by a gentle, twisting motion with your palm over the cork. You should hear a barely audible pop and see a mere wisp of "smoke." Loud pops and gushing Champagne are vulgar—and an awful waste of good wine.

➤ If the cork is difficult, push gently on alternate sides with your thumbs. When the cork begins to move, cover it with your palm.

Conducting Your Own Wine Tasting

You may have the impression that wine tasting is something to be undertaken only by those who are deemed (or who deem themselves) professional experts. This notion is far from the truth. You're learning more about wine each day. Perhaps you've mapped out your storage space and your collection is growing. Now is the perfect time to conduct your own wine tasting.

What Is a Wine Tasting?

A wine tasting is a gathering of people for the purpose of tasting and sampling wine. The occasion can be serious or strictly laid-back. Professional wine tastings are held for people in the wine trade, and consumer wine tastings are meant for amusement, entertainment, and education. Holding a wine tasting can be an enjoyable experience that advances your knowledge about wine and facilitates a lively social event. You do not need to be a wine expert; you *do* need to be a good host.

Contrary to what you might expect, conducting a wine tasting is simple. You merely need to select the wines, the wine glasses, and the people. Having something to nibble on between wines is helpful as a palate cleanser, but food is not a necessity. Having a theme to your tasting is a good idea, though, so you have a point of comparison. For example:

➤ A tasting of Chardonnays

➤ A tasting of Bordeaux

➤ A tasting of different wines from the same vintage

➤ A tasting of wines selected within a specified price range

The possibilities are almost limitless. Another alternative is to choose a certain number of red (or white) wines from different regions or countries to explore regional differences. Or you can focus on wines from an emerging wine country or region. When you're feeling confident, you can throw caution to the wind and go for a tasting that encompasses a wide variety of wine styles. Variety can be a theme in itself. For your first effort or two, however, you should stick with a more limited palate.

HEY!

Important Things to Know

The logistics of a wine tasting are not complicated. To gauge the number of bottles you need, assume that one bottle will easily serve 12 people, 15 if necessary.

Stand-Up Tastings

Conducting a stand-up wine tasting is easy. You start by setting up your table or tables. If you do not have a table large enough to accommodate several wines, a few smaller tables will do. With no seating arrangement, you don't need to worry about guests complaining that they were not at the "right" table. Wine bottles don't seem to care. You need white tablecloths to provide a proper background for viewing the color of the wines (paper tablecloths are fine), and enough wine glasses to suit your theme. I suggest two glasses per person at the very least, and they should be good-sized glasses so guests can fully assess the bouquet. The only odd thing you need are spittoons: buckets of some kind for spitting out wine or emptying glasses as you go on to taste other wines.

Remember the rule of lighting: Bright incandescent lighting enhances your sensory appreciation of the wine. Fluorescent lights impart a cast to all wines and ruin the appearance of reds in particular by making them appear brown, the sign of an overaged wine.

Sit-Down Tastings

The first rule of a sit-down tasting is to determine how many people you can comfortably handle in seating arrangements. The glasses are set out on the table. The wines are poured in flights (groups), for example, three wines at a time. Consider the following Bordeaux tasting:

➤ First flight:
   Cru Bourgeous Petit Château

➤ Second flight:
   Third and fourth growth, Cru Classé from the Médoc

➤ Third flight:
   Second growth Cru Classé from the Médoc

➤ Fourth flight:
   First growth Cru Classé from the Médoc

Another example is to compare Chardonnays from California, France, and Australia:

➤ First flight:
   Two wines from each country, under $8 each

➤ Second flight:
   Same kinds of wines, priced at about $15

➤ Third flight:
   Same kinds of wines, $25 to $35. In this flight, you might compare a Premier Cru Mersault with a Premier Cru Chassagne Montrachet, along with the two wines each from California and Australia.

Important Things to Know

HEY!

Wine tastings can be vertical or horizontal. No, this description does not refer to whether your guests stand upright or recline on divans. A *vertical* tasting is one that features several vintages of the same wine (for example,

Château Palmer in each vintage from 1979 to 1991). A *horizontal* tasting features wines of a single vintage from several different properties, usually of a similar type, such as 1993 California Chardonnay.

To Eat or Not to Eat

You want to be very careful in the selection of food. This rule applies both to the nibbles you choose for the wine tasting and to any food being prepared in a kitchen nearby. Cheeses are a natural with wine, but for wine tastings, the more neutral the cheese the better. Very aromatic cheese can clash with the wines' fragrances and taste. No browsing the gourmet grocery for blue-veined Roquefort or runny Camembert. The same rule applies to cooking odors from any food you choose to serve after the tasting. Wine tasting is one situation where food is not an enhancer. If possible, have food brought in after the tasting is finished. Plain bread or unsalted crackers are your best choices to accompany a wine tasting. Better yet, forget the food and go for plain water.

Important Things to Know

I prefer a neutral or mineral water because it cleans the palate without imparting a taste of its own. Some city water is over-treated with chemicals that can affect your ability to taste. Likewise, the hard water indigenous to parts of the Midwest and Southwest can influence your taste.

Blind Tastings

One way to taste wines is the "blind" approach, which means that the labels are concealed and unknown. Regardless of one's experience and professed impartiality, we all know that seeing a label can influence judgment—it's simple human reasoning. For example, perhaps someone tells you that the label is prestigious, or you have sampled the wine before and liked it. It takes a courageous soul to run counter to consensus—or worse, your own earlier judgment.

The only requirement is to cover the bottles and code them so the tasters are unaware of the contents. The slender paper bags used by wine and liquor merchants are perfect. Ask your retailer for a few bags. Aluminum foil works well, but it reveals the bottle's shape—and you want to eliminate all clues. Decanters are ideal; no clues here.

Important Things to Know

If you use decanters, always make a list of what wine went into what decanter. Getting the wines confused would be an awful mistake.

After a time, your interest in wine tasting may develop to a point where you want to discover more than which wines appeal to you. You can make the tastings more interesting and concentrate on fine-tuning your abilities through blind tastings. This leaning tends to develop on its own, as you find yourself guessing a wine's origin, vintage, region, winemaking style, or even brand. Wine tasting is like listening to music. You may not realize it at first, but your subconscious is processing information: composer, period, style, and so on.

You can use blind wine tastings to test your expertise as a safeguard against developing personal prejudices or a false sense of security. A blind wine tasting can be a chance to show off, but it can also be a very humbling experience. Basically, a blind test is a chance to show yourself where you stand.

Testing Your Palate

Experiment with these blind tasting strategies:

➤ A triangulation test is easy. All it requires is two wines and three glasses. Pour one of the wines into two glasses; pour the other wine into a single glass. The taster's task is to pick the two glasses filled from the same bottle. Piece of cake, right? This test sounds like a snap, but even experienced tasters get mixed up.

➤ Another good tasting test is working with pairs. Pour two wines with some dissimilarity into four glasses. The taster has to match pairs. You can use this exercise for any number of pairs. You also can vary the rules. Challenge the taster by simple matching or more complex tasks such as matching by vintage, country, or region.

Important Things to Know

In the beginning, testing is easier if you taste wines that are substantially different. As your palate develops, choose wines that are increasingly similar.

The important thing is to not make tasting a chore. Think of the test as a game of knowledge and sensory skill. But don't take tasting so seriously that you wind up ruining your enjoyment.

A Few Last Rules for the Wine Tasting

➤ Serve each wine at an appropriate temperature. Serve whites, rosés, and Champagnes slightly chilled; serve reds at room temperature.

➤ Fill the glasses—preferably all of the same size—to the same level so you don't prejudice the taster by providing too much or too little.

➤ Group together and taste wines of the same type.

➤ Taste sweet wines in progression according to sweetness. A very sweet wine, if tasted early, can make less-sweet wines seem dry.

➤ Limit the number of wines being tasted. Most people can taste only 10, maybe 12, wines and still maintain clear and meaningful judgment.

➤ Generally when mixing wines by type, sequence them so that the lighter, drier versions precede the heavier ones. At least, taste the whites and rosés before the reds.

Keeping Notes

Whether you're a novice taster or you can boast of notches on your taste buds, trying to recall a particular wine from memory can be a frustrating experience. Many wine enthusiasts jot down notes, not only at organized tastings, but at any social occasion where the wines are worth noting. (Do not, however, sit at a formal dinner party with a notepad—especially if you want to be invited back.) You can make the notes detailed or abbreviated using symbols. Tasting notes can be an invaluable aid, both to help you remember your impression of a wine and as a personal record of your wine-tasting education.

No hard and fast rules exist for describing a wine. Ultimately, your own perception is what counts. But you should include certain aspects of tasting:

➤ **Olfactory and taste perceptions.** Aroma, bouquet, fruitiness, etc.

➤ **Structure.** Balance of alcohol/sweetness/tannins/acidity

➤ **Texture.** The feel of the wine in your mouth

You'll also want to chronicle the development of your tasting experience from the first impression to the lingering aftertaste. For in-depth information, see Chapter 3.

Your Wine Journal

There is no single or right way of organizing tasting notes. Some people love index cards. Some prefer blank notebooks that they can arrange in their own way, and others prefer the wine journals sold for this purpose. If you're a fan of electronic organizing, software is available (check wine accessories catalogs), or you can set up your own.

If you have already established a cellar or you are beginning your collection, a cellar log is a useful tool. The log enables you to chart the development of your wines from the date of purchase (along with the price) through the first sampling (with a note of when to sample next) through the time that particular wine remains only as a memory. Again, you can set up your own cellar log or purchase a formatted journal or software.

Scoring Systems

If you become really serious about wines, eventually you will want to develop a scoring system for your tastings. This method is a good way to catalog particular favorites. Professionals and advanced wine buffs use several systems, but they tend to be unnecessarily complicated. My advice: Keep it simple. You can use the traditional star system, giving a wine five stars, or three, or one-half. You can use a letter system (A, B, C, etc.), although it may seem too much like a report card. Choose your own icons, if you like: *I give this wine a four-and-one-half bottle rating.* Just don't get too cutesy. A page covered with pictures of grapevines or corkscrews may prohibit you from reading your own ratings.

Important Things to Know

HEY!

Never downplay the importance of preference in rating your wine. Ultimately, wine evaluation is a personal matter, with no right and wrong responses. Our impression boils down to two things: what we perceive and what we like in a wine. We may very well be able to perceive a particular wine's high acidity or residual sugar, or its light or heavy body. What we like—how much a wine appeals to our taste—is a matter of individual taste perception and preference.

Comparing your own evaluations with those of others is the best way to learn about wine and your own perceptions and preferences. Understanding *why* another taster's preference is different from yours is more important in terms of learning about wine than knowing which wine is the better one. The best wine for you is the one you prefer. Knowing why you prefer one wine over another is the essential point.

As you develop more experience, you may find that your preferences change. This situation is common when you share your tasting experience with someone whose palate and expertise are more sophisticated than yours. Your "wine mentor" can help you to isolate some subtle sensations you may have missed. Or your mentor can help you to articulate those nuances that you just "know." A word of caution, however: Not every experienced wine taster is a good wine teacher. Above all, never feel that you must adjust your preferences because one wine buff prefers a wine you don't.

The Least You Need to Know

➤ Keep your wine-storage place dark, cool, humid, and between 50 and 70 degrees Fahrenheit.

➤ Conducting your own wine tasting is a good way to learn more about wine.

➤ Serve only bread, crackers, or a mild cheese at a wine tasting.

➤ Limit a wine tasting to 10 or 12 wines.

➤ A blind wine tasting is a tasting where the identities of the wines are concealed.

➤ Keeping a wine journal is a good way to remember what wines you tasted and what you thought of them.

Chapter 25

The Art of Matching Wine with Food

> **In This Chapter**
>
> ➤ The basic rules for matching food with wine
>
> ➤ Going beyond the basic rules
>
> ➤ Becoming your own food and wine matching expert
>
> ➤ Some food and wine matches

Whether you realize it or not, you've probably already had some practice in matching wine with food. Maybe you stuck to the traditional rules: "I'm having filet of flounder, so I'll have a light white wine to go with it." Or maybe you were spontaneous: "Serving this Beaujolais for brunch with eggs Florentine was a brilliant idea! Who would ever have thought it would work?"

On the minus side, you've probably had some experience that didn't work. Perhaps you chose a Salade Nicoise with vinaigrette, only to have a friend arrive with a bottle of full-bodied red wine. Or maybe you've absent-mindedly munched smoked almonds as you've sipped your wine. What harm could they possibly do?

If you evoke each experience in your mind and taste buds, one thing becomes clear: Certain wines and foods go very well together, and certain wines and foods clash.

The Basics of Wine and Food Matching

Some wines and foods are simply not compatible. For example, try tasting a very dry wine with a sweet dessert. You can chalk up such faux pas as learning experiences. Matching a wine with the wrong food can make both items taste bad, like the bone dry wine and the pastry torte. Or the food can neutralize the wine's flavor. You were expecting subtle complexities, a symphony of finesse. You intended to show off your noble wine at its peak. And what did you taste? A very expensive jug wine!

Important Things to Know

HEY!

All wine lovers agree that wine is the natural accompaniment to a meal. A meal without wine is a meal without salt and pepper. But would you put salt on a wedge of Camembert or pepper on chocolate ice cream? Matching wine with food is like adding condiments to a dish. Your aim is to bring out the product's full potential, not alter or mask its distinction.

Perfect wine and food matching is rare. Success requires a great knowledge of food and a lot of good luck. Even the greatest chefs do not make a dish exactly the same on each occasion (maybe that's what makes them great chefs). Just a smidge extra of this or a dollop of that is enough to mar—or if luck is smiling, enhance—the intended combination. Wine can be quirky too, as you've already gathered. It may not be quite as full or as fruity as you thought, or those tannins may not have settled.

General Rules for Matching Wine and Food

To understand the rules of this game, firsthand experience is definitely required. You may diligently study art history, but your reaction to seeing van Gogh's Sunflowers up close is probably much different from reading about his brush strokes. Despite all the great things you've read, you may or may not like the painting, depending on your personal preferences. Just as in art, it's your taste preference, and ultimately your own judgment, that counts in wine-matching.

To hone your skills for wine-matching, you need to develop a taste memory for wine. You already have a taste memory for food. Think of a pear, a banana, rib roast, or your favorite flavor of ice cream. Chances are you can evoke coffee, cola, or orange juice in a flash.

Now try this test with wine. Evoke the experience of Beaujolais, Cabernet Sauvignon, Chardonnay, or another wine. Visualizing the wine first may help, or you may associate it with a particular occasion—an occasion where the wine and food were well-matched.

The trick is to evoke the wine and food memory and play a matching game. Whenever you taste a wine, think of what flavors go with it to build in your taste memory. This concept may seem strange at first—what type of food goes with a wine that evokes *tar*? The idea is not really that strange when you think of the terms we use to describe wines (for example, fruity, herbaceous, creamy, tart). Immediately, certain foods come to mind that have these same qualities. These similarities do not mean that wine and food need to have the same traits. You can work in two ways: You can match wine with foods that have similar characteristics, or you can decide that opposites attract. Use these three basic categories as a guide:

➤ **Components.** Sugar, acid, bitterness, sourness, and so on.

➤ **Flavors.** Peachy, berrylike, herbal, buttery, minty, vanilla, and so on.

➤ **Texture.** Medium-bodied, thin, velvety, viscous, and so on.

The first category, components, is the trickiest. These elements directly affect our taste buds. Sweetness is perceived by the tip of the tongue, sourness by the sides, saltiness by the middle, and bitterness by the back of the tongue. The components of both food and wine stir the sensory buds in these areas:

➤ **Sweetness.** This one is easy. Sweetness is residual sugar in wine; natural or added sugar in food.

➤ **Saltiness.** Some foods are naturally salty (briny oysters or mussels); most have added salt. Saltiness is generally not associated with wine; however, Manzanilla Sherry is said to have the tang of the salty air.

➤ **Sourness.** Sourness in food is related to high levels of acidity, which can be natural (lemons, limes) or added (salad dressings). In wine, sourness is directly related to acidity.

➤ **Bitterness.** Bitterness is a component you want to taste only sparingly in food or wine. Strong coffee and tea are pleasantly bitter. In wine, a bitter taste or finish can mean a winemaking flaw, like too much tannin. But the right amount of tannins can afford an interesting bitterness like fine espresso.

Keep in mind these few essentials when you are matching by contrast or similarity:

➤ Acidic foods are a good combination with acidic wines.

➤ Acidic wines go well with salty foods.

➤ Acidic foods can overpower low-acid wines.

➤ Salty food and high-alcohol wine taste bitter in combination.

➤ Salty food and sweet wine are a good match.

➤ Sweet wine and sweet food go well together (the preferable way is a sweeter wine and a less sweet dessert).

➤ Bitter food with bitter wine is just plain bitter.

Important Things to Know

You must pay attention to the possible similarities and contrasts in wines and foods. After a while you develop an instinct as to what wines go with what foods. Usually your decision is based on a flavor, texture, or component of the food. Singling out a key element is an important facet of choosing wines for a dish.

After you have your components in mind (and palate), pay attention to similarities and contrasts. Ultimately, the judgment is yours, but a few basic guidelines always help:

➤ When thinking of flavor similarity, use your taste memory to evoke each specific flavor. For example, Gewürztraminer is usually characterized as a spicy wine, but not in a "hot-spicy" way. Spicy foods, however, can be anything from curries to cardamon. Never generalize about flavors.

➤ Food and wine that evoke similar flavors probably will go well together—like almonds and Fino Sherry.

➤ Some foods have no real similarities (wines do not taste like fish, garlic, or pork). Adding condiments, fruits, cream sauce, tomato sauce, and so on to such foods can give you matching cues.

White Wine, White Meat and Fish? Red Wine, Red Meat?

Like all conventions, the *white with fish/red with meat* rule started out with the best intent. Meat is heavier than fish, so a meat dish needed a robust wine that could stand up to it. On the other hand, light, acidic white wine is similar to the lemon juice we squeeze on fish. Additionally, tannins can mingle unpleasantly with fish and leave a metallic finish. So this concept is not just blind tradition—it has a sense of logic. However, these rules go back to the last century, and our wines and eating habits have changed. A century ago, the only white that could hold its own with red meat was a big white Burgundy—an expensive addition to any meal. For most people, white wine meant light wine. Reds were robust, full-bodied, and rich. Rhônes were as much in fashion as Bordeaux, and Bordeaux was heavier than it is today. People also drank Port with dinner. Red Burgundy of last century was beefed up with the addition of heavier southern reds, a practice that is no longer legal.

Now that we have a selection of New World wines, we have relatively inexpensive alternatives to white Burgundy, such as Chardonnay from California or Australia. And the reds have gotten lighter. Connoisseurs have discovered a range of light, red wines like Chinon, Barbera, and Rioja. Just as many other rules of late have changed, so have the rules of wine matching.

Our diets have changed as well. Cooks are more experimental about the sauces on fish or chicken, some of which are quite amenable to red wines. In our health-conscious times, beef dishes have gotten lighter, too.

The rule of white wine with fish and red wine with meat is a good general rule—as far as general rules go. But as we all know, following rules all the time is no fun.

Consider the rule of serving white wine with white meat. Here is one variation that works well and is not too radical:

➤ White meat/white sauce/white wine

➤ White meat/brown sauce/red wine

Some people don't follow color-coding (or rules) at all. Selected red wines are excellent with fish, and some whites are great with meat. You might consider these pairings and their variants:

➤ Serve red meats rare (broil, grill, sauté) with red wine.

➤ Cook red meats rare but with unusual spices or methods (like deep-frying) and serve with white wine.

➤ Red meats cooked for a long time can work with either red or white wine.

White Before Red? Youth Before Age?

The traditional order of serving white wine before red is subject to change, too. Again, this theory goes back to the light/heavy distinction. The white wine is usually lighter; however, a light-bodied red precedes a full-bodied white. Rosés are generally the lightest of all, so if a rosé is on your table, open it first.

The rules for choosing your sequence of wines are as follows:

➤ Light wine before heavy wine

➤ White wine before red wine

➤ Dry wine before sweet wine

➤ Simple wine before complex wine

Of course, there are always exceptions to confuse us. If you are serving a light red wine and a rich, full-bodied white, be colorblind—use the "light before heavy" rule. If your cuisine calls for all whites or all reds, use the other three rules as your guide.

As your guests arrive, you'll want to offer them an apèritif. A white wine, sparkling wine, or Champagne, usually inexpensive to moderately priced, is the ideal ice-breaker. If the party is especially elegant, add a few extra dollars to your bottle. Just don't get carried away. The apèritif is the opening act, not the headliner.

The guests are sitting down at the table. Now is your chance to prove how skillfully you can marry wine with cuisine. Don't worry—choosing wines is not an esoteric practice like ancient breathing techniques. For full details on matching wine with food, see Chapter 25.

How Much Wine Do I Need?

This category has no hard and fast rules. The amount of wine depends on the type of party, the preferences of your guests, the number of wines served, the pace of service, and the number of hours you expect the party to last. These few simple guidelines make your decisions easier:

➤ For an informal party, figure on two-thirds of a bottle of wine per guest, which is usually the average by the party's end.

➤ For a formal dinner party, the simplest rule is a full bottle of wine per guest. If you think this amount will have your guests weaving their way home, don't worry. You are gearing your service to a leisurely pace, integrating wine consumption with several courses of food. Always have plenty of water on hand, and check to see that water glasses are refilled as readily as wine glasses.

Each guest should have a separate glass for each wine. This method enables your guests to savor the flavor of each wine and to drink at their own pace. Once again, the glasses don't need to be styled differently.

Dry wine before sweet wine is another rule. This one is harder to challenge, because sweet wines are often served with dessert. Occasionally you may find an iconoclast chef who serves a sweet Sauternes with an appetizer, followed by a medium-dry, full-bodied, low-acid wine. This option can work, but in general, dry before sweet is one rule your taste buds do not want you to break.

Another traditional rule is to serve young wines before old. This rule may be due more to the vintage mystique than sensory experience. The fact is that you may be able to appreciate the subtle nuances and complexity of an older wine early in the dinner, before your palate is subject to those fruity and tannic youngsters. On the other hand, if your vintage item is a Port or Madeira, nothing can follow those acts! The same principle works with a rich, intense, aged Bordeaux. Serve the younger, lighter wines first.

From the Depths of the Sea

Just like there are light and delicate wines and robust and full-bodied wines, so there are light and delicate fish and robust and full-bodied fish. There are quite a few viscous fish too, although *oily* is a more suitable word. Then there are shellfish: from lobster and shrimp to clams, oysters, and mussels. In each group, certain wine pairings work, and certain pairings don't work.

These guidelines can help you decide on a wine to serve with fish:

➤ If you serve red wine with fish, choose one that is young and fruity.

➤ Choose a high-acid wine, either white or red.

➤ Stay away from oaky whites and tannic reds.

➤ Simple fish dishes work with light whites and light reds.

➤ Use only very light reds with shellfish (better yet, follow the rules and serve white).

➤ Avoid red wines with fishy or oily fish.

Light and Delicate Fish

Fish like sole and flounder are delicate in taste and texture. These fish are definitely white wine fish. The only red that should come anywhere near these fish is a light Beaujolais. Rosés are usually light and may be enjoyable, especially for a summer meal.

Salmon and Other Kings of the Sea

It's no coincidence that the menu often says "Salmon Steak." Tuna steak is less common, but they both have similar qualities. Both are robust, oily, and substantial in body. These fish can easily overpower many whites. White Burgundy or full-bodied California Chardonnay are your best white matches. Fish in this category can stand up to red Burgundy or similar wines.

Bluefish, mackerel, anchovies, sardines, or herring—all oily fish—are best kept with acidic white wines like a French Muscadet or Chablis.

Lobster, Shrimp, and Crabs

These succulent shellfish deserve something special—and it's generally white. The succulent and delicate meal of a lobster calls for big white Burgundy or California Chardonnay. A fine Champagne works well too. Lobster Newburg goes well with a French Chablis, a white Burgundy, a white Rhône wine, or a California Chardonnay. Grilled prawns or scampi go well with a California or Australian Chardonnay or a big white Burgundy like a Meursault. Curried shrimp calls for a spicy wine like an Alsatian Gewürztraminer. Soft-shell crabs go nicely with a French white Bordeaux or a California Sauvignon Blanc. For crab cakes, try a California Sauvignon Blanc, Chenin Blanc, or Italian Pinot Grigio. For steamed crabs, like the Dungeness, try a German Riesling Kabinett from the Mosel, a Washington Dry White Riesling, or a California French Vouvray. The rich and delicate meat of the Alaskan king crab calls for a white wine with considerable finesse like a French Puligny-Montrachet from Burgundy or a Premier Cru Chablis.

Clams, Oysters, and Other Delights

Oysters and Chablis are a traditional combination. The flinty acidic flavor of a young simple Chablis perfectly offsets the briny mineral taste of the oyster. So does a light and crisp Muscadet, particularly one that is "sur lie."

Speaking of delights from the sea, what better match for caviar than Champagne? Of course the two go together—both make a sizable dent in your wallet. This is one match where snob logic makes sense. If you opt for the real caviar (which includes beluga, the most expensive, and also sevruga and osetra), go for the real Champagne. The perfect match for caviar is a crisp, bone-dry French Champagne. At the risk of being called a wine traitor, I consider another perfect match for caviar to be chilled vodka.

Chicken, Turkey, and Other Birds

White wine is frequently served with fowl. Most big reds overpower broiled or grilled dishes. However, this is another instance where the sauce or spices can help you decide, if you like to experiment. For roast or broiled chicken, you might try a California dry Chenin Blanc (white) or a simple (non-reserva) Spanish Rioja (red). For fried chicken, a red Italian Chianti or simple Spanish Rioja is a good choice. Coq au vin goes well with a

Cote de Rhône or a Gigondas, both red. For chicken pot pie, consider an Italian Orvieto (white) or a French Beaujolais-Villages (red). Chicken Kiev with its rich butter interior calls for a good French white Burgundy or California Chardonnay. Roast game hens go well with an Italian Chianti or a simple French Burgundy. What goes with roast turkey depends on the stuffing, but usually a California Chardonnay or French white Burgundy is a safe bet. For an apple or prune stuffing, you may want to consider a California dry Chenin Blanc, White Riesling, or a French Vouvray. A Sauvignon Blanc from California goes well with an oyster stuffing. For a chestnut or walnut stuffing, try an Alsatian Riesling, a California Pinot Noir, or a French Beaujolais-Villages. A California Zinfandel is a nice match for a sausage stuffing.

Pasta and Casseroles

For pasta dishes, going ethnic with wine is always tempting. Pasta is Italian, so the wine should be Italian too, right? Maybe. If you are trying to create an atmosphere where your guests can imagine they see Mount Vesuvius over the horizon, by all means bring out the Chianti or Orvieto. But like everything else, pasta dishes have changed. Today we eat cold pasta with cherries. We mix all shapes of pasta with our favorite vegetables, some of which are indigenous to California, not Calabria. Now you have your wine match—pasta with California veggies and a California wine. Next question, California red or white?

For pasta or any casserole, break it down into components. Does the dish contain beef, lamb, chicken, fish, or pork? What if the dish is vegetarian or encased in thick cheese? What type of sauce are you serving, and what types of herbs and spices will you add? For lasagne, you may want to try an Italian Chianti. For ravioli, try a white Italian Pinot Grigio or an Italian Dolcetto d'Alba or similar light red wine. For a meat sauce, try an Italian Montepulciano d'Abruzzo or an Italian Chianti. For alfredo sauce, an Italian Pinot Bianco or Vernaccia is worth a try. Italian Orvieto (white) or an Italian Chianti (red) goes well with carbonara sauce. For clam sauce, try an Italian Gavi or Soave. An Italian Verdicchio goes well with a pesto sauce.

Picnics and Other Diversions

Some people think of rosés as picnic wines. They're light and outdoorsy and perfect for summer refreshment. Paté goes well with a simple Bourgogne Blanc or Rouge or a sweet wine like a Sauternes. But then, you may have some bold, full-flavored dishes on your picnic table. If a barbecue grill is in the picture, the complexion can change entirely. Try a California Zinfandel or an Australian Shiraz.

Salads are great picnic foods. Traditional wisdom says never serve wine with a salad. The dressing will ruin any good wine. Contemporary logic says that's not always so. You can match wine and salad and enjoy both. Just observe the basics:

➤ Always serve an acidic wine.

➤ Stick with light-bodied wines.

➤ If the salad has something sweet, try a wine with a mild sweetness.

➤ Avoid complex or subtle wines.

Eggs are another food that the purists say never serve with wine. Of course observing this rule would ruin the Sunday brunches of many trendy restaurants, but I personally don't like Mimosas with omelets. I do advise these options:

➤ Low-alcohol wines, like a Riesling from Germany, go best with eggs.

➤ Use the ingredients with which you prepare the eggs (cheese, meats, spices) as your flavor guide.

➤ Beaujolais is a very good complement to egg dishes.

Then you have cheese—a great picnic food or a course favored by wine lovers as an essential part of a fine meal. Red wine and cheese is the maxim, and among the red wines, Burgundy is my favorite with cheese. Proceed with caution:

➤ Firm, dry cheeses go very well with red wine. So does chevre (goat cheese), although to my taste the tang of a chevre is not compatible with any wine; it makes the wine taste of the cheese.

➤ Smelly cheeses overwhelm red wine.

➤ Salty cheeses, particularly blue-veined types, can overpower red wine. These are best served with a Port or similar wine.

➤ Soft or double and triple cream cheese go well with a red wine like a Burgundy or a white wine like a Chardonnay or Pinot Grigio.

The Least You Need to Know

➤ The old maxim—*red with meat, white with fish*—is a good guide to simple wine/food matching.

➤ Some red wines *can* go with fish and white meats.

➤ Some white wines can go with white meats like veal or pork.

➤ Oysters go well with a Chablis or Muscadet.

➤ You can become your own wine/food matching expert by developing a taste memory.

Chapter 26

Wine and Your Health

In This Chapter

➤ Health benefits of having a glass of wine a day

➤ Wine and heart disease

➤ Consuming wine in moderation

➤ Considering the temperance warnings

Does a glass or two of wine a day keep the doctor away? You've probably heard of the "French Paradox" that says *yes*. It seems the French, despite having a diet drenched in fat and smoking pack upon pack of those foul-smelling cigarettes, suffer 40 percent fewer heart attacks than their American counterparts and live an average of two and a half years longer. To what is their good fortune attributed? Surely not their friendliness toward foreigners. Au contraire. Some say it's due to the traditional French practice of enjoying red wine at mealtime.

Not surprisingly, such claims have been quite controversial. Even potential supporters have demanded to see more evidence on the subject. But the evidence has been coming in—from France, Italy, Spain, and Greece (the "Mediterranean Diet"), and also from Scandinavia, the Netherlands, the U.K., and the home of the skeptics, the good old United States.

HEY!

Important Things to Know

According to the French National Institute of Health and Medical Research, a moderate intake of alcohol cuts the risk of coronary heart disease by as much as 50 percent. This study has another angle. In addition to the French having far fewer deaths from heart attacks, their death rate from atherosclerotic cardiovascular disease—hardening of the arteries—is roughly half that of the U.S. What it the key to this amazing phenomenon? Many experts believe it's the moderate consumption of alcohol, specifically red wine.

A Glass of Wine a Day Keeps the Doctor Away

As you are probably aware, nothing is unusual about our culture regarding alcohol as a drug. The good news is that alcohol has recently been classified as a friendly drug for the first time. Indeed, the latest version of the Federal government's Dietary Guidelines for Americans gives thumbs up to light-to-moderate consumption. We are constantly bombarded with messages about the dangers of alcohol abuse (and yes, alcohol can be abused). But it can also be handled responsibly. Cultural messages seem to imply that we are incapable of moderation. Slogans like "Just Say No," the youth-oriented message that lumps alcohol in with hard drugs, makes it seem like we have only one purpose for drinking alcohol: To get drunk. Unfortunately, the slogan works well as a self-fulfilling prophecy and disregards the fact that most wine drinkers do not drink wine to get drunk.

In Mediterranean countries like France, Italy, Greece, and Spain, wine is an integral part of the family meal. Children who grow up consuming wine with their parents can hardly regard it as a "forbidden fruit." What forbidden thrill is there in sipping a drink poured for you by your mother? By watching their parents and other adults consume a glass or two of wine as part of an enjoyable social experience, young people are provided with a model for responsible drinking.

By the same token, youth are also provided with a model for responsible eating. Mediterranean dining is far more leisurely than our own. Combined with vino, the relaxed atmosphere of the Mediterranean dinner table has a dual effect:

➤ It acts as a stress reducer, which not only makes you feel good but has a positive effect on the cardiovascular system. Stress can raise your blood pressure by constricting your arteries. It can also make blood more likely to clot and raise levels of the bad LDL cholesterol. Few people are unaware that alcohol soothes the perception of feeling stressed. Alcohol also acts as a vasodilator, enhancing blood flow by relaxing the muscle tissue of arteries. Alcohol decreases the potential for blood clotting in coronary arteries and increases the level of HDL cholesterol (the good cholesterol) in the blood. Good food and wine, consumed slowly and leisurely and in the presence of good company, are a powerful (and very pleasant) stress-reducing trio. You don't have to consult your doctor for that. Just consult your own experience.

➤ The longer length of the meal may affect the absorption and metabolism of fats (remember, the French diet is no lower in fats than our own), the effects of fat on blood clotting, and insulin levels, along with the absorption of alcohol. As most of us know, consuming alcohol with a meal affects the absorption of the alcohol itself. Provided that you enjoy the company, a leisurely meal is a pleasant experience in itself. Add a bottle of your favorite wine, and you and your bloodstream will both be happier.

Important Things to Know

HEY!

Drinking wine with a meal may provide you with alcohol at just the right time—when the wine's potentially beneficial properties are needed to counteract the effect of the fats you take in. Drinking with dinner ensures that the protective effects of alcohol are strongest in the evening, when fatty foods are making their way through your bloodstream. This protective effect lingers into the next morning—the time when most heart attacks take place.

Wine and Heart Disease

Certain positive effects on the heart and cardiovascular system are associated with all alcoholic consumption, wine or otherwise. Moderate drinking can help you because it tends to

➤ Decrease the level of bad cholesterol and raise the level of good cholesterol in the blood.

➤ Decrease the tendency of blood to clot in arteries and increase the ability to dissolve clots after they have formed.

➤ Decrease the tendency of arteries to constrict during stress.

➤ Lower blood pressure.

➤ Increase coronary artery diameter and blood flow.

Wine Makes You Live Longer

I've already discussed the complexity, the multidimensionality, the breed, the bouquet, and all those other factors that separate wine from other beverages. Now wine can take credit for something else. Some of the components in wine are part of a group called *phenols*, which have antioxidant properties. Phenolic compounds exist in grape skins and seeds, and they contribute to wine's subtle nuances of flavor, aroma, texture, and color.

These nifty phenolic compounds are far more prevalent in wine than in fruits or fruit juices. For example, red wines have about five times higher phenolic levels than fresh grapes. The compounds tend to concentrate in the plant seeds, skins, and stems—parts that are discarded in the making of most juices. In winemaking, however, these parts are fermented along with the juice, especially in the red winemaking process. This process helps to explain why red wine tends to be more beneficial than white. Don't despair if you prefer white wine. Both red and white wine drinkers reap the cardiovascular benefits of the vinified grape.

One recent study identified specific phenolic compounds as the ingredients that inhibit the oxidation of the harmful LDL cholesterol. One of the antioxidants, quercetin, is also believed to be anti-carcinogenic. Also found in onions and garlic, quercetin has the ability to inhibit the action of the cancer gene. Quercetin is initially inactive in food, but it is stimulated into cancer-fighting action by fermentation or by bacteria in the intestinal tract. Studies have shown that high consumption of quercetin-containing foods lowers the incidence of digestive (stomach, intestinal) and other cancers.

Unfortunately, few health officials seem to support this fact. Instead, they have been quick to indict alcohol, if not as the major player, then at least as a conspirator, in the risk of various cancers. The government fails to inform us, however, that the risk of cancer is associated with heavy drinking. In fact, alcohol is responsible for barely 3 percent of all cancers in the United States, and in many cases other factors are involved. Even where alcohol in the form of beer and spirits is implicated, wine still appears to come out the good guy. In short, wine has a protective effect on health and longevity, in addition to flavor and fragrance, balance and breed, and just plain old-fashioned enjoyment.

What Is Moderate Consumption?

Moderate consumption is usually defined as 25 grams of alcohol per day; the vinous equivalent is two to two and a half 4-ounce glasses of wine per day. Some sources accept a higher level as moderate. A ballpark figure might be 1.5 to 3.5 glasses a day. Fifty grams (five glasses) on a daily basis, however, is generally considered heavy drinking. Thus, two regular servings of wine a day is OK for most people.

The rate of metabolism for alcohol varies from one person to another and affects the daily level of consumption that's moderate for you. Body weight is an important factor. But before you start thinking that maybe those extra pounds you were planning to shed now have a useful purpose, forget it! Body composition is also a factor. Lean body weight is what assists in the metabolism of alcohol. Body fluids exist in inverse proportion to body fat (the more lean body mass you have, the higher percentage of fluids; the more fat you have, the less fluid). Alcohol seeks out bodily fluids. Therefore, the concentration of alcohol will be weaker (more diluted) in a person with a higher fluid content.

In general, women have lower body weight than men, and a higher percentage of body fat. Of course, notable exceptions exist. If you're not sure of your body composition or weight, you can get on a scale, take a pinch test, or look in the mirror. But the best guideline for anyone is to recognize that the ability to metabolize alcohol varies a great deal among individuals. My advice is "know thyself." The lower your lean body mass, the lower your consumption should be. Table 27.1 provides an indication of how long it takes people of varying weights (with average lean body mass) to metabolize varying quantities of alcohol consumed.

Table 27.1 How long your body takes to metabolize alcohol (the minimum recommended amount of time to wait between drinking and driving)

Body Wt. (lbs.)	1 drink	2 drinks	3 drinks	4 drinks	5 drinks	6 drinks
100-119	0 hours	3 hours	3 hours	6 hours	13 hours	16 hours
120-139	0 hours	2 hours	2 hours	5 hours	10 hours	12 hours
140-159	0 hours	2 hours	2 hours	4 hours	8 hours	10 hours
160-179	0 hours	1 hour	1 hour	3 hours	7 hours	9 hours
180-199	0 hours	0 hours	0 hours	2 hours	6 hours	7 hours
200-219	0 hours	0 hours	0 hours	2 hours	5 hours	6 hours
Over 220	0 hours	0 hours	0 hours	1 hour	4 hours	6 hours

Potential Health Benefits of Moderate Consumption

The evidence keeps coming in—and it all tends to reflect favorably on wine drinking. Studies consistently show that regular moderate alcohol consumption reduces the risk of heart disease in some people by 25 to 45 percent, and overall mortality by 10 percent. What's more, the risks are lowered even more for wine drinkers.

Wine Wisdom
According to a survey of hospitals in the top 65 U.S. metropolitan areas, 52 percent offer a wine service to patients whose condition permits wine consumption.

If you're worried about liver cirrhosis, the scourge of alcoholics, remember that the people who experience cirrhosis are heavy drinkers. Regions of France with the highest wine consumption have the lowest rates of cirrhosis, lower than figures from the U.S.

If this fact isn't enough, wine drinkers have even been found to age more gracefully than nondrinkers. You know the old joke about how giving up alcohol doesn't really make you live longer—it just feels that way. Well, it's not a joke anymore. Keep up the wine drinking and you may live longer and be happier.

Heeding the Cautions

With all the warnings bandied about by anti-alcohol forces, it is difficult to tell which requires more caution: listening to the voices of temperance or imbibing the wine itself. Essentially, warnings about the consumption of alcohol refer primarily to heavy consumption—of wine or any other alcoholic beverage. One notable example is the warning on the label for pregnant women. Fetal Alcohol Syndrome (FAS) is an unfortunate and avoidable condition that can result in profound mental and growth retardation resulting from a pregnant mother's alcohol consumption. However, figures from the Center for Disease Control (CDC) report only 135 FAS cases each year. Women who give birth to FAS babies are heavy binge drinkers who abuse alcohol throughout the pregnancy. Low socioeconomic status, poor prenatal care, cigarette smoking, and poor overall health are all significant factors; even among women who have all of these risk factors, the incidence of FAS is still markedly low.

Does this situation really merit such drastic warnings and scare tactics? Many women say no, and so do a growing number of physicians. Let's go back to those Mediterraneans for a moment. French and Italian women face no such warnings on wine bottles and happily continue drinking wine at mealtime to no ill effect. The main thing in consuming wine if you are pregnant—and for all women and men in any situation—is to make an informed decision.

The fact is, despite all those warnings, we are not the irresponsible revelers the temperance voices suggest. In reality, American wine drinkers are a moderate lot. Statistics reveal that the average wine drinker consumes three to five glasses of wine per week, and usually no more than 1.5 glasses on any given occasion. Additionally, we tend to have healthy lifestyles. Very few wine drinkers smoke (cigarette smoke ruins the taste and aroma of wine). And many wine drinkers exercise regularly and consume a produce-rich diet— habits we have in common with the Mediterraneans.

Wine drinkers may like to jog or hike, but we also drive cars. A word of caution is necessary on that topic. Wine has been implicated in only two percent of all arrests for drunken driving, but even that figure is too high. Regardless of what beverage you are enjoying, accidents caused by drunk driving are tragic and avoidable. Legal intoxication is usually set at 0.08 to 0.10 blood alcohol level, but coordination and judgment are impaired well before that. Use your judgment before it is affected.

Wine affords many pleasures, but it does require some caution. I advise you to consider the following "Thou Shalt Nots," the Wine Drinker's Commandments:

➤ Do not drive anything immediately after drinking: cars, bicycles, motorcycles, boats, airplanes, or anything else that moves. In England, which has a very tough drunk driving law, some people have resorted to riding horses.

➤ Do not swim, surf, or water-ski when consuming.

➤ When drinking, do not participate in athletic activities requiring balance and perception on land or water; this includes rollerblading, skateboarding, skiing, gymnastics, and many others.

➤ Do not use firearms or other weapons if you've been drinking.

➤ Do not use power tools, particularly power saws, mowers, drills, or the like, after drinking.

➤ Do not drink wine with antihistamines or similar medication; drowsiness frequently results. For any other over-the-counter medicines, check the label for guidelines.

➤ Do not drink wine with prescription medicine without first consulting your health care provider or pharmacist.

➤ Do not drink wine when under a physician's care except with explicit permission.

➤ Last but not least, being a responsible party host means arranging a ride or ordering a cab for any of your guests who have had too much to drink.

The Least You Need to Know

➤ A glass or two of wine a day can be good for your health.

➤ Consumption of red wine may improve your good cholesterol level.

➤ Do not drive, swim, use power tools, or take antihistamines when you drink alcoholic beverages.

➤ Be a good party host by arranging a ride for any of your guests who have had too much to drink.

Recommended Wines

The following lists are my recommendations of wines that are nationally distributed and represent consistent quality and good value. The wine region follows the wine name in parentheses. Prices are for regular 750ml bottles unless indicated otherwise. Prices are full markup retail prices—you should find these wines at lower prices at discount stores.

Recommended Red Wines Under $8

Belle Jour (France) $7.99 (1.5L)

Bodegas Montecello (Spain—Rioja) $6.50

Casal Thaulero Montepulciano D'Abruzzo (Italy) $7.99 (1.5L)

Castello di Gabbiano Chianti Classico (Italy) $7.99

Château Gourgazaud (France—Minervois) $7.50

Château Pitray 1994 (France—Bordeaux) $7.99

Concha y Toro Cabernet Sauvignon/Merlot (Chile) $7.99 (1.5L)

Dessilani Spanna (Italy—Piedmonte) $7.99

Fetzer Valley Oaks Cabernet Sauvignon (California) $7.50

La Vieille Ferme (France—Côtes Ventoux) $7.50

Los Vascos Cabernet Sauvignon (Chile) $6.99

Monte Antico (Italy—Tuscany) $7.99

Napa Ridge Winery Cabernet Sauvignon (California) $7.99

Rosemont Estate Shiraz/Cabernet Sauvignon (Australia) $6.99

Serradayres (Portugal) $5.99

Vendange Cabernet Sauvignon (California) $7.99 (1.5L)

Recommended White Wines Under $8

Alianca Vinho Verde (Portugal) $4.99

Boucheron Blanc de Blanc (France) $6.99 (1.5L)

Casa Lapostolle Sauvignon Blanc (Chile) $6.50

Château Bonnet Blanc (France—Bordeaux) $6.99

Château du Cleray Muscadet (France) $7.99

Concha y Toro Sauvignon/ Semillon (Chile) $6.99 (1.5L)

Domaine de Pouy (France) $5.99

Fetzer Sundial Chardonnay (California) $6.99

Hogue Fumé Blanc (Washington State) $7.99

Joseph Brigl Pinot Grigio (Italy) $6.99

La Vieille Ferme Blanc (France) $6.99

Louis Latour Chardonnay (France—Ardeche) $6.99

Moreau Blanc (France) $7.49 (1.5L)

Rosemont Estate Semillon/ Chardonnay (Australia) $7

Vendange Chardonnay (California) $7.99 (1.5L)

Recommended Red Wines $8-$15

Beringer Knights Valley Cabernet Sauvignon 1992 (California) $14.99

Ceretto Dolcetto D'Alba 1994 (Italy—Piedmont) $13.99

Château Meyney 1993 (France—St. Estèphe) $14.99

Domaine Sorin 1994 (France—Côtes-de-Provence) $10.99

Filliatreau "Grand Vignolle" Saumur-Champigny 1995 (France—Loire) $13.99

George Duboeuf Beaujolais Villages (current vintage) (France—Beaujolais) $8

Guigal Gigondas 1993 (France) $14.99

La Rioja Alta Vina Alberdi Reserva 1991 (Spain—Rioja) $12.99

Louis Latour Côte-de-Beaune-Villages 1993 (France—Burgundy) $12.99

Markham Merlot 1994 (California) $14.99

Melini Borghi D'Elsa Chianti (Italy) $10.99 (1.5L)

Mouton Cadet Rouge (France—Bordeaux) $14.99 (1.5L)

Penfold's Bin 389 Cabernet Sauvignon/Shiraz 1993 (Australia) $14.99

Robert Mondavi "Woodbridge" Cabernet Sauvignon (California) $12.99 (1.5L)

The Monterey Vineyard Classic Cabernet Sauvignon (California) 10.99 (1.5L)

Villa Antinori Chianti Classico Riserva 1993 (Italy) $13.99

Recommended White Wines $8-$15

Beringer Chardonnay Napa Valley 1994 (California) $11.99

Château Cruzeau Blanc 1994 (France—Bordeaux/Graves) $10.99

Chartran-Trebuchet Rully "La Chaume" 1995 (France) $14.99

Domaine Aubuisiers Vouvray Sec "Le Marigny" 1995 (France) $11.99

Fernand Girard Sancerre "La Garenne" 1995 (France) $12.99

Livio Felluga Pinot Grigio 1995 (Italy) $12.99

Paul Pernot Bourgogne Blanc 1994 (France—Burgundy) $13.99

Rosemont Chardonnay "Show Reserve" 1994 (Australia) $13.99

Trimbach Riesling 1993 (France—Alsace) $13.99

Turning Leaf Sonoma Reserve Zinfandel (California) $14

Von Simmern Eltviller Sonnenberg Kabinett (Germany) $13.99

France—Recommended Wine Producers (Châteaux) of Bordeaux, Red Wines

In the following section, the Château name is followed by the district in parentheses.

Ausone (St.-Emilion)

Batailley (Pauillac)

Beauséjour-Duffau (St.-Emilion)

Bon Pasteur (Pomerol)

Branaire-Ducru (St.-Julien)

Calon-Ségur (St.-Estèphe)

Canon (St. Emilion)

Canon-La-Gaffelière (St.-Emilion)

Certan de May (Pomerol)

Chasse-Spleen (Moulis)

Margaux (Margaux)

Clerc-Milon (Pauillac)

Clinet (Pomerol)

Cos d'Estournel (St.-Estèphe)

Cos Labory (St.-Estèphe)

Daugay (St.-Emilion)

de Fieuzal (Graves)

Domaine de Chevalier (Graves)

Ducru-Beaucaillou (St.-Julien)

Duhart-Milon-Rothschild (Pauillac)

d'Angludet (Margaux)

Ferrand-Lartique (St.-Emilion)

Figeac (St.-Emilion)

Forcas-Hosten (Listrac)

Gazin (Pomerol)

Giscours (Margaux)

Gloria (St.-Julien)

Grand-Mayne (St.-Emilion)

Grand-Puy-Ducasse (Pauillac)

Grand-Puy-Lacoste (Pauillac)

Gruad-Larose (St.-Julien)

Haut-Bages-Libéral (Pauillac)

Haut-Bailly (Graves)

Haut-Batailley (Pauillac)

Haut-Brion (Graves)

Haut-Marbuzet (St.-Estèphe)

La Conseillante (Pomerol)

La Fleur de Gay (Pomerol)

La Mission-Haut-Brion (Graves)

La Dominique (St.-Emilion)

La Fleur Pétrus (Pomerol)

La Lagune (Ludon)

La Louvière (Graves)

Lafite-Rothschild (Pauillac)

Lafleur (Pomerol)

Lafon-Rochet (St.-Estèphe)

Lagrange (St.-Julien)

Langoa-Barton (St.-Julien)

Latour (Pauillac)

Latour à Pomerol (Pomerol)

Le Pin (Pomerol)

Le Tertre-Roteboeuf (St.-Emilion)

Les-Ormes-de-Pez (St.-Estèphe)

Léoville-Las-Cases (St.-Julien)

Léoville-Barton (St.-Julien)

Léoville-Poyferré (St.-Julien)

Lynch-Bages (Pauillac)

L'Angélus (St.-Emilion)

L'Arrosée (St.-Emilion)

L'Eglise-Clinet (Pomerol)

L'Evangile (Pomerol)

Montrose (St.-Estèphe)

Moulin-Pey-Labrie (Canon-Fronsac)

Mouton-Rothschild (Pauillac)

Palmer (Margaux)

Pape-Clément (Graves)

Pavie-Macquin (St.-Emilion)

Petit-Village (Pomerol)

Pétrus (Pomerol)

Phélan-Ségur (St.-Estèphe)

Pichon-Longueville Baron (Pauillac)

Pichon-Longueville-Comtesse de Laland (Pauillac)

Pontet-Canet (Pauillac)

Prieuré-Lichine (Margaux)

Rausan-Séglas (Margaux)

Smith-Haut-Lafite (Graves)

Talbot (St.-Julien)

Troplong-Mondot (St.-Emilion)

Trotanoy (Pomerol)

Valandraud (St.-Emilion)

Vieux Château Certan (Pomerol)

France—Recommended Wine Producers (Châteaux) of Bordeaux, White Wines

In the following section, the Château name is followed by the district in parentheses.

Bouscaut (Graves)

Carbonnieux (Graves)

Clos Floridène (Graves)

Couhins-Lurton (Graves)

de Fieuzal (Graves)

de Malle (Graves)

Doisy-Daëne (Bordeaux)

Domaine de Chevalier (Graves)

Haut-Brion Blanc (Graves)

La Louvière (Graves)

La Tour-Martillac (Graves)

Laville-Haut-Brion (Graves)

Loudenne (Bordeaux)

Pape-Clément (Graves)

Pavillon Blanc de Château Margaux (Bordeaux)

R de Rieussec (Graves)

Respide (Graves)

Smith-Haut-Lafitte (Graves)

France—Recommended Wine Producers (Châteaux) of Bordeaux—Sauternes/Barsac

In the following section, the Château name is followed by the district in parentheses.

Caillou (Barsac)

Climens (Barsac)

Clos Haut-Peyraguey (Sauternes)

Coutet (Barsac)

Doisy-Daëne (Barsac)

Doisy-Dubroca (Barsac)

de Fargues (Sauternes)

Filhot (Sauternes)

Gilette (Sauternes)

Guiraud (Sauternes)

La Tour Blanche (Sauternes)

Lafaurie-Peyraguey (Sauternes)

Rabaud-Promis (Sauternes)

Raymond-Lafon (Sauternes)

Rayne-Vigneau (Sauternes)

Rieussec (Sauternes)

Sigalas Rabaud (Sauternes)

Suduiraut (Sauternes)

France—Recommended Wine Producers of Burgundy, Red Wines

Armand Rousseau

Barthod-Noellat

Bernard Dugat

Bertrand Ambroise

Bouchard Père et Fils

Bouré Père et Fils

Bourée-Noellat

Chanson Père et Fils

Claude et Maurice Dugat

Comte Lafon

Comte de Vougüé

Daniel Chopin-Groffier

Daniel Rion

de l'Arlot

Domaine de la Romané-Conti

Dujac

Faiveley

George et Chistophe Roumier

Haegelen-Jayer

Henri Jayer

Hospices de Beaune

Hubert Lignier

J. F. Coche-Dury

Jacques Prieur

Jean Chauvenet

Jean Grivot

Jean Gros

Jean et J. L. Trapet

Joseph Drouhin

Labouré-Roi

Leroy

Louis Jadot

Louis Latour

Marquis d'Angerville

Michel Lafarge

Michel Prunier

Mongeard-Mugneret

Philippe Leclerc

Pierre Gelin

Ponsot

Ramonet

Remoissenet Père et Fils

René Engel

René Leclerc

Robert Arnoux

Robert Jayer-Gilles

France—Recommended Wine Producers of Burgundy, White Wines

Albert Grivault

Antonin Rodet

Ballot-Millot et Fils

Bernard Morey

Bouchard Père et Fils

Château de Meursault

Château de Puligny-Montrachet

Colin-Déléger

Comte Lafon

Domaine de la Romanée-Conti

Domaine de l'Arlot

Domaine Leflaive

Etienne Sauzet

Faiveley

Francois et Jean-Marie Raveneau

Georges Déléger

J. F. Coche-Dury

J. Moreau et Fils

Jacques Prieur

Jean Dauvissat

Jean-Marc Boillot

Jean-Philippe Fichet

Joseph Drouhin

Leroy

Louis Jadot

Louis Latour

Marc Colin

Marc Morey

Michel Niellon

Michelot-Buisson

Patrick Javillier

Philippe Testut

Pierre Boillot

Ramonet

Remoissenet Pere et Fils

René et Vincent Dauvissat

Thierry Matrot

Verget

France—The Wines of Bordeaux, the 1855 Classification of Great Growths of the Médoc (Grand Cru Classé)

First Growths (Premiers Crus)

Château Lafite-Rothschild (Pauillac)

Château Latour (Pauillac)

Château Margaux (Margaux)

Château Mouton-Rothschild (Pauillac)

Château Haut-Brion* (Pessac, Graves)

* This wine, although a Graves, is classified as one of the five First Growths of the Médoc in recognition of outstanding quality.

Second Growths (Deuxiemes Crus)

Château Rausan-Ségla (Margaux)

Château Rauzan-Gassies (Margaux)

Château Léoville-Las Cases (St.-Julien)

Château Léoville-Poyferré (St.-Julien)

Château Léoville-Barton (St.-Julien)

Château Durfort-Vivens (Cantenac-Margaux)

Château Lascombes (Margaux)

Château Gruaud-Larose (St.-Julien)

Château Brane-Cantenac (Cantenac-Margaux)

Château Pichon-Longueville-Baron (Pauillac)

Château Pichon-Lalande (Pauillac)

Château Ducru-Beaucaillou (St.-Julien)

Château Cos d'Estournel (St.-Estèphe)

Château Montrose (St.-Estèphe)

Third Growths (Troisiemes Crus)

Château Giscours (Labarde-Margaux)

Château Kirwan (Cantenac-Margaux)

Château d'Issan (Cantenac-Margaux)

Château Lagrange (St.-Julien)

Château Langoa-Barton (St.-Julien)

Château Malescot-St.-Exupéry (Margaux)

Château Cantenac-Brown (Cantenac-Margaux)

Château Palmer (Cantenac-Margaux)

Château La Lagune (Ludon)

Château Desmirail (Margaux)

Château Calon-Ségur (St.-Estèphe)

Château Ferrière (Margaux)

Château Marquis d'Alesme-Becker (Margaux)

Château Boyd-Cantenac (Cantenac-Margaux)

Fourth Growths (Quatriemes Crus)

Château St.-Pierre (St.-Julien)

Château Branaire (St.-Julien)

Château Talbot (St.-Julien)

Château Duhart-Milon-Rothschild (Pauillac)

Château Pouget (Cantenac-Margaux)

Château La Tour-Carnet (St.-Laurent)

Château Lafon-Rochet (St.-Estèphe)

Château Beychevelle (St.-Julien)

Château Prieuré-Lichine (Cantenac-Margaux)

Château Marquis-de-Terme (Margaux)

Fifth Growths (Cinquiemes Crus)

Château Pontet-Canet (Pauillac)

Château Batailley (Pauillac)

Château Grand-Puy-Lacoste (Pauillac)

Château Grand-Puy-Ducasse (Pauillac)

Château Haut-Batailley (Pauillac)

Château Lynch-Bages (Pauillac)

Château Lynch-Moussas (Pauillac)

Château Dauzac-Lynch (Labarde-Margaux)

Château Mouton-Baronne Pauline (Pauillac) (formerly known as Mouton-Baron Philippe)

Château du Tertre (Arsac-Margaux)

Château Haut-Bages-Libéral (Pauillac)

Château Pédesclaux (Pauillac)

Château Belgrave (St.-Laurent)

Château Camensac (St.-Laurent)

Château Cos Labory (St.-Estèphe)

Château Clerc-Milon-Rothschild (Pauillac)

Château Croizet-Bages (Pauillac)

Château Cantemerle (Macau)

Italy—Recommended Wine Producers of Piedmont

Aldo Conterno

Aldo & Ricardo Seghesio

Alfiero Boffa

Alfredo Prunotto

Angelo Gaja

Antoniolo

Azelia

Bartolomeo

Batasiolo

Bersano

Bruno Giacosa

Bruno Ceretto

Ceretto

Cerutti

Cigliuti

Clerico

Enrico Scavino

Fontanafredda

Francesco Rinaldi

G.D. Vajra

Giacomo Conterno

Guiseppe Mascarello

Luciano Sandrone

Manzone

Marcarini

Marchese di Gresy

Moccagatta

Paolo Conterno

Pio Cesare

Poderi Rocche Manzoni Valentino

Produttori di Barbaresco

Renato Corino

Renato Ratti

Roberto Voerzio

Vietti

Italy—Recommended Wine Producers of Tuscany

Altesino

Ambra

Azienda Agricola La Torre

Badia a Coltibuono

Barbi

Biondi-Santi

Caparzo

Case Basse

Castello dei Rampolla Sammarco

Castello di Ama

Castello di Gabbiano

Castello di Querceto

Castell'In Villa

Ciacci Piccolomini d'Aragona

Costanti

Dei

Felsina Berardenga

Fontodi

Frescobaldi

Il Poggione

Isole e Olena Collezione de Marchi l'Ermo

L. Antinori

Lisini

Melini

Monsanto

Monte Vertine

Nozzole

Ornellaia

P. Antinori

Pertimali

Podere Il Palazzino

Poggio Antico

Ruffino

San Felice

San Giusto a Rententano

Soldera

Villa Banfi

Villa Cafaggio

Germany—Recommended Wine Producers

Alfred Merkelbach (Mosel)

August Eser (Rheingau)

Christian Karp-Schreiber (Mosel)

Dr. Burklin-Wolf (Pfalz)

Dr. Loosen-St.-Johannishof (Mosel)

Dr. Thanisch (Mosel)

E. Jakoby-Mathy (Mosel)

Egon Müller (Saar)

F. W. Gymnasium (Mosel)

Freiherr von Heddesdorf (Mosel)

Freiherr zu Knyphausen (Rheingau)

Fritz Haag (Mosel)

H. & R. Lingenfelder (Rheinpfalz)

Heribert Kerpen (Mosel)

Immich-Batterieberg (Mosel)

J. F. Kimich (Rheinpfalz)

J. J. Christoffel (Mosel)

J. J. Prüm (Mosel)

Josef Deinhart (Mosel)

Klaus Neckerauer (Rheinpfalz)

Koehler-Ruprecht (Rheingau)

Konigin Victoria Berg-Deinhard (Rheingau)

Kurt Darting (Rheinpfalz)

Mönchhof (Mosel)

Schloss Schönborn (Rheingau)

Selbach-Oster (Mosel)

von Brentano (Rheingau)

von Kesselstatt (Mosel)

von Simmern (Rheingau)

Weingut Karlsmuhle (Mosel)

Willi Schaefer (Mosel)

Spain—Recommended Table Wine Producers

CVNE

Bodegas Muga

Domecq

Frederico Paternina

Jean Léon

La Rioja Alta

Marqués de Caceres

Marqués de Grinon

Marqués de Murrieta

Marqués de Riscal

Miguel Torres

Montecillo

Pesquera

René Barbier

Rioja Santiago

Vega Sicilia

Spain—Recommended Sherry Producers

Emilio Lustau

Gonzalez Byass

Osborne

Pedro Domecq

Sandeman

Vinicola Hidalgo

Portugal—Recommended Porto Producers

Churchill

Cockburn

Croft

Delaforce

Dow

Ferreria

Fonseca

Graham's

Niepoort

Offley

Quinta do Noval

Ramos-Pinto

Sandeman

Smith-Woodhouse

Taylor Fladgate

Warre

Portugal—Recommended Table Wine Producers

Carvalho, Ribeiro, Ferreira

Casal de Valle Pradinhos

Caves do Barrocas

Caves Dom Teodosio

Caves San João

Caves Velhas

Condo do Santar

Ferreira

J. M. Da Fonseca

João Pires

Luis Pato

Porta dos Cavalheiros

Quinta do Carmo

Quinta do Cotto

Quinta da Cismeira

Quinta do Confradeiro

Quinta da Lagoalva de Cima

Quinta de la Rosa

Sogrape

Tuella

Vasconcellos

Australia—Recommended Australian Wine Producers

Berry Estates

Browen Estate

Brown Brothers

Château Tahbilk

Hungerford

Lindemans

Mildara

Orlando

Penfolds

Peter Lehmann

Rosemount

Rothbury Estate

Seppelt

St. Hurbert

Taltarni

Tyrells

Wolf Blass

Wyndham Estates

Wynns

Yarra Yering

California, Oregon, and Washington State—Recommended Cabernet Sauvignon Producers

Arrowood

Beaulieu

Benziger

Beringer

Burgess

Cain Cellars

Cakebread

Caymus

Château Montelena

Château St. Jean

Château Souverain

Château Potelle

Clos du Val

Cuvaison

Dalla Valle

Dehlinger

Dry Creek

Duckhorn

Far Neinte

Farrari-Carano

Fetzer

Flora Springs

Franciscan

Gallo—Sonoma

Geyser Peak

Grace Family Vineyard

Heitz

Hess Collection

Joseph Phelps

Justin

Kendall-Jackson

Kenwood

Mount Veeder

Newton

Opus One

Ridge

Robert Mondavi

Robert Pecota

S. Anderson

Shafer

Silverado

Simi

Spring Mountain

Stag's Leap Vintners

Stag's Leap Wine Cellars

Sterling

Vichon

ZD

325

California, Oregon, and Washington State—Recommended Merlot Producers

Arrowood

Benziger

Beringer

Cain Cellars

Château St. Jean

Château Souverain

Cuvaison

Duckhorn

Ferrari-Carano

Frog's Leap

Gary Farrel

Joseph Phelps

Kenwood

Matanzas Creek

Robert Keenan

Robert Mondavi

Robert Pecota

Sterling

Whitehall Lane

California, Oregon, and Washington State—Recommended Pinot Noir Producers

Acacia

Adelsheim

Au Bon Climat

Beaulieu

Benziger

Bouchaine

Calera

Carneros Creek

Caymus

Château Souverain

Conn Valley

David Bruce

Dehlinger

Domaine Drouhin

Etude

Gary Farrell

Kendall-Jackson

Meridian

Robert Mondavi

Robert Sinskey

Robert Stemmler

Saintsbury

Sanford

Santa Cruz Mountain

Wild Horse

Williams-Selyem

ZD

California, Oregon, and Washington State—Recommended Zinfandel Producers

Benziger

Beringer

Caymus

Château Souverain

Château Montelena

Château Potelle

De Loach

Dry Creek

Ferrari-Carano

Fetzer

Franciscan

Frick

Gallo—Sonoma

Grgich Hills

Guenoc

Gundlach-Bundschu

Hop Kiln

Kenwood

Lytton Springs

Quivira

Rabbit Ridge

Ravenswood

Ridge

Robert Mondavi

Rosenblum

Seghesio Winery

Sutter Home

Topolos

Wild Horse

California, Oregon, and Washington State—Recommended Chardonnay Producers

Acacia

Arrowood

Au Bon Climat

Bargetto

Benziger

Beringer

Bouchaine

Burgess Cellars

Cakebread

Calera

Carmenet

Carneros Creek

Chalone

Chappellet

Château Montelena

Château St. Jean

Château Ste. Michelle

Château Souverain

Château Woltner

Clos du Bois

Cronin

Cuvaison

De Loach

Dehlinger

Ferrari-Carano

Flora Springs

Franciscan

Freemark Abby

Gabrielli

Gallo—Sonoma

Girard

Gloria Ferrer

Grgich Hills

Hanzell

Hess Collection

Iron Horse

J. Lohr

Joseph Phelps

Kendall-Jackson

Kenwood

Matanzas Creek

Meridian

Mirassou

Murphy-Goode

Napa Ridge

Newton

Pahlmeyer

Qupé

Rabbit Ridge

Robert Mondavi

Robert Sinskey

Rombauer

S. Anderson

Saintsbury

Sanford

Simi

Sonoma Cutrer

Sonoma-Loeb

Stag's Leap Wine Cellars

Vichon

Williams-Selyem

ZD

California, Oregon, and Washington State—Recommended Sauvignon Blanc Producers

Araujo Estate

Benziger

Beringer

Cain

Cakebread

Caymus

Chalk Hill

Château Potelle

Château St. Jean

De Loach

Dry Creek

Duckhorn

Ferrari-Carano

Fetzer

Flora Springs

Geyser Peak

Grgich Hills

Guenoc Winery

Iron Horse

Kendall-Jackson

Kenwood

Matanzas Creek

Murphy-Goode

Napa Ridge

Navarro

Preston

Quivira

Robert Mondavi

Robert Pepi

Seghesio

Simi

Spottswoode

Stag's Leap Wine Cellars

Vichon

California, Oregon, and Washington State—Recommended Sparkling Wine Producers

Codorniu

Culbertson

Domaine Carneros

Domaine Chandon

Domaine Ste. Michelle

Gloria Ferrer

Handley

Iron Horse

Korbel

Maison Deutz

Mirassou

Monticello

Mumm Napa

Piper Sonoma

Roderer Estate

S. Anderson

Scharffenberger

Schramsberg

The Best-Known Grosslage Wines of Germany

These wines are from the large Grosslage district; however, they have generic names that appear to be a single vineyard name (einzellage). These wines are mostly simple everyday wines and should be inexpensive. Don't confuse these names with single vineyard names.

Mosel-Saar-Ruwer

Bernkasteler Badstube

Bernkastler Kurfürstlay

Erdener Schwarzlay

Graacher Munzlay

Krover Nactarsch

Piesporter Michelsberg

Trierer Romerley

Wiltinger Schwarzberg

Zeller Schwarzer Katz

The Nahe

Kreuznacher Kronenberg

Neiderhausener Burweg

Rudesheimer Rosengarten

Rheingau

Hattenheimer-Deutelsberg

Hochheimer Daubhaus

Johannisberger Erntebrigner

Rauenthaler Steinmacher

Rudesheim Burgweg

Rheinhessen

Bingener Sankt-Rochuskapelle

Niersteiner Gutes Domtal

Niersteiner Rehbach

Niersteiner Spiegelberg

Oppenheimer-Krotenbrunnen

Oppenheimmer-Guldenmorgen

Rheinphalz (Palatinate)

Bockenheimer Gafenstuck

Deiderheimer Hofstuck

Durkheimer Hochmess

Foster Mariengarten

Wachenheimer Schenkenbohl

329

Wine Words

acidic   A description of wine whose total acidity is so high that it imparts a sharp feel or sour taste in the mouth.

acidity   Refers to the nonvolatile acids in a wine, principally tartaric, malic, and citric. These acids provide a sense of freshness and an impression of balance to a wine. Excessive acidity provides a sharp or sour taste; too little results in a flat or flabby character.

aftertaste   The impression of a wine after it is swallowed. It is usually described as the "finish" of a wine. It ranges from short to lingering. A lingering aftertaste is a characteristic indicative of quality.

aged   Describes a wine that has been cellared either in cask or bottle long enough to have developed or improved. As a tasting term it describes the characteristic scent and taste of a wine that has so developed while in its bottle.

astringent   A puckering, tactile sensation imparted to the wine by its tannins. A puckering quality adds to the total sense of the wine, giving it a sense of structure, style, and vitality. Tannins are an essential component in red wines, which are made to improve with age while in bottle. Red wines lacking in tannins are generally dull and uninteresting. Wines vinified for prolonged aging are harshly tannic when young, but mellow when the wines age and the tannins precipitate to form a sediment in the bottle.

Auslese   Literally, "picked out" (i.e., selected). Under the new German wine law, Auslese wine is subject to all regulations included in Qualitätswein mit Prädikat (quality wine with special attributes). Auslese wine is made entirely from selected, fully ripe grapes, with all unripe and diseased grapes removed. No sugar may be added. The wine is especially full, rich, and somewhat sweet.

balance   Refers to the proportion of the various elements of a wine; acid against sweetness, fruit flavors against wood, and tannic alcohol against acid and flavor.

Barrel-fermented   Refers to the fermentation of a wine in a small oak cask as opposed to a large tank or vat.

Beerenauslese   "Berry-selected," i.e., individual grape berries picked out (by order of ripeness) at harvest for their sugar content, quality, and their amount of Edelfaule (noble rot).

Blanc de Blancs   Describes a white wine made from white grapes. The term refers to both still table and sparkling wines. The words "Blanc de Blancs" do not signify a quality better than other white wines.

bodega   In the Spanish wine trade, a wine house, wine company, wine cellar, or even wine shop.

body   The tactile impression of fullness on the palate caused by the alcohol, glycerin, and residual sugar in a wine. The extremes of "body" are full and thin.

Botrytis cinerea   A species of mold that attacks grapes grown in moist conditions. It is undesirable for most grape varieties, or when it infects a vineyard prior to the grapes reaching full maturity. Vineyards are treated to prevent its occurrence. When it attacks fully mature grapes it causes them to shrivel, concentrating both the acidity and the sugar, and resulting in an intensified flavor and a desired sweetness balanced by acidity. This is beneficial and highly desirable for white varieties such as the Johannisberg Riesling, Sauvignon Blanc, Semillon, and Chenin Blanc, from which unctuous, luscious and complex white wines are made in various wine regions of the world.

breed   A term used to describe the loveliest, most harmonious and refined wines that achieve what is called "classical proportions." The term is elusive to definition, but wines that deserve such acclaim are unmistakable when encountered.

cooperage   Refers to the wooden barrels and tanks used for aging wines.

Cru Bourgeois   Refers to red Bordeaux wines from the Haut-Médoc that rank just below the Grande Cru Classé wines of the 1855 Bordeaux classification.

Cru Classé   "Classified growth." Refers to those wines originally classified as Grand Cru Classé in the 1855 Bordeaux classification.

crush   Commonly used to refer to the grape harvest or vintage. Most specifically refers to the breaking of the grape stems, which begins a fermentation process.

cuve   A large vat, usually made of wood, used for the fermentation of grape juice into wine.

cuvée   Refers to the contents of a wine vat. More loosely used to refer to all the wine made at one time or under similar conditions. Sometimes refers to a specific pressing, or batch of wine. Sometimes used as part of a brand name or trademark, or as wine label nomenclature to refer to a batch of wine.

dosage   A small amount of sugar, champagne, and brandy that is added to Champagne right after degorgement. The final sweetness of the wine is determined by this step.

éleveur   Refers to a wine firm that cares for wines in their barrels and bottles them, frequently blending to provide better structure and balance. Often, this firm is also a négociant or shipper.

estate-bottled   Refers to a wine that has been bottled at the vineyard or winery in which it was made. Has legal significance in several countries, particularly France, Germany, and Italy, but is not controlled in others. Basically it connotes wine that was under the control of the winemaker from vineyard to bottle. It does not ensure the excellence of a wine, although it once did, as a general rule, many years ago.

fermentation   The process of converting sugar into alcohol, usually by the action of yeast on the juice of fruit, such as grapes. It is a complex process in which the yeast produces enzymes that convert the sugar into alcohol, carbon dioxide, and heat.

finesse   A quality of elegance that separates a fine wine from a wine that is simply good. It is a harmony of flavors and components rarely found in wine. The term is hard to define, but a wine with finesse is unmistakable when encountered.

fining   A clarifying technique that introduces an electrolytic agent, such as egg white, powdered milk, blood, diatomaceous earth (bentonite), or gelatin, to attract the solids and settle them to the bottom of a cask. Beaten egg whites or bentonite are the most frequenly used agents.

finish   The aftertaste of a wine when it has been swallowed. Usually consists of both flavor and tactile sensations from the acidity, alcohol, and tannins of the wine.

flor   A film of yeast or bacteria, usually in the cask on top of a wine, but also found in unhygienically bottled wines. In Spain it refers to a specific yeast that grows in Jerez and imparts a delicate, nutty quality to its wines. When Sherry is affected by this yeast, called Saccharomyces fermentati, it is called *fino*.

fortified   A wine to which alcohol has been added to raise its alcoholic strength. These wines usually range from 15 to 21 percent alcohol.

Free-run juice   The juice that is released from the grape as it is being crushed, before the pulp and skins are pressed. This juice, generally less harsh than press wine, is used for the finest wines. Free-run accounts for about 60 percent of the juice available from the grape for fine wine. This juice is separated immediately from the skins for white wine but is combined with the skins and pulp for reds. It is drained off the solids prior to the pressing of the remaining grape material.

French oak   The wood from the great oak forests of France, particularly from Nevers and Limousin, which impart a distinctive and mellow character to wine aged in barrels made from them. Also used as a term to describe the flavor imparted to wine by barrels made from this oak.

generic wine   A broadly used wine term signifying a wine type, as opposed to a more specific name, such as a grape variety or the actual region of production. Such names have frequently been employed on American wines using famous European place-names such as Chablis, Burgundy, Rhine, Champagne, or European wine types such as Claret or Sherry.

Goût de Terroir   The specific taste characteristic imparted from the soil of a particular wine district.

Goût de Vieux   The distinctive taste of an old wine.

Grand Cru   Great growth. Refers to a classification of French wines considered to be superior in quality. Used in Bordeaux, Burgundy, and Alsace.

hybrids   New grape varieties genetically produced from two or more different varieties—usually defined as varieties from different species, although the term is loosely used to include vines "crossed" within the same species.

hydrogen sulfide   A chemical compound that is a natural by-product of fermentation and imparts the smell of rotten eggs. With proper handling it dissipates prior to the finishing of a wine, but remains in poorly handled wines.

jug wines   Refers to inexpensive, everyday drinking wines, usually bottled in large bottles known as jug bottles. Most wines in this category are generics, but occasionally varietals also appear in jug bottles.

Kabinett   Refers to a legally defined quality level of German wines that is governed by the German government. Kabinett wines are the lowest rank of Qualitätswein mit Prädikat wines, stringently defined as to geographical region of origin, natural sugar content, and other attributes.

Late-Harvest   Refers to a type of wine made from overripe grapes with a high sugar content. Generally, Late-Harvest wines have been made from grapes deliberately left on the vine to achieve high sugars and concentrated flavors. White wine grapes are frequently affected by Botrytis cinerea, the noble mold, which further concentrates the grape and imparts its own unique, honeyed character. Most Late-Harvest wines are unctuously sweet, luscious in flavor, and are meant to be drunk with dessert or by themselves rather than with a meal.

lees   The sediment that results from clarifying a wine following fermentation in casks or tanks after separation from the skins and pulps. Usually consists of dead yeast cells and proteins. Wines are left on their lees to gain character and complexity; improper procedures can result in wines with unattractive flavors.

legs   The "tears," or streams of wine, that cling to the glass after a wine is swirled. Legs are usually a sign of a wine with body and quality and are caused by the differences in evaporation rates of alcohol and other liquids in the wine.

Limousin oak   The great white oak of the Limoges Forest in France, which is considered to be among the finest oak for aging wines and brandies. It imparts a mellow, complex vanilla character, with subtle nuances particular to its species, which adds complexity and elegance to a wine aged in casks made from it.

Maceration Carbonique   The whole-berry, intercellular fermentation by bacterial, rather than yeast action on the grapes in an airtight container. Imparts a fresh, fruity, jamlike quality to wines so treated, which are light in body and meant to be consumed when young.

Maderized   Refers to a wine that has lost its freshness or has spoiled due to oxidation in the bottle, either from storage in an excessively warm area, or simply because of overage. Maderized wines tend to smell like the wines from Madeira, hence the term. They have a sharp, yet sweet, caramelized character that is not attractive. Maderized white wines darken in color to amber or brown.

Maltre de Chai   In France, refers to a winery's cellarmaster, who is charged with tending the maturing casks of wine. Frequently he is also the winemaker. This position is the most important in a winery.

malolactic fermentation   The secondary fermentation that occurs in some wines due to the action of certain bacteria on the wine, which transform the hard malic acid to softer lactic acid. It also imparts new subtle flavors which, depending on the wine type, may or may not be wanted. It is usually undesirable in white wines, which require malic acid for freshness.

Méthode Champenoise   The traditional method of making sparkling wine and the only one permitted in the French district of Champagne where it was invented. It is the most labor-intensive and costly way to produce sparkling wine but also imparts a character and refinement not obtainable with other methods, particularly with regard to the quality of the bubbles produced. A shortcut to the Méthode Champenoise is called the transfer process, which eliminates the riddling and degorement steps—which are the most costly and time-consuming—and produces wines that are sometimes indistinguishable from the more complicated method.

middle body Refers to the part of the taste sensation that is experienced after the initial taste impact on the palate. It provides the core of the taste on which assessments are usually based. The first, or entry, taste and finish should both be in harmony with the middle body. A wine with a weak middle body generally gives the impression of being incomplete.

Mis en Bouteilles Sur Lie "Put in bottles on its lees," refers to the practice of bottling a wine directly from the barrel, immediately after fermentation without racking. The wine (almost always white) retains a fresh, lively quality, often with a slight petillance due to carbon dioxide absorbed during fermentation that had not completely dissipated when bottled. "Sur lie" wines often experience a malolactic fermentation in the bottle, which also contributes to the petillance or "coming alive" in the bottle in the year after bottling.

must Refers to the unfermented grape juice produced by crushing the grapes. It is a loosely defined word and equally defines grape juice, crushed grapes, or the juice after pressing.

Qualitätswein Literally "quality wine," which, under the German wine law, is one grade above Tafelwein ("table wine") and one grade below Qualitätswein mit Prädikat (quality wine with special attributes). Quality wine must come from a single district, and among other qualifications, must be of a minimum alcoholic strength.

racking Refers to the traditional way of clarifying a wine by transferring it from one cask to another and leaving the precipitated solids behind.

residual sugar Refers to the unfermented sugar remaining in a wine. It is usually described in terms of the percentage by weight, and is detectable when it exceeds three quarters of one percent. Above two percent it tastes quite sweet.

robe Refers to the color of a wine in general, and, more specifically, to the wine's color when the glass is tipped at an angle.

Sec Literally means "dry," and refers to a dry wine. Its use is not legally defined, and it frequently appears on wine labels of wines that are off-dry or even somewhat sweet.

sediment Refers to the deposit precipitated by a wine that has aged in the bottle.

Solera Refers to the traditional Spanish blending system used in making Sherry. The Solera, itself, is a series of Sherry casks containing wines of various ages which are fractionally blended by transferring part of the contents of a younger cask into an older one.

sparkling   Refers to a wine that, under pressure, has absorbed sufficient carbon dioxide to bubble, or "sparkle" when poured into a glass.

Spätlese   In German nomenclature, refers to a wine made from fully ripe grapes.

Spumante   Refers to Italian sparkling wines.

tannin   Refers to an astringent acid, derived from the skins, seeds, and wooden casks, which causes a puckering sensation in the mouth. Tannin is an essential preservative for quality wines. A moderate puckering sensation caused by the tannins adds to the pleasurable character of a red wine.

Tonneau   A Bordeaux measure of wine, equivalent to four barrels, or one hundred cases of wine.

transfer process   Refers to a shortcut method of making bottle-fermented Champagne. In this process, the wine is filtered rather than riddled and disgorged.

Tröckenbeerenauslese   The highest Prädikat a German wine can carry. It signifies that the wine is made entirely from late-picked, individually selected grape berries that have been allowed to shrivel on the vine, usually after being attacked by the Botrytis cinerea, the noble rot, which imparts a special quality to the finished wine.

unfiltered   Refers to a wine that has been bottled without being clarified or stabilized by filtration. Such a wine might be clarified by fining, however. When bottled without any cellar treatment, such a wine is labled as "Unfiltered and Unfined."

unfined   Refers to a wine that has not been fined as part of its cellar treatment. Also infers that the wine has not been filtered and has received a minimum of treatment.

varietal   Refers either to a wine named after a grape variety, or one that is made entirely from a single grape variety. As legally defined, such a wine need be made only from 75 percent of the named grape.

varietal character   Refers to the recognizable flavor and structure of a wine made from a particular variety of grape.

vinifera, vitis vinifera   Refers to the species of grape varieties known as "the wine bearers," which are responsible for all the finer wines of the world.

vinosity   Refers to the characteristic flavor of a wine as a result of fermented grape juice. It is distinct from any other flavors such as those of the unfermented grape, oak cask, or other flavor components.

viticultural area   A delimited region in which common geographic or climatic attributes contribute to the definable characteristic of a wine. Although it is called by different names in various countries, it is usually referred to as an Appellation of Origin. In the

United States, such an appellation is called a viticultural area, and is defined by geography alone, as opposed to requirements regulating the varieties of grapes grown, yield, or nature of wine produced.

volatile acid   Refers to the acid component of a wine that can be detected in the aroma. In wine this is acetic acid, the acid of vinegar. It is always present in wine, usually undetectable or at low levels that add to the complexity and appeal of a wine. When excessive, it is an undesirable defect.

Index

J-K

L

M

X-Z

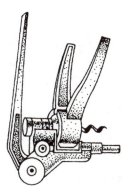

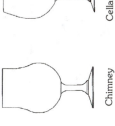
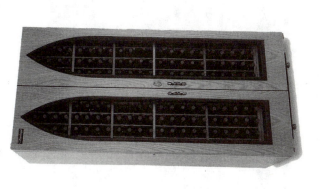

Philip Seldon's Wine Advisor Computer Software will make matching wine with food a breeze, and it's FREE* with the purchase of The Complete Idiot's Guide to Wine!

*$4 shipping and handling required (U.S. Dollars), along with your sales receipt for the purchase of *The Complete Idiot's Guide to Wine.*

Yes, if you want recommendations for compatible wines to go with your food, Philip Seldon's Wine Advisor program is for you. It will take all the trials and tribulations out of finding the right wine to go with a particular dish.

Here's how it works:

➤ First you select a food item from a list.

➤ If you want, you can narrow the selection by price range, wine type, country of origin, or wine district.

➤ Your computer prints out a list of recommended wines.

➤ You take this list to your retail wine store and ask "Which of these wines do you have in stock?"

➤ You decide which one of these wines you want, and then you buy it!

That's all there is to it. All you need is an IBM-compatible computer, 80386 or better, Windows 3.1 or Windows 95, and a minimum of 4 megabytes of memory and 10 megabytes of available disk space.

Philip Seldon's Wine Advisor program gives you detailed information and descriptions of more than 2,000 wines from most of the popular wine districts at all price ranges. Each wine is rated on an "A-B-C-D-F" scale so that you can get the best wines. You can also choose a wine by district without making a food choice.

Please clip out the following coupon and mail it, along with your check or money order, to

Philip Seldon's Wine Advisor
201 E. 87th Street
New York, NY 10128

Philip Seldon's Wine Advisor program is an exclusive product of Philip Seldon. Shipping/handling charge and availability are subject to change without notice.

-- cut here --

YES, send me my copy of Philip Seldon's Wine Advisor. I have enclosed $4 for shipping and handling and a copy of my sales receipt for *The Complete Idiot's Guide to Wine.*

Name _____

Address _____

City/State/ZIP _____

Tel No. _____